Chris Bromham Autobiography

A Strange T

B

Chris B

Text copyright © 2014 Christopher John Bromham

All Rights Reserved

I have tried to recreate events, locales and conversations from my memories of them. In order to maintain their anonymity in some instances I have changed the names of individuals and places, I may have changed some identifying characteristics and details such as physical properties, occupations and places of residence.

Thanks to my wonderful and ever supportive wife, Anna-Marie, for her patience and belief in me.

My beautiful daughters Natalie and Natasha and my two incredible Grandsons, Corey and Colton for putting the light back in my life.

My good friend Chris Barry for his endless support over the years.

Ann Tawe-Jones for her keen eye and guidance.

Darren Cassidy for his knowledge and advice.

My son Shane Bromham for design of the front cover

Son in law Paul Evans for the editing of the book and creation of the book cover.

My Father and Mother in Law, Phillip and Joan Davies, for accepting this broken man into their family.

Last, but by no means least, my beautiful late wife, Donna. Who was constantly by my side with her love and support in everything I did.

"Table of Contents"

CHAPTER 1: STORMY BEGINNINGS

CHAPTER 2: INTRODUCING MY FATHER

CHAPTER 3: BOMBS, BOBBIES AND BATHTIME

CHAPTER 4: DEATH AND BACK AGAIN

CHAPTER 5: A STUPID DUCK IN FRONT

CHAPTER 6: NEVER A TYRESOME MOMENT

CHAPTER 7: THE PENIS AND THE PLIERS

CHAPTER 8: MOVING THROUGH THE GEARS

CHAPTER 9: MANY LESSONS LEARNED

CHAPTER 10: AT THE CROSSROADS

CHAPTER 11: YOU HAVE TO START SOMEWHERE

CHAPTER 12: BECOMING SOMEBODY ELSE

CHAPTER 13: ADRENALIN VERSUS INCHES

CHAPTER 14: RIDING HIGH

CHAPTER 15: DREAMS

CHAPTER 16: TO PARADISE

CHAPTER 17: ...AND THEN TO BROMLEY

CHAPTER 18: THE HAZY EIGHTIES

CHAPTER 19: TWELVE WORDS

CHAPTER 20: A LOST LIGHT

CHAPTER 21: THE AFTERMATH

CHAPTER 22: PICKING UP THE PIECES

CHAPTER 23: THE FAN CLUB, THE DOGS, MY DAUGHTER AND HER SON

CHAPTER 24: A STRANGE TWIST OF FATE

CHAPTER 1: STORMY BEGINNINGS

On a wretched winter's morning in late 1946 a grimy steam locomotive heaved its sombre procession of groaning carriages towards Swansea's now-razed Victoria Station.

Among its few dozen travel-weary passengers sat a petite, demurely-attired lady called Violet and her three young children: Jack (named after his late father), Gwen and Peter.

Violet's story, like so many from that dark and uncertain period of austerity and hardship, makes for pitiable reading; rendered a widow by the events at Dunkirk six years earlier she'd been forced, consequently, to raise a family in her humble Hampshire home without any form of reliable income.

This, you should realise, was the age before child allowances, social security, family tax credits or any welfares of the sort. In those days whatever you owned you made the best of. What you didn't own you didn't miss and couldn't dare dream of holding in your hands unless you truly believed you could earn it.

How times and values have changed.

While the train lurched through the town Violet must have been in fearful awe of the bleak backdrop which would have appeared to sprawl for miles beyond the dusty, nicotine-glazed windows.

Building after building, as far as the dull blanket of drizzle would have permitted her drowsy eyes to gaze, remained a shadowy and bombed-out ruin.

There would have been people strolling here and there, some with dogs perhaps, some with friends, some carrying their paltry rations of bread and meat for the coming week, some pushing their new-borns through innumerable heaps of rubble and debris.

The port, once the pulsating gateway to Swansea's booming copper industry, lay hushed; monstrous cranes with their dangling cables, like mourners weeping tears in a noiseless graveyard, maintained an eerie vigil around the listless docklands.

And yet, for Violet, that cheerless panorama of devastation and decay was somehow meant to represent a new beginning.

Her motivation for migrating to Swansea, of all places, should be clarified; she and Dolly, her aunt who'd lived for many years in the town, had corresponded throughout the War and for some time previously. On learning of Violet's mounting despair with her existence in Hampshire Dolly offered her temporary lodgings in her own house, along with the real prospect of paid work.

Violet could in no way refuse such a charitable invitation to start hers and her family's life afresh so, after cramming their worldly possessions into several battered suitcases and trying in the plainest of terms to explain her desperate circumstances to three sobbing and bewildered youngsters, all four boarded the train from which, their journey being almost over, they were shortly to disembark.

Were they excited about what lay ahead? Maybe they would have been an hour or so earlier, but even their most resilient shards of optimism would surely have been blunted by their first demoralising glimpse of post-war Swansea.

Were they apprehensive, frightened even? Of course they were. After all, how could they *not* have been? Let's not forget they'd forsaken familiarity, miserable though that might have been at the time, for somewhere that was totally alien to them.

So, when Violet struggled down from her carriage on that freezing day, encumbered as she was with her children and their meagre effects she was, quite literally, stepping into the unknown.

Assistance, though, was not slow in arriving.

William Isaac Bromham, a brawny miner from the nearby village of Skewen (pronounced 'Skew-win') placed himself, with a gallant twinkle in his eye, completely at Violet's disposal.

With his offer of help most gratefully accepted he ensured that she and all that travelled with her made it safely onto the bustling platform and out of the station.
Violet and William were mutual strangers until that moment. Isn't it remarkable, though, how often the most unassuming display of human kindness can develop into the first act of love?

Sadly, it's also remarkable that that first act of love can all too frequently turn out to be the last.

Nevertheless, they became acquainted and their friendship grew. Friendship blossomed into a fondness of sorts, and that fondness resulted in a marriage of sorts.

So, within weeks of arriving in South Wales Violet had accepted the proposal of a man who, at the time, she perceived as her devoted protector and, following a modest ceremony at Swansea's registry office, moved herself and her family into William's tiny bungalow on Skewen's Ormes Road.

Even by today's benchmarks such a leap from faltering courtship to eternal wedlock might have appeared hasty and even, it could be argued, foolhardy.

However unenviable we consider Violet's predicament to have been, we should acknowledge that the availability of a permanent and secure home for her three precious children would have clouded any misgivings that she may have had.

Not surprisingly, the well-documented stresses experienced by five people seeking to survive in such a confined space as William's bungalow emerged quickly and began to take their inevitable toll.
He started exhibiting aggressive and often violent tendencies, probably stemming from the toxic combination of the inconvenience of having to house his step-children, the additional strains that would have brought upon his already-scant salary and, more damagingly, Violet's flirtatious nature.

Ill-feeling and jealousy would fester into arguments, arguments would flare into blazing rows and those rows, with ever-increasing predictability, would climax with the defenceless Violet finding herself on the receiving end of a physical beating.

It must have been glaringly obvious to them both that their marriage was one of convenience; a sham, no less, and one in which Violet, through the unshakable maternal desire to provide shelter for her offspring, had become ensnared.

In the hope of at least releasing some of the pressure which was building due to the overcrowding in the place, and thereby possibly salvaging something, *anything*, from her near-impossible situation, Violet decided to send Jack, her eldest, back to Hampshire to live with his grieving grandmother (Violet's mother-in-law). As was described earlier she'd lost her own son at Dunkirk and Violet must have intended that 'donating' Jack would have gone some considerable way to resolving two distinct emotional crises.

Jack, poor lad, must have been shell-shocked and possibly even traumatised by the speed of events but, despite that, he was given no opportunity to object or to have any meaningful opinion on the matter.
So, before he could even exchange final farewells with his newly-made friends he was driven the six miles to Swansea Victoria and sent on his way with little more than a change of clothes, a few shillings and some food for the long and lonely trip back to Hampshire.

Despite the two good deeds she undoubtedly thought she'd contrived at that time, abandoning Jack so cruelly left a deep-seated guilt which gnawed at Violet for the rest of her days. They managed to stay in touch as the years came and went but, inevitably, as their worlds drifted ever-further apart their cherished reunions became more intermittent before ceasing altogether.

For the record, Jack lived into his forties before succumbing to cancer.

Back in Skewen, any lessening of the tension generated through Jack's departure would have been short-lived since, soon after he left in 1948, Violet fell pregnant with William's first son, Stuart.

Three years later she gave birth to Graham, and then Michael came along in 1953.

So, to recap, that's five young and hungry mouths which required feeding, (after Jack, Violet's next-eldest child, Gwen, was a mere thirteen years of age when Michael was born), a turbulent relationship between two adults who in all likelihood despised each other by that point, barely enough room to pick up a cat let alone swing one, and a single derisory wage.

The one thing that household most certainly didn't want was another pregnancy.

That, though, was precisely what happened.

On July 20th, 1957, with the help of Edwina, her friend-cum-part-time-midwife, and after a few too many hours of excruciating labour (William was most likely listening to the horse racing on the radio at the time and, therefore, far too busy with more pressing matters to offer any support), Violet introduced that already-bulging bungalow on Ormes Road to its newest resident.

That child would have cried, the room around Violet would have been sanitised in the hours following the delivery and, gradually, everyone would have drifted away to give her the chance of some much-needed rest.

It wouldn't have crossed her mind, of course, that the baby boy she cradled so lovingly in her exhausted arms might go on to hold seven world records.

She couldn't possibly have imagined that he would one day perform on a live link-up to the United States of America, or gain mention in a television programme hosted by a Hollywood giant.

Neither would she have had any inkling of the boundless determination he would show as, one by one, he struggled to realise his many ambitions.

His life would be punctuated with some of the most extraordinary highs and lows, either achieved or borne against seemingly-insurmountable odds.

To all of that and more, she would have been wholly oblivious.

She could see only an ordinary new-born through her moist and dead-beat eyes, and so she gave him an ordinary name; Christopher John Bromham.

To everybody that knows me though, I'm just plain Chris.

CHAPTER 2: INTRODUCING MY FATHER

In harmonious accord with Skewen's staunch working-class values of the late 1950s I was given my first job within twenty-four hours of being born.

It's appropriate now to relate the circumstances of how that job came about and, more significantly, the gratuitous and malevolent manner with which it was taken away.

This, then, is how it began.

My beloved mother, as might be anticipated, was altogether spent after urging me into the world in excruciating instalments. So, eager to seize the chance to drive a wedge between herself and my father whilst killing that second bird with the same stone and reducing the risk of yet another unwanted pregnancy, she had me sleep beside her in the big matrimonial bed.

My father, who probably reasoned along not too dissimilar lines, consented to that pact and subsequently slept in a low-to-the-floor single bed next to ours but with a strategically-deployed chest of drawers in-between.

That subtle but prudent precaution was unquestionably Mum's doing.
At first the new routine chugged along fairly well. Yes, there were the inevitable day-to-day quarrels and Mum's regular beatings (life, in other words, drifted blithely by) but the sleeping arrangements seldom featured on my father's erratic radar.

Incredibly, it took nigh on four years for his carnal frustrations to simmer and come to the boil.

Being only three years of age I was blissfully unaware of the problems that my continued but loathsome tenancy of that bed was causing. I savoured, you must realise, the unconditional love of a compassionate mother and a gorgeously-warm place to sleep, and shouldn't that be all that any child ever needs?

The trouble was, it wasn't *my* bed and, in truth, it wasn't really Mum's either.

It was *his*, and the tenuous lease was about to expire.

Everything unravelled in the space of a dizzying week or so.

I can recall only the vaguest of details from my life prior to these events but, as you'll soon come to appreciate, I can convey much of what occurred afterward with disturbing clarity (perhaps, though, with a few gaps having being filled in by Mum down the years).

This is what I/she remembered.

Before busying herself with rustling up the family's teatime meal Mum always gleaned immense pleasure from preparing a magnificent open-hearth coal fire in the living room.

My brothers (Gwen, I believe, had flown/escaped the nest a few months before) had finished school on that particular day but each in turn had come home, changed their clothes, grabbed a drink or a speedy sandwich and rushed back out. That meant that, cosily swathed in my woolly blanket and lolling in the larger of the room's two armchairs I had that glorious fire, and the spellbinding black-and-white television, to myself.

I can only assume I was watching *Bill and Ben* at the time, or it might have been *Andy Pandy*.

Anyway, edging above the delightful voices crackling from the television I could make out Mum's echoing from the kitchen. I then recognised my father's (he must have arrived home from work through the back door only minutes before), followed by Mum's again, then my father's once more.

With each volley the fractious exchange became louder and more vindictive, and it wasn't long before the television's comforting tones were entirely overwhelmed.

Slowly but as surely as always, the bungalow reverberated with yet another ferocious row.

Even at the tender age of almost-four I could somehow grasp that something bad was about to happen so I pulled my blanket tight around me.

After an explosion of swearing from my father I winced with the gut-wrenching sounds of glass smashing, two slaps, a desperate cry from Mum, and the door to the living room being flung open with such force that its handle crunched into the wall behind me. In a feeble attempt to hide I tried to tug the blanket over my head but, before I could, the armchair had been swung around and, utterly petrified, I found myself gazing into my father's rage-filled face.
"Get *out* of my f----- chair, you little *bastard*!" he shouted as, with one of his rugged hands clasped firmly around my ankle and the other squeezing my wrist, he yanked me halfway to the ceiling.

At that moment Mum came dashing into the room and, howling uncontrollably, sought to grab my father's muscular arms with whatever strength she had left.

"Please, Will," I can still hear her begging. "He's only a child for God's sake! Don't hurt him, *please*!"

He promptly released my leg and, with his free palm, struck my mother across the face with a ferocity that propelled her back towards the kitchen door.

With my solitary source of protection gone, and with both of his enormous hands available again, he hoisted me up so that his wrathful eyes were staring into my terrified ones which was like being face-to-face with a wild animal which was teetering on the verge of tearing its prey limb from limb.
"I hate you, you little *bastard*!" he snarled, and I can still recollect him frothing at the sides of his mouth as he spoke. "I absolutely f------ *hate* you!"

I was kicking out frantically and flapping my arms, which was my way of pleading with that grotesque man-monster to put me down.

Unfortunately, my wish was duly granted.
He shook me so severely that I became giddy and then threw me across the room toward the fire.

Whilst you're endeavouring to summon a mental image of this chaos, don't forget that I hadn't yet turned four years of age.

Instinctively I screamed as any similarly-petrified infant would have done but, instead of landing on the flaming coals, all I felt thudding into my spine and shoulder was the hard and uneven stonework at the side of the hearth.

I slumped onto the carpet with a numbing pain coursing through my arm and ribcage.

There I lay, stunned, winded and gravely vulnerable, and unable to make a sound. I tried crying out but with each futile effort the agony within my torso was heightened once again.

My hearing, though, was fine.
"And as for you, you *bitch*," he roared, turning his frenzied anger back onto Mum who was poleaxed by the kitchen door, "don't you *ever* pull a stunt like that again! Do you understand? I've warned you about that before, haven't I? If you *ever* lay a single finger on me again I'll break both your f------ arms! I've sweated my arse off all f------ day down that stinking shithole of a mine, and what do I find when I get home? I find *that* little bastard sitting in my chair watching some stupid f------ puppets while you're cooking some disgusting pile of *shit* that I wouldn't even give to a *pig*!"

On each of the words 'shit' and 'pig' he powered his right foot into my mother's abdomen as she struggled to crawl, bless her, back to the sanctuary of the kitchen.

"Yeah, go on! Get back out there where you belong, bitch! And this time, do me a proper meal, not some garbage you'd lob in the bloody trough for *your* worthless tribe!"

I hadn't moved from where I'd collapsed. I was in dreadful pain but, luckily, I was conscious and still able to breathe freely.

I then have a chilling memory of emitting a frightened yelp and straining to wriggle free as my father, after snatching my aching arm, jerked me upright and slung me into the kitchen towards Mum who, by that time, had managed to raise herself onto her own hesitant feet.

"There you go!" he sneered. "If you haven't got any decent meat, stick *that* little bastard in the oven! And stop that pathetic crying before I give *both* of you something to fucking cry about!"

He slammed the kitchen door, and that was the end of that.

My mother, whilst propping herself against the draining board, hugged me closely and wept. I wept with her.

She was hunched over me like some decrepit old woman and I can distinctly recall that her every breath was inhaled and then exhaled with a wheezy groan.

"You'll be alright tomorrow, love," she stammered through her tears while checking my head and the ugly red patches on my back. "You've got a few bumps and scrapes, but you'll survive."

Despite the soreness in my chest and shoulder it wasn't long before, like so many occasions previously, I faded toward sleep wrapped snugly in her trembling arms.

The final things I glimpsed before drifting off at the end of that horrendous afternoon were the remains of the plate of food which my father had thrown across the kitchen floor, a shattered drinking glass near the clothes horse and a single drop of blood trickling from Mum's left nostril.

Thankfully, and perhaps surprisingly, the place was peaceful for the next couple of days. There wasn't much talking going on and Mum, probably through wandering around in her own private soul-searched world, barely spoke to any of us.
My father, as I understand it, spent the next few evenings taking his accustomed strolls around Skewen which gave us all, and especially my mother, some well-deserved respite from his unremitting torrent of abuse.

Alas, it didn't last.

One night around the end of that week my brothers and I had shuffled off to our beds leaving

Mum to read her book in the living room.

My father stormed home after one of his walks in an absolutely appalling mood. He'd involved himself in some squabble or other with Mr Lloyd, our next-door neighbour and, judging by the way he was shouting at Mum, he'd ended up with by far the worse of the situation. His festering indignation, from what I'd strained to glean with the side of my head pressed onto the safe side of Mum's bedroom door, then focused upon me.

"Are you listening to me, woman? I want that little bastard out of my bed *tonight*! Nearly four bloody years I've had to sleep like some tramp in that single, and I'm getting bloody pissed off with it! I don't give a toss how you do it, but get him *out*, *now*!"

Naturally, it was the ever-venomous 'that little bastard' which made my heart skip. To him, at any rate, *that* was my name; the number of times he called me 'Chris', certainly with any paternal affection, I can count on one hand with change left over.
I apologise in advance for not being able to share Mum's response but, as I'm sure you've gathered by now, her placid voice didn't have anywhere near the aggressive potency of my father's and so, to my ear at least, it remained muffled by the door's thick panels.

"Don't you *dare* f------ answer me back!" he thundered on. "This is *my* house, *not* yours, and *that* in there is *my* f------ bed! I want that…that *thing* out of it tonight! Understand? Or do I have to hammer it into you instead?"

This was obviously serious; not only was Mum one false word away from yet another pummelling, but *I* was extremely close to losing one of the few shreds of comfort that I enjoyed in that house, aside from her of course, so I carefully teased the door off the latch to muster what she was saying.

Through the slenderest of gaps between my door and its frame, and also amidst the living room's murky light, I could make out Mum cowering on the edge of her cushion with my father looming over her with such menace that she appeared to be less than half his size.

"But where is he going to sleep, Will?" she appealed. "There's no space in the boys' bedrooms, and I'm not going to be able to prepare a bed for him this late at night! We don't have any spare sheets or blankets!"

That sounded good to me; my brothers, as I would soon find to my cost and which I'll describe in more detail later, had no affection for me whatsoever so my life would have become intolerable if I'd been forced to pitch up with *them*.
Nonetheless, my father was on the brink of totally losing it. Like everyone else, I'd learned to recognise the signs after a while.

"Does it look like I honestly give a stinking shit *where* he sleeps? Well, does it? He can sleep out the f------ coal bunker freezing his bollocks off and rolling in the stale cats piss for all I care! Do as you're f------ told and get him out of my bed, NOW!"

Mum endeavoured to stand up in a vain attempt to pacify my father but, before she could lift herself completely, he thrust his palm squarely into her shoulder which caused her to crumple back down. She thrashed her arms as if to defend herself against the expected clobbering but, on a whim, he dragged her from the chair like a rag doll and flung her onto the floor.

No sooner had she heaved herself back on to her knees that the malicious onslaught began.

Punch after brutal punch rained down on my helpless mother, who squealed each time my father's clenched fist was rammed into her slender frame. If a blow was lost through a valiant parry he made doubly sure that the one following reached its mark.

Before long she'd capitulated into the foetal position; my father, having traded clouts for kicks, didn't relent.

She was no longer squealing; instead, each time he booted her she emitted a low, hollow grunt.
I'd seen and heard enough but, in spite of my immaturity and slightness of build, I was determined to do something. So, I threw open the bedroom door and recklessly launched myself onto my father.

I swatted at his legs and his waist but that didn't distract him from lashing out against Mum.

Ominously, she wasn't even grunting anymore.

Clearly irritated by my laughably-weak attack he picked me up by the throat and slapped me hard before hurling me across the room. He then moved toward me with his fingers gnarled like an eagle's talons, but I scampered swiftly behind the sofa.

He growled and swore and jerked the sofa away from the wall but, by that time, I'd already scurried into the kitchen on all-fours.

I expected him to hound me out but, bravely choosing a less mobile target, he directed his reinvigorated fury on Mum.

I was so worried for her, and I knew that anything I was going to do to help had to be done very quickly.

I then spotted a rounded butter knife, perched near the edge of the table.

Almost without thinking I grabbed its metallic haft, charged as fast as I could back into the living room and plunged the blade into the back of my father's leg.
There was a horrid, almost endless silence.

He stopped kicking out, looked up to the ceiling with clenched teeth, and emitted a strangled cry.

I cowered behind the sofa again but with the knife held fast in my unsteady hand.

The steel hadn't actually penetrated my father's calf.

Had I the good judgement to have been standing still when I stabbed at him it might well have done but, in my growing panic, I'd only succeeded in cutting into the fabric of his trousers and slicing across his skin rather than through it.

I had, however, drawn a few specks of blood.

He let out another stifled wail.

From bitter experience I knew what was coming next so, gripping the knife ever-more tightly, I buried my head between my knees. I sensed a gust of wind blast past me but, by some miracle, the flaying I dreaded didn't materialise. My father had instead made straight for the bedroom, cursing incessantly as he limped away, and we didn't see him again until the next morning.

Mum, though, was in a terrible state.
A full half-hour must have passed before she was able to sit up unaided and, even then, she was only able to do so by arching her back onto the skirt of the sofa.

She didn't stand, and didn't try to. To be honest, I don't believe she could have.

For an hour or more she sat mulling the ebbing fire's sputtering flames, not saying a word, not sharing a thought, barely moving a muscle.

She flopped an arm around my shoulder and lightly stroked my hair but, still, she wouldn't speak.

I'd hidden the knife under my thigh because I was worried she might have been angry with me for what I'd done but, as I only found out years later, she wasn't even aware of my actions that night.

The room had grown cold but she didn't seem to care, and neither did I. I was just so relieved that he'd cleared off for the night and, in all likelihood, pampered his trifling wound with the First Aid kit that she kept in a bedroom drawer.

What of Mum herself?

Well, my father was as merciless and as cunning as he always prided himself on being whenever he was disposed to give her a good walloping.
He would, for example, seek to avoid striking her on any part of her body where the evidence of an assault might be seen and, because of that cowardice, I don't remember seeing *any* bruises on her skin that night.

Rather, he would amuse himself by thumping her repeatedly either in her midriff or on the top of her skull.

I rarely saw any of the contusions beneath her clothing but they were always there and, I would strongly suspect, in considerable number.

But, *c'est la vie*.

My father had reclaimed his prized bed and, for him, that was the principal objective. I sincerely hope, having punched and kicked my mother possibly to within sight of death, that he was thoroughly satisfied with the way he'd procured it.

As far as my own situation was concerned he wasted no time the next day in moving the low bed, his bane for almost four years, into the bedroom occupied by Graham and Michael.

Well, I say 'moving' but 'chucking' offers a more accurate depiction because he dismantled the bed where it stood and tossed the pieces, one by one, into my new room for my brothers to reassemble for me.

They were both pretty pissed off with that new set-up and repaid me deliberately and, on occasions, quite nastily over the coming years.
Aside from getting the essential shopping Mum didn't venture outside the door during the following week, since it took that long for her friable self-esteem to show some signs of returning.

Her bingo friends called a few times, perhaps in the hope that she would join them down the now-demolished Ritz for a few houses but they were rebuffed icily on the doorstep by my father with a put-on "She's got a bit of a chill at the moment", or "she's having an early night", or "she's got a bit of a headache".

Yes, bloody right she had a bit of a headache! Bastard!

They hadn't the slightest suspicion as to what was happening and were not likely to provided he kept fobbing them off with a pack of lies, a self-effacing grin and the oh-so-caring-husband charade.

So, he was back in his bed, which meant I'd lost my job but at least the pitter-patters from *my* tiny feet were the last that would be heard in the bungalow.

There were no more unsolicited pregnancies but, sadly, my father's brutality didn't stop. He would beat both me and Mum with near-mechanical regularity for years to come, and rarely with just cause.

Not there is such a thing as 'just cause' when it comes to domestic violence, but I'm sure you'll understand what I'm striving to say.

I claimed the little butter knife as my own and I still have it to this day but, no matter how frequently or how savagely he would beat either me or Mum, I never wielded it again.

CHAPTER 3: BOMBS, BOBBIES AND BATHTIME

Those shocking incidents were still lucid in my mind when, in September 1961, I started in Coedffranc (pronounced 'Coyd-frank') Infant's School.

Mum would walk me there first thing in the morning, return to collect me at three o'clock and, after a short detour for an ice-cream (on sunny days at least, or on days when she'd received her nominal weekly allowance from my father), we'd trudge over the railway bridge, up the hill and then head back to Ormes Road.

For those precious hours without any of us under her feet she, along with her furniture polish and bottle of Dettol disinfectant, would tear like a tornado through the bungalow cleaning out nooks and crannies that I didn't even realise existed.

She was submissively dedicated to her housekeeping and kept the place as palatial as she could but, with four boys living there and a pugnacious husband lurking in the background, that couldn't have been a straightforward task.

In addition my father was a heavy smoker (rarely would we see him without a cigarette either dangling from his mouth or clasped between his stained fingers) so, while she bustled around with her daily sweeping, spraying and scrubbing every door and window would be thrown open 'to let the fresh air blow through'.

That was fine during the week when my father was in work and we were stuck in school. It wasn't much fun at weekends though, especially during the winter when my brothers and I invariably had to swaddle ourselves in sweaters, scarves and bobble hats, and pray she would hurry up and get it done!

Impulsively and obliviously onward she would wash, sluice and brush, contentedly singing along to either *Stranger on the Shore* by Acker Bilk or (later) *Keep On Running* by The Spencer Davis Group, both drawn from our limited assortment of seven-inch singles.

Whenever I hear either of those tracks, even after so many years have flown by, all that's triggered in my memory is the sound of Mum's crooning and the pungent tang of Dettol!

So, you might imagine my relief when, after shepherding me home from school, she would habitually let me occupy myself in the garden while she rounded off her blitz on the bungalow.

Now, a word or two of explanation is required here.

Our back yard was, in its own right, rather unusual.

At around one hundred feet long (that's about one-third the length of a football pitch) it was constructed on three tiers with stone steps between the levels.
You may have already calculated that that's a more-than-acceptable size for a kick-about but I should also record that it was inclined at something like forty-five degrees!

Those distinctive facets aside, the garden would have been no different from that owned by Mr and Mrs Average.
It was a bit wild, weedy and unloved, with grass consistently long enough to hide an elephant in. We also had an apple tree, a chicken pen, an outside toilet (which will figure later), the mandatory clothes line and, finally, a stack of wood strips which might have become a fence one day so, taking everything into account, not too many entertainment possibilities for the inquisitive child.

But I was lucky.

My feature of choice in that garden, namely the path which ran its full extent, led to the back gate and, beyond that, to the most spectacular adventure playground that any six-year-old could have wished for.

Drummau (pronounced 'Drummer') Mountain soars to almost nine hundred feet above the northern fringes of Skewen and there's scarcely a place in the village where its tree-covered slopes can't be seen. Our home was at its foot with only the narrow and winding Drummau Road in between.

The other kids from Ormes Road and beyond all made for that mountain, building themselves dens, lookouts, tree swings and the like, and we'd only go home when our stomachs rumbled loudly enough for our mothers to hear.

It was on that mountain that I met my first true friends. They included Tom, who was five months older than me, and his brother Jonathan who, I recollect, was nearly twelve.

On one particularly memorable day Tom bounded up to me during morning play-time at Coedffranc and asked me if I'd meet him after school at Drummau Mine, one of our most-frequented haunts on the mountain.

He had a fiendish smile on his face. I know I was young but, still, I should have known better.

He also asked me to bring my toy soldiers which I thought was strange but, keen to go along with something I assumed would be a damn good laugh, I joined up with him later that afternoon all the same.

Drummau Mine was actually a redundant facility located on the mountain's shallowest gradients, and about two hundred yards from Ormes Road. Replete with coal tips, overturned railway wagons and derelict outbuildings (which, with hindsight, definitely *weren't* safe enough to even stand beside, let alone play in), it was a mischief-maker's paradise.

Tom, who was already there by the time I arrived, was excitedly watching Jonathan spooning some white, bead-like powder from a squat plastic bottle.
"Ooh, is that sherbet?" I asked.

"Nah," Jonathan replied casually. "It's sodium nitrate."

Those were new words for me but I could see they weren't to Tom who was grinning like the Cheshire cat while observing his brother carefully measuring out one little mound.

Naturally my curiosity had the better of me. "What does it do?"

"I'll show you in a minute," said Jonathan. "Did you bring your soldiers?"

I revealed my stash of French legionnaires that I'd taken along, plus the few cowboys and Roundheads thrown in for good measure.

"Well done!" he chirped. "Can you pass me one of those behind you?"

He gestured toward my feet and to a bundle of thin aluminium tubes which looked suspiciously like old television aerials. No sooner had I handed one of them over than, cautiously, he started filling it with the powder.

"Nearly ready?" Tom pressed him.

"Yep! Nearly ready! You can start burying them now."

Tom let out a cheer, beckoned me over to the highest of the three coal tips and started planting his own pocketful of soldiers.

"So what's going to happen now?" I asked, copying Tom's example by pushing my figures into the tip's face.

"We're going to blow them up!"

"Blow them up! But you can't do that! These are the only ones I've got!"

"Don't worry," Tom said. "They'll be fine. They're not *really* going to be blown up. They're just going to be… erm…"

"But I don't want them to be blown up!"

"All ready!" Jonathan said, elbowing us out of his way and thrusting the primed tube into the midst of a horde of Red Indians and German paratroopers. He took a match from the box in his pocket, lit the fuse (his hand was wobbling quite markedly I remember) and, after an anxious dash, took shelter behind one of the coal wagons. Tom quickly followed and, in spite of my reluctance to leave my figures stranded in the tip, I wasn't far behind.

We gazed with anticipation as the fuse gradually sparked and fizzled away to nothing.

"COVER!" Jonathan yelled without warning.

We turned away, closed our eyes and shielded our heads with our forearms.

KA-BOOM!

That, I confess with some gratitude, was the nearest thing I've ever experienced to being within twenty yards of a detonated bomb.

There was a sharp clatter like a brief but intense shower of hailstones as a tremendous barrage of coal fragments, minute rocks and other debris rained down on our wagon-shield. That heralded a shrill rushing noise similar to a swarm of angry bees approaching at speed but, thankfully, that died away relatively quickly.

My eyelids were still rammed shut but I could feel a warm, tingly cloud of dust hugging me like a shawl; that took longer to recede, but recede it finally did.

I coughed, spluttered and spat (as, I heard, did Tom and Jonathan) before plucking up enough courage to take a peek.

The first thing I noticed was that the sky appeared considerably darker than it had been *before* that fuse was lit!

Tom was clambering back onto his feet but Jonathan was already peering over the top of the wagon. They were both filthy and covered in glistening slivers of rock and coal, and their hair had turned grey with the swirling dust; I assumed with due dread that I looked much the same.
"Um, I think the soldiers have had it," Jonathan bleated.

Tom and I both scaled the side of the wagon so that the three of us were peering over its corroded and flaking rim.

Only then did I discover for myself what sodium nitrate did, and my heart plummeted.

The tip's height had been reduced by about a half; its diameter, as you might guess, had roughly doubled.
What began the day as a stately but otherwise unsightly cone poking out from the foliage at the base of Drummau Mountain would end it as a pathetic and podgy hump, like the remains of a tower that some fool had tried to build from dry sand.

That, I fathomed, accounted for the rushing sound I'd heard; we'd actually caused a minor landslide.

"My mate Gwyn's going to kill me," Tom moaned, brushing down his clothes. "Those were his soldiers!"

"My *mother's* going to kill me," I whinged. "This is a brand new pair of trousers!"

Sifting through the truncated tip for our fallen heroes we became aware of raised voices from beyond Drummau Road.

"Shush! Who's that?" Jonathan hissed, clearly more than a tad panicked.

We each stopped excavating and listened.

Even above the breeze which was ruffling the nearby branches I could make out agitated tones and phrases like "The mine's blown up!", "Get help, there might be somebody up there!" and "I've only just put the washing out, and now it's plastered in bloody soot!"
"Shit!" Jonathan squealed. "We're in serious trouble! Come on! We've got to get out of here!"

"What about my soldiers?" I complained. "I've only found five so far!"

"Stuff your poxy soldiers! We'll have to come back for those another time! Don't forget, Tom's lost a few as well, and so have I!"

He grabbed his bottle of sodium whotsit and jogged warily down the overgrown dirt track which led back to Drummau Road. At the noise of the approaching police siren he charged back up again.

"Bollocks! Shit! Bastard!" he shrieked, rocketing past us like an Olympic sprinter and barely giving either of us a glance before vanishing into the woodland above the mine.

The siren's wail grew louder and we could also see a blue flashing light so, with the curtest exchange of terrified looks, we hastily trailed Tom to his hideaway.
Panting nervously the three of us watched the action unfold from a distance of fifty yards or so.

Perhaps 'action' was not the most suitable word to have employed there, but let me tell you what happened so that you can decide for yourself.

The police car brought two officers to the scene.

They stretched and yawned when they got out and kicked the coal chips around for a minute or two. They repeatedly said "pesky kids" and other such things, unearthed some toy soldiers and a couple of television aerials which they slung into the undergrowth, did their best to act bemused, wrote stuff in their notebooks, and then they buggered off.

That was my first and only *serious* entanglement with the Law and, in spite of my delight at not being spotted, I have to admit that I didn't enjoy it one bit.

"That was *way* too close for comfort," Jonathan mumbled.

Still quaking in our shoes, Tom and I both agreed.

Having shaken as much dust and muck off ourselves and out of our hair as we could, we sheepishly made our separate ways home.

As for me, well, I most certainly *wasn't* in the happiest frame of mind as I pouted my way back to Ormes Road. Despite swabbing away the loose dirt my clothes (including my new trousers) were still absolutely stinking which meant, as a bare minimum, a humungous telling-off from Mum.

And what if my father was home as well?

Luckily he wasn't as it turned out, but I don't dare contemplate the clobbering that surely would have come my way *had* he been.
On top of that my throat had become incredibly sore after leaving the mine; swallowing had become difficult and painful.

Then, of course, there were my absent soldiers…

Mooching along as though my feet were cast from lead I shuffled into our back garden and, soon afterward, sulked my way through the back door.

"Oh my good *God*," Mum screeched when she saw the state I was in. "Where the *hell* have you been? You've been up that bloody mine again, haven't you? How many times have I got to tell you about that place? It's not safe! Mrs Lloyd next door said that there was an explosion or something up there earlier! I just hope *you* didn't have anything to do with it, that's all! Right, get those clothes off *now*, all the way down to your shreddies! You're father's working late so don't worry about making a mess. I'll mop it up later. I'm boiling water so that your brothers can have a bath, and you can bloody well join them! Just leave your shirt and trousers by the back door. Are *those* your *new* trousers as well? Oh, for God's *sake* Chris! I'll need to shake those through before I even try to wash them! And they're ripped at the knee! Look!"

While I stripped off, and took the opportunity to conceal my five dust-caked soldiers on the cluttered window sill, she again mentioned the blast at the mine and described how, according to Mrs Lloyd, one of the coal tips had apparently collapsed and blown a load of dust down the mountainside.

Yes, didn't I know it!
So, I realised that I could either be a weak-willed coward and lie to my mother about what had taken place, *or* I could show her that I was becoming a responsible young man who would own up to his transgression, tell the truth and accept the consequences.

After not many seconds of reflection I decided it would undoubtedly be best to lie.

Improvising quickly I 'divulged' that I'd heard a big boom when making my way home from the tree swing near the mine and then grappled with the dust cloud on Drummau Road.

She said that she was glad I was home in one piece, but told me not to go up there again.

I didn't mind that because I knew that she'd forget it in a couple of days; I was basically thrilled to have perjured myself off the hook when, really, I should have had my arse kicked from there to high heaven!
There was, however, a bath to be endured and *that*, without question, would have been punishment enough in anyone's book.

This, you'll remember, was the early 1960's.

Our bungalow had no plumbed-in bathroom suite, and therefore no plumbed-in bath, of the type that's taken for granted today. It's true that many homes *did* have that refinement, but ours wouldn't be joining them for several years yet.

Instead, *we* boasted a sullied tin tub which Mum placed within sight of the living room fire, but not so close to it that we'd end up being steamed like lobsters in a pot!
She'd then struggle to even half-fill it despite making goodness-knows-how-many precarious journeys *from* the kitchen, stabilising by its handle a saucepan brimming with scorching water, and then making the same number of trips back.

On that and every other bath day my brothers and I, and wearing only our underpants, formed an orderly queue in front of the tub.

They, as always, established and enforced that order - eldest to youngest, with *no* exceptions.

Stuart, being the most senior on parade (Peter had left home by that time), dropped his Y-fronts and dived in first.

Graham was next, and he was followed by Michael.
As each washed themselves, with Mum's help now and again for those trickier-to-reach areas, the crust on the water's surface became that much more displeasing to the eye.

Also, all of that waiting around in line might well have caused a bladder or two to fill, so where better to have a thunderous pee than right there in the tub where a bit of splashing would disguise any wrongdoing?

I can quite categorically state that the economy-class toilet paper from those days would *not* have been included on Her Majesty's shopping list and, let's face facts here, young kids are not brilliant at keeping their bums rosy and fresh but, hey!

No worries!
A few discreet wipes in the old tin tub will bring everything up as shiny as new!

And what communal bath-time wouldn't be enlivened by an in-house fart-fest? Entry is free so let's hear and see if you can bubble through your finest brew!

So now, here's a short quiz for *you*, my dear reader, to make sure you've been paying close attention: Can you remember who was last in line for a scrub on that day, as he was on all bath days?

Do you need a clue? No, I thought not.

By the time it was *my* turn to brave that scum-covered, filth-infested swamp it was almost totally opaque, no hotter than lukewarm and utterly revolting.

Still, in I went.

I absolutely detested having that grimy, tepid bath water being poured down my back, especially as I knew it was laden with my brother's 'additives'.

Perhaps they did it on purpose. It wouldn't have surprised me if they had.

Mum, to her credit, would always boil up more water which made the whole ordeal marginally less tortuous but, even so, I still had to swirl the water around to find a clean(ish) scoop to rinse my face with.

She was washing my hair and the back of my neck on that noteworthy day when she touched a tender area beneath my chin.

I flinched, and she frowned.
She examined my neck and gently massaged the areas on either side.

"Does that hurt?" she whispered, evidently concerned.

I nodded.

"Have you got a sore throat?"

I nodded again.

She made me face the table lamp and open my mouth as wide as I possibly could. By applying firm pressure on my cheekbones she pivoted my head up and down and left and right so that she could see everything she needed to see.

"Hmm,' she mulled. "I think we should get you over to the clinic. Come on, out you get! And while you're drying yourself off I'll get you something for that throat of yours."

Maybe she *wanted* me out of that slough quickly. Then again, maybe she could see that *I* desperately *needed* to get out.

Either way, my feet hit the hearth rug and, in a flash, I was shrinking inside a lovely soft towel which had been warming by the fire.

That was the only thing about my bath time that I looked forward to.

She brought me a change of clothes and also a mouthful of gloopy and beetroot-coloured medicine, ready and poised for immediate swallowing upon a large tablespoon.

Once I'd dressed she gazed at the back of my mouth again. "Yes, they're a bit red and inflamed aren't they?" she pronounced as if auditioning for a part in *Dr Finlay's Casebook*. "I'm worried that it may be your tonsils."
I had no idea what 'tonsils' were but I was greatly comforted that Mum seemed to know.

Her sickly medicine had successfully fended off the rawness in my throat, but only for an hour or so.

When my father came home from work she mentioned to him that I needed to visit the doctor.

Apparently, from what she told me when I was older, he was completely indifferent to the issue with my 'tonsils' and actually said, and I quote: 'if that little bastard has to go into hospital then at least that'll be one less mouth to feed for a few days.'

Having had his irascible opinion on the matter he scoffed his evening meal without so much as another word and then set out on one of his evening ambles around Skewen.
"Who's for a bit of telly then?" Mum shouted almost as soon as he'd closed the front door.

Within moments of that call each available seat in the living room had been eagerly occupied, and the only sound to be heard came from the wood-encased television set in the corner.

If *that* had been removed you could have heard a pin drop.

After squeezing myself as inelegantly as ever between Graham's and Michael's elbows, I sat in my usual cleft on the sofa.
Mum reclined in her armchair watching, well, whatever was on at the time, but I soon became aware that she was squinting over at me.

Once or twice I returned her glances; she looked troubled.

I guessed at the time that she was meditating about my 'tonsils' and my yet-to-be-confirmed visit to the clinic, but I had a far more pressing problem to ponder.

I still hadn't worked out how I could get my soldiers back.

CHAPTER 4: DEATH AND BACK AGAIN

Sure enough, Mum was dragging me to Skewen's antiquated clinic that very next day.

I can still describe its drab waiting room nearly half a century on; bare-walled with unsightly cracks in the discoloured and blistering paintwork, a grubby pane which looked out on a withered tree and a pile of empty cardboard boxes, a single low-power light bulb dangling precariously at the end a brown cable, a well-scratched table with two dog-eared magazines and some adults and children who, like myself, were desperately seeking something interesting from that lot to gawk at.

No-one spoke; even breathing was restrained, and eye-contact was a no-no.

"Mrs Bromham and Chris?" the resident doctor's elfin assistant called from the half-open door to the surgery.

On hearing my name I gulped (and it hurt as well!), Mum rose up and sighed heavily as if to say 'at last', and in we trooped.

I wasn't keen on the doctor. He was a bit chubby, obviously getting on a bit and his breath was rancid. He wasn't gentle either and kept peering and poking around inside my mouth as if he were trying to remove the final blob of jam from a jar with a spoon that was slightly too short.

His diagnosis, when it eventually came, was that I was suffering with a severe bout of tonsillitis and, as a consequence, he immediately referred me for an operation to have the offending glands removed (a *tonsillectomy*, I understand it's called).

Everything moved along really quickly after that. Indeed, it had to, as he'd wasted no time in informing Tonna Hospital (which, I gather, is still up and running) that I'd be arriving there at ten o'clock the following morning!

To begin with though, Mum was quite melancholy and said next to nothing as she whisked me back toward Ormes Road.

She still took me for an ice cream as a treat 'for being such a good boy' and, contrary to custom, got one for herself also. She bought me a larger-than-usual carton of my favourite vanilla, perhaps inwardly conceding that *that* would have been more effective than her own mawkish medicine at dulling the horrendous pain at the top of my throat.

I can't remember if it did the trick but it certainly would have tasted a good deal better, that's for certain.

We arrived home later that afternoon to find my father perched upon the edge of his armchair with some betting slips on his lap, a few more strewn on the floor and a choking fog of cigarette smoke swirling around his head. He was also having some sort of hissy fit while bellowing at a horse race on the television.

Naively assuming that he might have had some passing interest in his family's health Mum informed him that I needed a tonsillectomy (I may as well use the word seeing as I've researched it) and that I'd be going into hospital that next morning.

I didn't hear his full response because, as always, I tended to make myself scarce whenever he was around. Still, I did catch a number of his unrefined catchphrases, like 'that little bastard!', 'I don't give a shit!', 'where's my dinner?' and 'now piss off and leave me alone!'

Once she'd closed the living room door Mum quietly muttered that *he* could piss off as well. None of my brothers were around so I asked her if I could go outside to play but, with her well-honed antennae probably relaying a fuzzy image of Drummau Mine, she replied with a vigorous 'no'.

I nagged for a little while, but it was wasted effort.

Her instincts were annoyingly astute and as reliable as ever, but I really wanted to recover those lost soldiers!

So, instead, she cooked me a bowlful of alphabet soup, probably judging *that* to have been less troublesome for me to swallow than whatever she'd prepared for my father, then started filling a carrier bag with everything that I'd be needing for my overnight stay.

You might have already guessed that I didn't sleep especially well that night. In fact, I can't imagine I slept at all so I must have been pretty shattered come the following morning.

Tonna Hospital was, and still is, two bus journeys away from Skewen.

The first journey, from the main stop on New Road to the centre of Neath, was one that I'd already done with Mum several times before. The second, from Neath bus station and up the hill to Tonna, was totally new to me.

On that first leg of the trip Mum was justifiably muted but, apparently, I didn't stop yapping all the way. Maybe that was my defence mechanism for fending off rising apprehension, but if that's really what it was then it didn't work.

By the time the second leg was underway I'd clammed up completely because my nervousness had begun to hold sway.

When we reached the hospital an accommodating receptionist, perhaps realising that Mum was agonising about what might lay ahead for me, actually chaperoned us to where we needed to be.
After following her through a warren of windowless corridors we found ourselves in the rather dismal children's ward. There we were met by the day nurse who, after she showed me to my bed, asked Mum to firstly get me into my pyjamas and then fill in a form.

Blah, blah, blah, the nurse mumbled on, struggling as she was to enlighten us with everything that was going to happen to me.

She barely warbled above a discreet drone and I'd long since given up straining to hear what she was talking about so, while Mum nodded to her every syllable with a discordant mix of politeness and trepidation, I occupied myself by gazing around my gloomy quarters from the discomfort of my lumpy mattress.

There were three other beds on that ward.

The one directly opposite held a boy who could hardly have looked more miserable, that alongside mine was empty and the remaining one, in the farthest corner of the room, had curtains drawn right around but someone on the other side was coughing and spluttering with considerable gusto.

I'd seen and heard enough; I wanted to go home.

Blah, blah, blah.

Another nurse, clearly irritated by the amount of time her colleague was spending with us, was zipping back and forth, huffing and puffing, and going to almost theatrical lengths to appear busier than she actually was.

Mum, quite naturally, in her attempts to absorb each word being patiently imparted to her, blanked those histrionics completely.

Nevertheless, while I perused the boy in the other bed who, by that time, was gawping shiftily back at me, I'd somehow managed to pick up on some fragments of what *our* nurse was saying.

For example, I knew what an injection was, but an injection in the back of the hand didn't sound particularly alluring.

I didn't understand what anaesthetic was, but I most definitely knew what four hours of deep sleep meant.

I also knew what sweets and lollies were, and I was old enough to recognise a bribe when baited with one.

Before long the nurse toddled off, presumably to be of marginally more use elsewhere, leaving Mum to her own scrambled thoughts and I to mine. She assured me that she wouldn't leave the hospital while I was having my operation, and I was so pleased about that.

What puzzled me at the time though was that she'd taken off her hat and coat and was sitting more or less serenely beside my bed.

Did that mean it was all going to be happening soon?

Yes, it most certainly did!

Half-an-hour later an older nurse started fussing around me and, after some soothing but largely superfluous words, gave me two large tablets and some tepid water with which to flush them down.

Within ten minutes I'd become quite groggy although I still have vague recollections of being laid upon a trolley bed by two jovial porters and being rolled out of the ward, around a corner, through some double doors, past an elderly woman with a walking stick, around another corner and along a narrow corridor (though perhaps not in that exact order).

I finally arrived in a cramped and olive-coloured room inhabited by three doctors and a rather stern-looking woman who was standing alongside a large tray of what looked like Mum's Sunday-best cutlery.

The room had that irrefutable 'not-nice-things-happen-in-here' kind of smell and I was growing anxious but, thanks to those pre-op drugs that I'd downed on the ward, I was also drowsy and my body felt extremely heavy. I would have gladly jumped off the trolley there and then were it not for believing I had slabs of slate across my chest and legs.

A friendly and bearded face edged into view right above my own.

It belonged to one of those doctors. I saw it only on that day and never again but, in my memory, his features have always remained as clear and as unambiguous as my own. "Hello Chris," the face said with a reassuring smile. "I'm your anaesthetist and I'm going to make sure that you have a nice deep sleep. Now, do you see that black spot on the ceiling, right there, above my head? I want you to focus on that and nothing else, okay?"

The spot was about the size of an old penny and, while I stared at it, I could sense my right arm being lifted up and my hand being gently cradled within someone else's.
Something then pierced the skin behind my knuckles, and that was followed by a cold, tingling sensation which spread up my arm and, more slowly, through my entire body.
"Keep looking at the spot, Chris," that unflappable voice kept telling me. "Keep looking at the spot. Good! That's really good! Now, can you count to ten out loud for me?"

Mum, who'd accompanied me into the room, later told me that as soon as I'd mouthed a garbled 'four' my eyelids dropped.

The briefest of moments later, or so I'd figured, they were wide open again.

I sat up with a jolt and recognised immediately that I was somehow back on the children's ward but, that time, Mum wasn't there.

The boy in the bed opposite glanced up from his *Beano* and gave me, to be fair to him, quite a sympathetic look.

"You don't need to worry," declared a female voice from behind the screen in the far corner of the ward. "You'll be alright now. You'll sleep much better tonight." With that the curtain was drawn back and the melodramatic nurse that we'd encountered earlier duly appeared carrying a kidney-shaped stainless-steel bowl overflowing with soiled tissues.

She noticed me and beamed.

"Well, hello Christopher!" she said cheerfully. "It's good to see you're awake! How are you feeling? You gave all the theatre staff a terrible fright! I'll get rid of this and then I'll come back and see if you need anything. Once the doctor has come around to see you I'll fetch you a nice cold ice cream to help soothe your throat. That'll perk you up, you poor love!"

With that, she was gone.

I then heard Mum's voice coming from the corridor outside the ward.

I tried to call out to her but my throat was still incredibly sore and the only noise that came out was a subdued whimper. I turned onto my side and sought to grab a box of tissues that had been left on top of my bedside cabinet, but only succeeded in bundling it to the floor.

Clearly alarmed the boy opposite again looked up from *The Bash Street Kids* or whatever it was he was reading just as Mum emerged at the doorway to the ward.
On seeing me awake she rushed over to my bed and threw her arms around me.

After what seemed like an age I sensed her muscles relax and her embrace soften. She collapsed into the chair at the side of my bed and, with tears streaming down her cheeks, gripped my hand more tightly than I think she'd ever done.

Looking positively exhausted and ghostly pale she shook her head with what I interpreted as disbelief.
I then had the haziest of hunches that something had gone wrong with my operation.
"Is your throat still sore, Chris?" she asked through the sobbing. "Do you want me to ask the nurse for some painkillers?"

The answer to *both* of her questions was an emphatic 'yes', but I didn't want her to leave the room again so, rashly, I shook my head.

The nurse, as she'd promised, then returned.

"It's all been quite a shock for you hasn't it, Mrs Bromham? Would you like me to get you a cup of tea? No? Okay. Chris will be fine now. I'll be sure to take good care of him. So, how is your throat now Chris? Is it painful? Yes, okay. Would you like something to help take that nasty pain away? You would? I thought you might! I'll speak to the matron about what he can have, Mrs Bromham, and then I'll be right back."

Mum nodded, said "Thank you" and, again, the nurse withdrew.

"The doctors have said that you'll have to stay in for at least two nights," Mum said to me. "You've lost a lot of blood and you're going to need plenty of rest."

She remained with me until a bell rang out in the corridor indicating the end of visiting time but, probably satisfied that I was in reasonable enough shape and in good hands, she made for home in slightly better spirits.

"I'll try and come back over tonight with a change of jimjams for you," she said as she was leaving. "Rest well my love, and maybe I'll see you later."
Still extremely weak I wanted nothing more than to sleep.

Outside the sky had become darker and gloomier, and I could make out the waning crescent moon behind a raincloud's silvery fringes; clearly, some considerable time had elapsed since I first lay down in that bed.

As far as my operation was concerned it wasn't until some years later that I discovered that the doctors had accidentally cut into the carotid artery whilst my tonsils were being removed, and that my heart had stopped.

I had, therefore, technically died.

However, I'm a philosophical man and so I can accept as readily as anyone that mistakes do happen.

After all, did they do it deliberately? Did they actually try to kill me?

No, of course they didn't, so who am I to apportion blame?
I'm just so indebted to those three doctors and the attendant nurse who must have worked so, so hard and over a number of hours to elevate my condition from 'deceased' to 'alive'.

Heaven only knows what was going through Mum's mind when *that* was transpiring but, speaking as a father who's experienced an equally traumatic episode in more recent times, she must have been beside herself with blind terror.
As I edged steadily and obliviously toward a deep but troubled sleep that early evening, having seen off the little lollipop that the nurse had brought and after reading a few pages of the *Beano* which the kid opposite had kindly let me borrow, my *own* mind began to wander.

Then, for some random reason, I thought of my father.

Why was he not here? I remember asking myself. *Why did he not come to see me?*

Ah, yes! I then realised why!

Father's prerogative! *He* had a choice!
He probably reckoned that he could either come and see me or slump into his comfy armchair, after returning home from the bookies of course, and indulge himself with the two-fifteen from Haydock Park.

Talk about a no-brainer!

Still, without me or Mum there to spoil his afternoon at least he could enjoy the race in peace.

CHAPTER 5: A STUPID DUCK IN FRONT

"You *will* be my Queen," proclaims Einar, the Viking lord, after tenderly taking Princess Morgana by the hand within the tower's tiny chapel. "I knew it the first moment I saw you. *You* knew it too. You knew it that night, on my ship."

"It's not true…" she argues.

"Yes!" Einar asserts. "It's *true!*"

"I don't love you!"

"You must love me exactly as I love you."

Longing to kiss her he edges closer but she resists, turning away her head in disgust.

"I *hate* you!" she shrieks. "It's *Erik* I love!"

With piquing revulsion Einar releases Morgana and withdraws, only to then snatch her by the wrist and pull her up the stone staircase to the tower's lofty ramparts.
"Where are you taking me?" she demands as Einar, prowling the parapet like a ravenous serpent, searches the now quiet battle scene below.

"To see Erik," he snarls, "for the last time!"

"Don't kill him!" Morgana pleads, revealing her necklace. "Look at this! It's from the pommel of the sword Requieter! It was given to Erik by his mother, Enid the Queen! Listen to me! Ragnar was his *father!*"

"Lies won't save him!" growls Einar, dismissing Morgana with an indignant flail of his hand.

"It's *true!* I *swear* it is! He is your *brother!*"

Einar, disregarding Morgana's withering appeals, spies a familiar figure walking beside one of the castle's ocean-facing watchtowers.

"ERIK!" he screams with an intensity powered by bestial fury.

Erik looks up to see Einar and Morgana, his betrothed, standing side-by-side on the ramparts high above. Believing his love to have been lost forever he charges, as valiantly as his war-drained legs will bear him, toward the chapel.

"Look at him!" Einar mocks. "How he hastens to his death! He can't *wait* to die!"

In her desperation to reach Erik Morgana attempts to flee, but Einar thwarts her.
"If I can't have your love," he roars, grabbing her coarsely by the shoulders, "I'll take your hate!"

He then hears anxious footsteps hurrying through the chapel. Moments later Erik emerges at the parapet's threshold, his sword long-since readied.
Einar, gently ushering Morgana to one side, draws his own blade.

The two warriors exchange not a word; each stares at the other with unfettered hostility.

Erik, awaiting Einar's attack, is pensive.

Einar, for his part, has rage rippling through every sinew in his muscular frame; he dearly wants to kill the man standing before him. He has *always* wanted to kill him.

And yet, for all that, it is Erik who lunges first.

Einar blocks the challenge with a confident sweep of gleaming steel. He then counter-attacks in turn, but Erik deflects the wrathful strike.

The redoubtable clamour of metal slamming against metal resounds around the castle's monstrous walls again, again and yet again as the bitter rivals in love tussle to the death.

Then, silence.

Einar stands, seemingly victorious, with his sword poised above his head.

Slumped, exhausted and gasping for air upon the rampart's slabs Erik clinches his hilt steadfastly within his hand but his trusted blade is shattered into two.

Einar's eyes widen; his breathing deepens and his grip tightens. He prepares at last to slay his adversary and dispatch him once and for all to the domain of the dead.

But, deep within the pained expression of the vanquished who expects a swift end and nothing less, he sees something.

Something intimate. Something of Ragnar, his father. Something of himself.

He pauses. His anger mellows. His guard drops.

Seizing an opportunity he couldn't have possibly divined Erik, with waning strength, thrusts his splintered foil deep into Einar's abdomen.

Anguished and defeated Einar gives out an agonised yowl before dropping his sword and crumpling backward onto the tower's crown of stone.

Erik is bewildered. "Why did he hesitate?" he asks Morgana but, deeply troubled by all that has transpired, she cannot speak.

Barely conscious and forced to confront his own mortality Einar reaches down for his weapon which lies beyond his grasp on the parapet.

A Viking departing this earth without his sword in his hand can *never* reach the mighty gates of Valhalla. Loath to see Einar, his enemy, succumb with that dishonour, Erik passes the blade.
The weakening Einar grasps it and, pointing the shard of gleaming metal wearily toward the heavens, stands for the final time.

"ODIN!" he yells before collapsing onto the rampart, dead.

Only then, and at the instant of his downfall, do a number of Einar's loyal henchmen appear and regard with reverence the body of their fallen master.

"Prepare a funeral," Erik commands them with palpable grief, "for a Viking!"

Did you enjoy that, dear reader?

My clumsy words probably didn't do it any justice whatsoever but it is, in my opinion, the most remarkable scene from *The Vikings*, one of the seminal movies of my life, and I hope you'll forgive me for wanting to share it with you.

For me, it portrays an incredible act of self-sacrifice; Einar (played by Kirk Douglas, my long-time idol) surrenders his own life because of his reluctance to kill Erik (that was Mum's favourite, Tony Curtis) who he realises, but only *after* the moment of redemption has slipped by forever, *is* his brother after all.

That illustrates perfectly the enduring bond that can still exist between two siblings where, as in the film, one is stubbornly unwilling to acknowledge the other until, regrettably, it's all too late.

That impassioned situation yields a poignant message and, unfortunately for me, a pertinent one as well.

Now, as you may recall, I had a trio of full-blood older brothers; Stuart (the eldest), Graham and Michael.

I also had a brutal father who, quite understandably, each of them was averse to provoking. Sadly, had they been as disinclined to emulate him as they were to cheesing him off then my formative years might have been a little more bearable.

As it was, they were nothing short of sheer hell.

Their gutless guideline for ensuring day-by-day survival on Ormes Road was: *If Dad does it, then that means it must be fine for us to do it as well.* So, twisting that amoral logic slightly, we have: *If Dad makes Chris' feel like he doesn't exist, then so can we.*

And they did, with enthusiasm.
Michael, for example, might stake his claim to be my "older" brother by pinning me on the floor and then spitting and blowing his snot into my open mouth.

You should realise that this was a regular occurrence, not an isolated one; Michael's persecution of me was a pastime rather than a character trait.

But I've no desire to be reproachful since the time for that has long gone.
Besides, they'd probably argue that my existence with them wasn't too bad at all and, in a sense, they'd be right. After all, for perhaps ten per cent of the time it bordered upon being sufferable and, for a small fraction of *that*, I even felt wanted.

The remainder of this chapter relates to one pivotal day of life-changing recklessness, drawn from that small fraction.

For this I'll only need to draw your attention to Stuart, and his all-consuming hobby at that time; motorbikes!

At the age of fourteen or thereabouts he'd bought the rusting carcass of a Bantam BSA with the noble but ambitious intention of rebuilding it virtually from scratch. Hardly an afternoon would go by when he wasn't in the back garden either washing it or buffing it or installing some new part that he'd acquired with his pocket money.

On fine days he'd manoeuvre it the fifty yards or so to the top of Ormes Road (and to the junction with Drummau Road), coast all the way down again and then bring it to a neat and accomplished halt outside the front of the bungalow.

You see, it didn't have an engine nor, as you'll soon discover, would it *ever* have one.

But that didn't matter to me at the time. I was just raring to have a go, and what frivolous six-year-old boy wouldn't?

So, on one of those singular occasions when Stuart seemed to be in a passably-agreeable mood I asked, without harbouring any real prospect of success, if *I* could ride his bike.

I was flabbergasted when he said yes!

So, and after throwing on my coat and shoes probably faster than I'd *ever* done, I was all ready to rock and roll!

My stomach was doing somersaults as we pushed the Bantam up the hill, not with worry but expectation. And, yes, we *did* actually chat like brothers are meant to do so, for *me* at least, it was a rare and precious moment indeed.

On reaching the top, and after turning around so that we faced down Ormes Road, Stuart held the bike steady so I could clamber on board safely.

I had to lean forward to reach the handlebars and my legs, which were literally shaking through impatience, were left to dangle as they weren't long enough to reach the foot pegs.

With his hands still squeezing the brakes Stuart vaulted on behind me. "Hold on tight then," he shouted. "Here we go!"

My heart was pounding nineteen to the dozen as the bike started to trundle forward then gradually pick up speed as Stuart relaxed his grasp on the brakes. The faster we went the further I was pushed back until I found myself being pressed against his chest.

Before long though we were back outside our front door, and it was all over.

Though short that ride was absolutely indescribable so, therefore, I shan't try.

What I *will* say is that I was gutted when, after no more than ten seconds of what was undoubtedly the greatest adrenalin rush of my life to that point, Stuart eased on the anchors to bring the bike, as he always did, to a measured stop in front of the bungalow.

Those of you who can remember tottering from the train after their first bowel-churning jaunt on a roller-coaster might best appreciate how I looked and felt when my woozy feet finally hit dry land.

"Thanks S…Stu," I spluttered with my eyes bulging and wispy hair totally windswept.

"No problem," he replied.
I waited briefly, hoping that he might take up my invitation to say 'any time', but he didn't.

Nevertheless, I was itching to do it all over again.

As the days passed I simply couldn't get that maiden ride on a motorbike out of my mind. I yearned to ask Stuart to take me out once more but, even at that age, I'd learned to be thankful for a one-off when it came my way.

Then, about a week later, my friend Robert and I were messing around in the back garden and admiring all the work that Stuart had done on the bike when a calamitous thought took root in my head.

Why wait for Stuart to offer? I pondered. *Why not simply take the bike out ourselves? He's gone out for the day so we'd have plenty of time to have some fun and also to return the bike to its place without him knowing that it had ever been moved!*

A good plan, huh? Hmm…

Anyway, Robert was all in favour of taking it for a spin (his zeal might have been curbed somewhat if Stuart had been *his* brother rather than mine) so, after a quick check around the bungalow to make sure Mum wasn't watching we lugged the bike round to the front and, subsequently, to the top of the Ormes Road.

Now, at that most elevated point there was an entrance to a narrow footpath which ran parallel to Drummau Road and led, after a fashion, back down to my home. It was also very uneven with gravel, hollows and large stones, and it also had a sharp drop into the gardens below.

Once we'd hauled the bike around so that it aimed down Ormes Road I glanced ahead at the boringly-smooth tree-lined tarmac and thought: *Nah! Seen it and done it! Let's give this path thing a whirl!*

I was eager to share my brainlessness with Robert who, on hearing my idea, had the look of a parachutist who's realised that he's left his backpack on the plane.

Still, he allowed himself to be sucked into my lunacy and so, between us, we carefully directed the bike at the path instead.

I mounted the seat as best I could and told Robert to give the bike a push then jump on once it had picked up some speed.

Bobsledders will, of course, be quite at home with the basic technique.

We'd travelled no more than a few yards along the path when the rear tyre started to lose traction while the front wheel was thrown into the air every time we hit a large stone.

"Slow down!" was Robert's frantically recurring cry as the bike started bouncing its way down the heavily-rutted track, it's inertia increasing all the while.

Naturally, I would've done *exactly* that if I'd been able to reach around the handlebars. I explained this to him. He wasn't pleased.

"You're a stupid duck in front!" he shouted. At least, that's what it sounded like given the limitations of his juddering voice box.

Our front tyre then hit a jagged rock and was thrown, along with the rest of the Bantam, completely clear of the path. We both screamed as the three of us, that's myself, Robert *and* the motorbike, were launched into the air.

I braced myself for the sickening *thud* but the impact, when it eventually came what seemed like a lifetime later, wasn't that bad. We dropped onto soft earth but then bumped and rolled our way to the bottom of the incline where a well-known patch of brambles and nettles finally brought us uncomfortably to rest.

I laid there for a moment completely dazed and entangled but then things got *really* painful as I felt the stingies and thorns chafing my bare skin.

"Ooh! Aargh!" Robert and I both groaned through gritted teeth as we gingerly tore ourselves clear.

We gazed at each other, both scuffed and scratched as we were from earhole to arsehole, both with blood leaking from innumerable cuts and grazes and both looking like a couple of hapless extras from a zombie B-movie.

"Where's the bike?" I panted while brushing myself down. Robert pointed up the incline to where the Bantam was resting on its side about halfway up. Its front wheel was still spinning.

I groaned with despair and, after Robert had called me that duck-thing again, hid my face within my filthy hands.

Once I'd gathered sufficient courage to look properly I could tell that, like us, the bike was plastered in mud and leaves and other stuff and, even from twenty-or-so feet away, I could see a cavernous dent in the petrol tank.

I could also see Stuart giving me a battering.

That was all in my head of course, but I feared it would become a stark reality soon enough.

I have to say that, with all due credit, I couldn't have shifted the bike back to the bungalow without Robert's help and, even now, I'm surprised he stuck around for as long as he did.

Still, that's friendship for you I guess.

Leaning the bike against the front wall we gauged the true extent of the devastation then, with Robert keeping guard over the ruin, I ran inside to get Mum's help.

"What the *hell* has happened to you!" she screeched above Acker Bilk with a flannel in one hand and her Dettol bottle in the other.

I burst into tears and blubbed: "I've crashed Stuart's motorbike!"

Mum pushed past me to see for herself and, when she saw what we'd done, gasped no more loudly than if Tony Curtis himself was standing there instead.

At that instant Robert took off and ran as fast as he could, abandoning me to face the music alone.

Still, that's friendship for you I guess.

That left me and Mum to push the bike around to the back so that at least it could be returned to where Stuart would expect it to be.

She cleaned up my wounds with some Dettol (*that* stung more than those bloody brambles, I can tell you!) and then it was a case of counting down the minutes to my brother's return and all the horrors that *that* would entail.

About an hour later, from the sanctuary-cum-hiding-place that was my bedroom I could make out the disquieting sounds of the back garden gate creaking open then swinging shut, followed by that of manly footsteps stomping down the path. Those footsteps paused somewhere near the two-wheeled-wreck and, about ten seconds later, the kitchen door was flung open.

"What the f--- has happened to my bike?" Stuart ranted as he thundered inside. "Has some little prick tried to steal it or something?"
I was utterly dumbstruck! He had no idea it was me!

I could just about hear Mum's rueful reply.

"Yes son. I'm *really* sorry. Somebody must have taken it when I went out shopping this morning. Chris and Robert spotted it dumped in the nettles by the path. The poor little buggers cut themselves to ribbons trying to get it out of there."

"If I find the bastards that took it I'll wallop ten sacks of shit out of them!"

I heard the back door open again and I assumed (correctly, as it so happens) that Stuart had blustered back outside to assess what, if anything, could be salvaged.

Shortly afterwards Mum gently cracked my bedroom door ajar.

"You won't ever do anything like that again, will you?" she whispered with the faintest hint of a warm, motherly smile.

I shook my head no less heartily than if she'd offered me raw tripe for supper.

"I love you Mum," I murmured.

"I love you too, boy. Now, do yourself a big favour and stay out of sight for a bit. He's absolutely tamping out there so don't give him a daft reason to start on you."

Yes, damn good advice that, and fervently heeded too!

It had been a truly awful day for me (and for Stuart of course) but, somewhere in the midst of my relieved young mind, a career-defining seed had been sown.
I would never again ride Stuart's motorbike, and neither would he for that matter, but I'd had my first taste of stunts and the excitement that goes with them and I was hungry for more!

Perhaps the closest I came during my early years to again experiencing the exhilaration of my blast on the Bantam was on something called a 'gambo'.

Now, for the unversed among you, a gambo was merely a long and otherwise-stationary plank of wood which had been cunningly adapted for movement.

All of the Ormes Road boys, including myself and all of my brothers, would gleefully contribute to that daring makeover.

Getting hold of a suitable plank was easy because Drummau Mine was strewn with them. Wheels of old prams which had been fly-tipped here and there on the mountain were perfect for the 'movement' aspect since their axles could be sawn through the middle, if necessary, to fit the width of the wood.

The steering mechanism was more convoluted but, from what I remember, that involved a hole being burned through the top and near the head of the plank and a metal rod which basically acted as a steering column being pushed through and held in place but still free to rotate.

A length of rope for steering was tied at each end of the front axle, just inside the pram wheels, and that was pretty much that!

The gambo would normally accommodate eighteen or so but, even then, we always had some latecomers who had to wait for a seat on the next ride.

Starting on the lowest slopes of Drummau Mountain we would joyously tear straight across Drummau Road and down one of the treacherously-steep and furrowed paths (yes, including the one that Robert and I came a cropper on!) until we reached the bottom and the driver shouted 'Brake!', at which point the soles of thirty-six shoes would be teased almost in unison onto the ground, thereby bringing the rickety contraption slowly to rest.

Not even that, though, could beat the sensation of riding Stuart's Bantam.

For my fiftieth birthday I made a pilgrimage to Fort-la-Latte in Brittany where, in 1957, the climax of *The Vikings* was filmed.

Yes, I walked along the ramparts where that final clash between Einar and Erik took place.

Yes, I stood at the spot where Einar finally fell and, yes, I thought back to my childhood and to the time when I first watched the movie at the age of five on what was, by modern standards, a pitiful little black-and-white telly.

Life with my father and brothers was usually difficult and often distressing but, as I mentioned earlier, I'm not seeking to dwell upon that sibling hatred because *out of those times*, and *most notably* the decisive adventure with the Bantam BSA, came the *dream*.

The dream of what I wanted to do with the rest of my life.

The dream of what I aspired to be.

The dream of finally gaining the respect of my brothers for the person I was and for all I would eventually achieve.

Well, I suppose two out of three isn't bad.

CHAPTER 6: NEVER A TYRESOME MOMENT

I despised being at school so much that I've sought to defer writing about it and for that I must apologise.

I shouldn't seek to evade my responsibilities any longer though, so here goes.

I remember mentioning in an earlier chapter that I embarked on my first grim years of so-called 'formal learning' at Skewen's Coedffranc Infant's School.

When I reached eight I was shifted across the yard to the Junior block and remained incarcerated there, with parole on weeknights and weekends, until I turned eleven.

Right from the outset I didn't believe I truly fitted in at Coedffranc, or that by traipsing there each day in the shadow of my own personal raincloud I would learn anything that I really wanted to know.

I had absolutely no interest whatsoever in the animals which lived on the foothills of the Andes, or in how a coal mine functioned, or in what the capital of Mongolia was. Motorbikes, Vikings and Kirk Douglas weren't on the menu so, through utter boredom, I simply switched my brain into stand-by mode instead.

Now, I know that probably sounds like a fairly shabby effort on my part but there's something quite significant I need to mention here.

I suffer terribly with dyslexia.

That became as problematic for me as it would have been for any similarly-afflicted child but, of course, there wasn't really any such creature as 'dyslexia' to tarnish our enlightened education establishment of the 1960's.

So, there was no tolerance and, consequently, no help available either.

In those days dyslexics were all-too-conveniently pigeon-holed as 'dense' or 'beyond hope'.

Unfortunately it was on the basis of such ignorant and irresponsible judgements that young lives like mine were so nearly destroyed.

From an early age we were made harrowingly aware of the importance of maths and English, so if we dared crash with those then all else tended to collapse like a house of cards as well.

And, boy!

Didn't I just struggle with maths and English!
The other Coedffranc kids would have a bloody good laugh at me if I was given a sum to do on the blackboard and I wrote my numbers backwards, or if I was forced to stutter my way through a page of *Janet and John* with the threat of a slipper being rapped across my arse if I didn't get it word perfect.

As a result, my confidence to cope with anything the school threw at me (which included the odd board duster) was obliterated before I had any real prospect of developing it.

So, while the non-dyslexic 'brighter' kids were doing their three *R*'s (reading, 'riting and 'rithmetic), I had to make do with the three *C*'s (corner, crayons and called thick).

That pretty much sums up the state of affairs for me during my time in Coedffranc.

Please don't misunderstand me here, because I'm not having a swipe at what is actually a very good school or any of the teachers that were forced to put up with me while I was there.

It's simply that, like many others around the country, I suffered badly with a condition that wasn't fully comprehended or legislated for and, as a consequence, I was as overlooked in Coedffranc as I would have been anywhere else.

Such was the world of the time, but Coedffranc Infant's School is still going strong and long may that be the case.

Despite absconding after the incident with Stuart's Bantam, which in all honesty I can't reasonably condemn him for, Robert remained one of my most dependable school-friends and I don't suppose I'd have retained my sanity without him.

He didn't provide 'support' as such because children of our age didn't really appreciate, at least not in the formal sense, what that was.

He was just 'there'.

No matter how angry or frustrated or upset I became with my day-to-day difficulties in Coedffranc, he was always 'there'.

We even used to stargaze together!

My back garden was so steep and so close to our bungalow that, on clear nights, we were able to jump from about ten feet up and straight onto the flat kitchen roof, where we'd spend many a peaceful hour staring at the moon and Venus and the tapestry of constellations as they drifted imperially overhead.

We'd chat about anything and everything, from spacemen to motorbikes (over which we'd have a chuckle or two!), and from the colour of little Janice's knickers that day to…yes! Of course! November the fifth!

Sadly, Bonfire Night is yet another of those unique community-driven spectacles which, in my opinion, has had much of its sparkle (no pun intended) eroded away over the years.

After all, give your archetypal modern kid a choice between standing around in the freezing cold watching a pile of old furniture burn while trying to cook a potato on the end of a stick, or spending five hours at their games console stealing virtual cars with their online mate from some-country-or-other and they'll be running inside and plugging themselves into the system before they can laugh in your face!
Back in the good old days Bonfire Night was a healthily competitive and socially unifying event.

The local lads would organise themselves into foraging teams with the goal of constructing a pyre grand enough to make everybody scoff with derision at all others.

Robert and I were in the same team, as were the other boys from not only Ormes Road but the next two roads as well.

As you've doubtless anticipated our main hunting ground was the mountain, and we always assembled our bonfire in the field next to Drummau Mine.

Now, I need to digress ever so slightly here and record that, some months before and with a pretext only *he* could explain, my brother Graham bought a mongrel bitch from the pet shop.

With surprisingly no objections from my father, 'Tess' (as Graham christened her) was allowed to stay.

Predictably enough, Graham soon lost interest in his new pet and, as a result, it was left to Mum to shoulder the burden of looking after her.

Nevertheless, for some strange reason that dog would follow me around wherever I ventured, including on one unforgettable rummage for our team's bonfire when Robert and I were scaling a largish tree in search of readily-gatherable twigs.

We'd climbed up to one of the sturdier branches and had decided to sit there for a short while to rest and catch our breath.

Tess was circling the girth below us and, with an occasional high-pitched yap, reminding us she was there.

Without warning those yaps had turned into low nasty growls so, naturally curious, we peered down to find out what had spooked her.

It was Robert who noticed a cat, about six yards from Tess, prowling around in the scrub and most likely on the look-out for food.

It gave Tess a cursory glance as it passed by but, probably judging her proximity as sufficiently large to make a brusque getaway if one was needed, it continued scavenging.

Tess then became aggressive.

Skulking toward the feline intruder she started barking uncontrollably but the wilful cat, instead of fleeing, held its ground.

It raised its hackles, hissed menacingly at Tess and began creeping in her direction.

I nervously watched the stand-off from our dicey vantage point some twenty feet above then, fearing our dog would have her eyes scratched out by a cat that, quite evidently, was not one to be messed with, called out "Tess! Leave!"
But it was too late; Tess had already flung herself at the seriously-pissed-off cat.

I then heard her wail, sickeningly.

She's been hurt! I shuddered.

In the commotion I freaked out and lost my grip on the branch.

I screamed as I fell.

The trunk was quite irregular so I knew that, provided I acted quickly, I had some marginal but precious leeway to check my plunge.

As it turned out, that was just as well.
Directly beneath me was a weather-worn stump with splintered fragments like wooden stakes sticking upwards and out.

I realised I was in huge trouble and so tried as best as I possibly could to alter the course of my fall and possibly even slow myself down.

But, strain as I might, it was to no avail.

Instinctively I knew that some part of my body was going to be skewered.

So, resigning myself to my fate, I forced my eyes shut and awaited the inevitable.

I heard the sound of cloth being torn before I clattered onto the ground, face up.

There was a peculiar silence; I could hear no rustling of leaves, no background noise from the village and no animals fighting.

I couldn't even pick out the rhythms of my own breathing, but at least I could sense no pain.

My vision was blurry although I could make out Robert scrabbling back down the tree.

It took a good number of seconds for my sound and vision to start sorting itself out so I can only assume he was calling out to me as he returned hurriedly to earth.

"Chris! Chris!" I suspect he was yelling as Tess came over to lick my face. "Talk to me! Are you okay?"

"Yeah, I'm okay," I replied groggily.

Only then did I start experiencing a throb in my right leg so, gingerly, I propped myself up on my elbows to see what damage I'd done.

My trousers were ripped above the knee and some blood had collected around the tattered fabric.

"You were lucky there," Robert gasped, helping me up and onto my feet.

"Stupid bloody mutt!" I roared at Tess who was sitting at my side, panting proudly and clearly seeking to incite some approval for seeing off the cat.

With my fervour for twig-collecting completely trashed for the day I limped my way down Drummau Road and, with Tess in tow, to the top of our back garden.

After Robert and I exchanged low-key goodbyes I hobbled down the steps and into the bungalow where Mum and my father were watching television in the living room.

He was about to gorge himself on his favourite snack; a doorstep-sized chunk of cheese wrapped in a thick slice of over-buttered brown bread. Typically he would dip that into his mug of tea, wait for it to soften then ram as much of the soggy mass into his gaping mouth as he could, making a racket like a pig sucking custard through a hosepipe in the process.

"Oh *no* Chris, what on *earth* have you done *this* time?" Mum demanded, waving despairingly at my leg.

"Nothing," I said, quite unconcerned. "Had a bit of a fall, that's all."

Clearly she was not convinced by my frivolous explanation, and scowled. "Drop your trousers for me would you, love?"
Grudgingly, and with some embarrassment, I did as she asked.

My father was about to shove some of his disgusting cheesy mush into his mouth when, on glancing over, he almost regurgitated whatever he'd already swallowed.

He tossed what remained in his hand into the fire and dashed from the room, probably to puke into the kitchen sink.

Mum had already turned as white as a sheet and, when I dared to look down, I understood why.

Running from the middle of my thigh and down to my knee was a yawning gash, about six inches long, through which my thigh bone was clearly visible.

I could even see my sinews twitching.

Yet, for some weird reason, there wasn't a huge amount of blood.

Mum, who was completely hysterical by then, ordered me to lie on the sofa before garbling some frenzied instructions to one of my brothers (I'm thinking that it might have been Graham) to sprint down into Skewen and call for an ambulance.

I'd begun to sweat profusely as the shock of what I'd done to myself finally started to kick in but, remarkably, I still wasn't suffering anywhere near the level of discomfort that my lesion probably warranted.

Still, I have to say that, when they arrived minutes later, the ambulance crew were truly excellent.

They quickly disinfected and dressed my wound where I lay, gave me a jab to dull the pain which certainly *was* intensifying by that stage and then, with an extremely anxious mother for company, I was whisked off to hospital.

Thankfully, and especially after my experience at Tonna three years previously, I was in and out within twenty-four hours.

After a couple of weeks of hobbling around the bungalow on my crutches, and not being of much use to anybody (so, nothing new there!), my bandages and stitches were removed and, apart from a prominent scar on my leg which I still have, the doctors declared me to be as good as new.

Not a moment too soon either, because the fifth of November was fast approaching and I wanted to see how our bonfire was coming along.

I have to admit that it did look in decent shape from what I can remember, but there were concerned rumblings within our camp that ours, at that moment at any rate, was *not* Skewen's crowning glory.

However, we were soon offered a golden opportunity to claim that accolade.

As a gesture of goodwill a local tyre depot gave us, along with the village's other bonfire-building squads, a choice of one tyre from their surplus or damaged stock.

Modern Health and Safety practitioners and Fire Prevention Officers will, quite naturally, be having kittens on reading that.

Anyway, some of the gangs picked bog-standard car tyres, others were a little more ambitious and plumped for one which had seen service on an old lorry or maybe even a bus.

So, what did Bromham and his crazy lot do?

We regretted our choice almost as soon as we'd made it, that's what *we* did!
You see, there used to be a firm in the United States (Illinois, to be precise) called the International Harvester Company, specialising in farm machinery such as tractors.

These tractors required tyres.

Immense tyres in fact, and probably not too dissimilar from the one that me and the rest of the idiots in my team drooled over when we spotted it leaning against a wall in the depot.

So, having made our absurd selection and been sent on our way with a furtive snigger from the manager of the place, we began the ridiculous task of persuading that monstrosity up the hill.

The thing measured approximately six feet in diameter (that is, taller than any of us as it lumbered along), two feet in width and it weighed, well, if I said half a ton then that would probably be an exaggeration, but you get my drift.

Our plan was to push it up Drummau Road then straight into our field where, hopefully, the boys assigned to sentry duty were still at their posts and watching over our hard-earned hoard like hawks.

Our dilemma, as we heaved the tyre ever-higher and ever-closer to its final resting place, was that Gravity seemed to have hatched a plan as well.

Lo and behold! Just as we attempted to negotiate the steep turn on to the field the tyre began to wobble and, ultimately, it broke free from our feeble control.
And off it went.
We could only gaze with helpless horror as it rolled back down the hill, gathering momentum and swaying erratically from side to side all the while.

A number of the older boys tried to pursue it.

I couldn't really understand why because it was blatantly obvious to me and everyone else that, despite our gallant efforts, Gravity had won and was apparently keen to have a right good gloat at our expense because the tyre was flattening whatever lay in its path and heading straight for the houses below.

Now, picture yourself in the following scene, if you will.

It's a lovely, quiet Saturday afternoon and you've just enjoyed a delicious lunch in your brand new and expensive extension.

You've cleared away your plate and cutlery, put the tomato ketchup back in the cupboard and retired to your living room to enjoy *David Frost at the Phonograph* on the wireless.

Unexpectedly, and above the great man's dulcet tones, you hear a strange rumbling in the distance.

With your brow befittingly furrowed you lower the volume on the radio and listen, as intently as is possible, in all directions.
Ah yes! It seems that the sound is coming from the back garden, maybe even from Drummau Road itself!

You decide to investigate, but wait a moment!

The noise has become less of a continuous 'rumble', and now appears to be more of an intermittent 'bounce'.

Not only that, it's unquestionably getting louder which probably means it's getting nearer as well.

Let's think now, where did you put your spectacles...
CRRRASH!

You've absolutely no idea what's happened but you somehow know that it's absolutely catastrophic.

Your best guess at that moment is that something has dropped on top of your house after falling from a flight inbound from America.

Amazingly, when you open the door from your living room and are faced with a heap of rubble that used to be your extension, glorious daylight where there was once a ceiling and a free but unwelcome souvenir from the International Harvester Company of Illinois, you realise that you're not a million miles from the truth.

As for us, well, we could only gawp with a collective and petrified hush as the tyre bounded its way down that guy's garden and annihilated the rear of his home.

His neighbours rushed out to see what had happened, and a number of them were gesticulating angrily towards our field but, being so brave and fearless, we'd long since taken cover in the long grass.

Had they clocked us earlier maybe, rolling the tyre up the hill?

Yes, quite possibly they had.

We weren't going to stick around to find out though because when the police arrived at what was formerly that man's house we unanimously agreed that it was time to scarper.

We panicked for days afterwards, wondering whether we'd get the dreaded knock on the door from the local bobby but, by some miracle, none of us did.

Our long-awaited night around the blazing bonfire was, as you might appreciate, somewhat muted.

Ours wasn't the best in Skewen that year after all but, considering everything that had happened, we inwardly conceded that we could live with that.

So, I now feel the need to issue two apologies.

The first, if indeed he is still with us, has to go to the desperately unlucky bloke whose house we half-demolished on that bizarre afternoon.

The second goes to yourself, dear reader, for enduring an account which had absolutely nothing to do with school rather than perusing one, as I'd originally promised, relating to my terrible time within it.

My quandary, though, is that there's little more that can be added to what I've already said about Coedffranc.

I absolutely hated it and couldn't wait to flee from there each day at three o'clock.

Yes, I know I've said that my life in school and also in our bungalow perhaps wasn't the most pleasurable but I'm proud to have played my part in fashioning the many acres surrounding Ormes Road into the most magnificent and magical place with its tree dens, swings, hideouts and everything else that we'd made for ourselves.

That was my world.

That, apart from a motorbike's saddle, was the only place I wanted to be.

Would that be classed as a misspent childhood?

Possibly, but at least I'm able to say that I *had* a childhood and, in any case, most of my significant learning was done when I moved into adulthood.
For example, I now know from watching Michael Palin's programmes that the foothills of the Andes are packed with llamas.

I know how a coal mine functions because, unfortunately, I ended up working in one.

I'm still not sure what the capital of Mongolia is, though.

I know that Mongolia is in the Sahara desert somewhere, but sadly that's as far as my geography knowledge will stretch.

Don't worry, I'm only kidding…

CHAPTER 7: THE PENIS AND THE PLIERS

The first thing I learned on moving to Rhydhir (pronounced 'Rid-ear') Secondary Modern School in 1968 was the meaning of the well-oiled phrase 'Same shit, different bucket'.

It was such a soul-crushing disappointment for me because, after the unmitigated disaster that was Coedffranc, I'd kind of geared myself up for a nice fresh start. At the time I simply refused to accept that I could loathe my new school any more than the old one.

How naive I was.

From my very first day in Rhydhir all of my misplaced optimism began to crumble horribly into dust. There were bigger classes with all new people keen to take the piss, harder maths (well, for *me* anyway), tougher books with much smaller print to try and read, lukewarm slop at lunchtime and horrendous teachers who were far more concerned with drilling us for their prized exams than they were with actually giving us something interesting to do and learn.

I even had French and Welsh to get to grips with when I was still fighting a losing battle with English!
It was a catastrophe just longing to happen, and I had five endless years of it to somehow get through.

I did, however, enjoy the art lessons and, without wanting to sound overly arrogant here, I considered myself to be moderately good at it. My art teacher was an exceptionally tolerant and mellow lady by the name of Mrs Evans, and she would always offer me more patience, understanding and encouragement in one of her lessons than the rest of her colleagues could collectively muster in a week.

"Chris," I remember her saying on one occasion after I'd drawn something-or-other particularly well, "*you* can be whatever you want to be in life. All it takes is a little self-belief and, if *you* have that belief in yourself, then *others* will believe in you as well."

Wonderfully uplifting words which I vividly remember to this day, and which have served as a poignant inspiration for all that I've gone on to achieve. At the time, however, armed as I was with smouldering anger, an immovable sense of injustice and the brash impetuosity of pubescent youth, I knew *exactly* what I wanted to be.

I wanted to be a truant, and the best one in the school what's more!

There were no timetabled classes for that unfortunately so, in the absence of any formal training, I had to pace myself a little at the outset, just until I found my feet. I then started to

refine my clandestine skills, missing certain lessons either by hiding out in the toilets or by secreting myself around the large, tree-lined sports fields next to the school.
As my proficiency and cockiness grew I'd move on to skipping back-to-back lessons, thereby allowing plenty of time to take the short walk into Neath and have a wander around the market or maybe even the guitar shop.

Not surprisingly it didn't take long for the local 'Mitch-Man' to start sniffing around.

Yes, sometimes I'd have my collar felt and get driven back to Rhydhir with a caution and a slip of paper, signed by him, which he was actually gullible enough to believe that I would hand to the school's clerk. Nevertheless, the Mitch-Man's early victories didn't deter me from bunking off and it wasn't long before I'd created a mental dossier of the clown's movements and a reliable working knowledge of his preferred stake-outs.

Now, to all like-minded children who are reading this and possibly even cheering me on, please be advised that, no matter how much of a tosser you think he is, the Mitch-Man *always* triumphs in the end.

In *my* case Mum was duly informed of my exploits and, because they didn't stop promptly enough for the liking of the education authority, she was hauled up before a court and fined. She was also told in no uncertain terms that if my truancy didn't cease with immediate effect then I would be removed from the family home and sent to a detention centre.

So, as a last-ditch precaution, and in spite of me constantly moaning about how much I despised the place, she would escort me to Rhydhir's main entrance each morning where I'd be surrendered to one of the suits in charge there.
I was naturally mortified at being treated like a naughty four-year-old and I had the mickey taken out of me no end but, believe me, I got the message quickly enough.

You probably won't need me to tell you that when my father heard about my antics he went absolutely wild.

Honestly, I must have wanted my head examined for being so dull! After all, if there was one thing we'd *all* discovered through living with him during those years, then it was *not* to present him with a cheap reason to have a nightmare in your face!

That, stupidly, was what I'd gone and done.

He roughed up Mum a bit as well for not informing him earlier about what I was doing, so I had *that* chomping away at my conscience as well. They didn't talk to each other for days afterward but, when the touchy stalemate *was* eventually broken, it was through that rarest of all events; my father needed Mum's help.

And, wow! *Didn't* he just need it!

Bear with me while I set up some of the background for you here.

I've already revealed that we had an outdoor toilet, situated between the bungalow and the first inclines of the back yard. Typically, such structures were constructed with bricks and cement (I'm sure that I've read that somewhere), with the nature of its roof left to the discretion of the architect.

Our toilet, though, was not typical.

Despite the obvious benefits that it brought to many of buildings of the time, including the rather basic requirement of ensuring they remained more-or-less upright, my father, who raised our lavvy with his own hands, was evidently not a huge fan of cement.

The walls of his creation, for example, were erected with bricks only. There was not the slightest trace of any mortar.

His bewildering theory was that each brick would be held solidly in place by the weight of the ones above it, and that the whole edifice would be fortified by a roof created from a rusty tin sheet nailed to a makeshift wooden frame and placed (as opposed to 'safely secured') on top of the bricks.

When you were sitting in there it could be a bit draughty between the old cheeks, to say the least!

Anyway, I was happily messing about in the garden that day with my new Action Man when my father, clearly in need of only a pee and nothing more substantial because he wasn't carrying his newspaper, appeared from the kitchen. He slipped into the loo, concealed himself with the wooden 'door', fumbled about for a few seconds then, as he always did, started humming *Calon Lân* to mask the noise of his urinating.

Those who are familiar with the song will know that there are some reasonably high notes tucked in there, but I doubt that any tenor has ever hit the levels that my father succeeded in reaching just after he tugged on the flush.

Both myself and Mum, who was pottering about near the kitchen door at the time, stared at the toilet with genuine alarm as the tranquil melodies of *Calon Lân* were rapidly transformed into agonised and blood-curdling squeals.

By that time my father had already kicked the door away and was hopping around within like a flea in a matchbox.

The inevitable then happened; the whole lot collapsed on top of him.

There was an uneasy quiet as he emerged from the rubble and rolled onto his back, screaming and swearing loudly.

"What the *fuck* are *you* staring at?" he roared at poor Mum, who had come out from the kitchen on hearing all the commotion and probably just wanted to be of some help.

It was a daft question, though, because she was staring at the same thing that I was.

There was my father, covered in dust, lying prostrate upon the mound that mere minutes ago had been the family privy, sporting numerous cuts and grazes to his head and hands, and with his penis poking out from his trousers like a worm grabbing a few gulps of fresh air first thing in the morning.
It was the just the sort of demeaning spectacle that cameras were invented for.

From what he was willing to impart to us later it seems that, on trying to 'get the snake back in the sack' after his pee, he'd jammed his foreskin in his zip. Sensibly enough he'd attempted to rescue it but had only prospered in getting it snarled up even more. In his blind panic he booted down the toilet door, tumbled backwards against the interior wall and, well, you now know the rest.

"Help me Vi,' he was pleading, with tears rolling down his cheeks. "I think I've cut my dick off!"

By that time all of my brothers had come out of the house, swelling the size of his captivated audience to five.

Our sniggering next door neighbour, Mr Lloyd, made it six.

"Fuck off!" my father yelled when he spotted Mr Lloyd sneering over the top of the wall. "I'm not a bastard cabaret!"

"Maybe not a cabaret," Mr Lloyd sniggered, "but I've always said that you're *something* beginning with 'c'…"

"You wanker! I promise I'll give you good bloody shaking one day and put you away!"

"Who are you talking to, Bromham? Me or your cock?"
My father growled furiously and Mr Lloyd, perhaps prudently, vanished behind the wall with a self-satisfied chuckle.

"Hey, Brenda!" we heard him chortle just before he shut his kitchen door. "You'll never guess what that silly twat next door has gone and done…"

In the meantime Stuart had galloped back into the house and had returned with, judging by his look of infantile achievement at any rate, the solution to my father's embarrassing plight.

My father, glaring with rapidly-escalating horror at the gleaming pair of pliers that Stuart was waving jubilantly in his hand, clearly thought otherwise.
"What the *hell* do you think you're doing?" he shrieked at Stuart.

"I'm just going to yank it free, Dad!"

"Like *shit* you are! You're not yanking anything! Look! It's only holding on by a little bit of skin!"

In his defence, my father had a point. His manhood was very badly distended and the skin was almost blue in hue, but worryingly it appeared that there were also quite a few streaks of fresh blood emanating from the zip area.

And yet, Stuart was adamant; he was determined to be the hero of the hour.

 "Hold him!" he chirped. "I'm going in!"

My father tried desperately to turn his body away but Graham and Michael were too quick for him and pinned him down by his wrists. In a flash Stuart had gripped the zip's slider and, without giving my father any prior warning at all, jerked the pliers as hard as he possibly could.

The noise which followed is almost impossible to describe in words but, to nudge you in the right direction at least, I'll just say this: Imagine Tarzan's call as he's swinging through the forest.

Then turn the volume right up and put the surround-sound on as well.

That's probably the best that I can do for you, I'm afraid.

Mum nipped back into the kitchen to fetch her largest clean towel so, while he lay on top of the rubble recovering from his narrow brush with total emasculation, he could at least do so with some dignity.

One by one my brothers wandered back into the house once the comedy had ended, probably so they could have a damn good cackle out of my father's earshot.

I can't criticise them for that, because I did exactly the same.
He himself tottered back inside about ten minutes later, supported by Mum with every step and shuffling along none too assuredly, it must be said. She helped him to slump into his armchair before judiciously removing his ruined trousers.

I remained in the living room, as did Stuart.

He and Mum then went to work immediately on cleaning and dressing my father's wounds and I was sent back and forth the kitchen to fetch everything that they needed whilst trying hard to not laugh out loud in the meantime.
"I think you should go to hospital for a doctor to take a look at this," Mum suggested.

"No chance!" my father snapped. "I'm not going to no bloody hospital! I'm not turning myself into a laughing stock!"

Mum persisted. "But I think you need stitches. It's a very bad cut."

"Listen to me, woman! If I turn up in hospital with… with *this*, then it'll be all over the bloody Evening Post by the weekend! I won't be able to show my face down that bloody mine ever again! Don't know why I'm worried though because that arsehole next door will spread it round the Labour Club when he's there playing his stupid fucking dominoes anyway! Look, just get it sorted out then bloody well leave me alone!"

I really thought that Mum deserved some thanks for offering to tidy up my father's nether region, but that was never really his way.
Still, things *were* at least a little easier around the bungalow for the next couple of weeks.

My father was much quieter and far less confrontational than he had been for many a long year.

He resorted, somewhat resentfully, to hiring a proper builder (i.e. one with a proven track record for using cement) to come and restore our toilet. He also resolved to never again wear trousers which had a zip and, to my knowledge, he never did.

Everything was going along really quite nicely until I had to balls it all up by encouraging my old nemesis, the Mitch-Man, to darken our door once again.

He was a touch more understanding that time though as I had been pretty good for over a month, but he did warn Mum that the detention-centre threat was still hanging over her like the sword of Damocles if I decided to slip back into my bad old ways.

I know that I didn't deserve any treats or favours for my behaviour but, on reflection, I do think that Mum sensed that something was seriously wrong in school (aside from my teachers' on-going conviction that I was 'thick'), and so she spent a few weeks giving me a little slack at home.

Astonishingly even my father was showing a superficial interest in me and what I was up to.

Better late than never, as the old saying goes.
To his credit though I think even he recognised that all was not well in my world and so, perhaps reluctantly accepting that brutality and violence wasn't after all the most effective

way to bring up a son, he actually did something which was so totally out of character for him that, even now, I can scarcely believe that it happened.

He took me to the pictures.

Can you believe that? The pictures!

It was just incredible, especially when you consider that the man had never even bothered to walk me down to the sweet shop before! There *was* an ulterior motive of course but, even at the age of eleven, I was more than happy to just savour the moment and ignore any covert subplot.

You see, for one night only the fleapit cinema in Neath was, due to popular but dubious demand, re-showing *One Million Years BC*.

Now, why *was* that I wonder?

Were local moviegoers hungry to see once more the innovative stop-motion technique that had brought the film's monsters juddering to life?

Nope!

Did they want to enjoy the thrilling battle between the Triceratops and the Ceratosaurus all over again?

No, of course they didn't.

All they wanted was to spend a blissful hour-and-a-half slobbering at Racquel Welch's knockers bobbing up and down like two skinheads fighting under a tiny fur blanket.

That didn't matter to me though. I was just so happy that, after so many years of barely a benevolent word from him from one day to the next, my father finally wanted to spend some quality time with me.

The great night out was, as I remember, on a windy, soggy and freezing cold Friday in the Autumn.

The bus ride into Neath was short (less than two miles even with the detours around the estates) but, probably through my excitement, it seemed to take an eternity.

I was prattling away to my father all the way without, I should say, eliciting a great deal of response.

That didn't bother me too much to be absolutely frank with you. After all, if your father says precious little to you even when you've both been living under the same roof for eleven years then you can't reasonably expect him to start nattering away when you're squashed together on an uncomfortable, smoke-filled and choc-a-bloc bus.
As far as *he* was concerned I was probably no less of a stranger than any of the motley assortment of randoms sitting around us.

At long last though we reached the bus station and, when it came to my turn to get off, I leapt out and splashed into a deep and inviting puddle.

I quickly remembered that my father was behind me and I swivelled around, half expecting a swift and evening-wrecking admonishment but, to my relief, it didn't come. Instead he offered something which, in *my* presence certainly, was so unusual as to have normally been considered totally out of the question.

He smiled.

And it wasn't an artificial or phoney smile either. There was sincerity and an indisputable warmth there, or so it seemed to me at least, and maybe even a fragile pride.

It remained there as well as we walked to the pictures, in spite of the rain which had started to fall more heavily.

He was chatting about whatever, and I was joyously jabbering back.

For the first time in my short life I actually felt as if I had a Dad!

We reached the ramshackle cinema just as the rain began to *really* hammer down.

In front of us a dozen or so of the local rank-and-file perverts were queuing for their tickets.

My gaze, though, had been drawn to the wall on my right, and to the most exquisitely colourful exhibition of sweets, chocolates and ice-creams that I'd ever slapped eyes on.

Dad noticed that I was gawping over at what was on display there. "Once we get our tickets," he whispered, and I noticed that there were only two in front of us by then, "we'll go over and you can have whatever you like!"
So, as soon as Dad had paid his couple of shillings or whatever it was I hurried over to the Pick 'n Mix and started eagerly filling my little paper bag with samples of everything, including my favourite sherbet bonbons.

Dad also bought a couple of drinks and a small bag of popcorn and, after showing me where the little boy's room was, just in case I needed to go, we took our seats in the auditorium.

Just in the nick of time as well!

Before I'd shaped my backside around the springs in my seat the sallow lights had dimmed, the dusty velvet curtain was drawn back and the giant silver screen came alive.

We had to sit through some boring *Pearl & Dean* stuff first, then a trailer for *Barbarella* which, judging by the cheers and Neanderthal grunts from the assembled clientele, was received most favourably indeed.

Then, finally, the film itself started.

I don't recall to much about it to be perfectly honest, and I haven't watched it since, but I do remember seeing a giant spider which scared me a bit, a girl trapped up a tree by some dinosaur or other and Racquel Welch being carried into the air by a flying thing before being dropped into the sea, thereby initiating that most valued cornerstone of modern Western culture, the 'Wet T-Shirt'.

The closing credits ran, the lights grew nearly-bright again, we all pushed and jostled our way back out into the rain, and that was that.

My long-awaited night with Dad, and also my first experience of prehistoric soft porn, was over.

We travelled home on the last bus back to Skewen.

Clutching my almost-empty Pick 'n Mix as a treasured keepsake, I began to feel tired.

Dad didn't say too much to me on the way home, so I guessed at the time that he was shattered as well as he hadn't been sleeping too easily since the calamity with his zip.

I was understandably dejected as we toiled up the hill and back to Ormes Road in the still-pouring rain, not only because my wonderful evening had drawn to a close, but also because another change had seemed to come over Dad.
His chirpiness from earlier in the evening had gone, his smile had vanished and his friendliness was no more.

I'd prattled on excitedly about the film all the way home but something told me, long before we came within sight of the bungalow, that it was time for quiet.

Dad, it seemed, was no longer 'Dad'.

He was just 'my father' again and even then, as we stepped through the front door, I worried that *that* was the last time that he would show me any fondness.

Sadly, and apart from one final occasion some eighteen years later, I was right.

CHAPTER 8: MOVING THROUGH THE GEARS

Within months the Bromhams were on the move!

I'm certain that that never-to-be-forgotten fiasco with the outdoor toilet had persuaded my father of the necessity to heave himself and his hillbilly clan into, as it was viewed *then* at least, the modern world.

So, after selling our cramped but wistfully-cherished Ormes Road bungalow he shifted us into a two-storey, semi-detached council house on the still-extant Southall Avenue, situated at Skewen's southern periphery.

It was strikingly larger than our previous home and, with its three bedrooms, could comfortably billet a family of five (Stuart was nearly twenty by that time and would soon be settling into his own abode). We were also blessed with *two* indoor loos so, if somebody had rendered one of them temporarily unusable after a big session with the Sunday crossword then, mercifully, the other could be utilised instead. There was a plumbed-in bath as well so the much-vilified tin tub could at last be thrown out, while Mum could finally indulge herself within her very own fitted kitchen.
Predictably enough, once the novelty of all these cutting-edge luxuries had worn thin, the numerous disadvantages become more apparent.

For example, I'd slowly but steadily lost contact with the majority of my childhood friends, particularly the chummy contact that I'd grown accustomed to and so often relied upon. Yes, I'd bump into them in Rhydhir of course, provided I wasn't being chased around Neath by the Mitch-Man, but our relocation meant estrangement from any new Drummau Mountain adventures which, in turn, led to my being progressively marginalised.

Unsurprisingly, it wasn't too long before I was snubbed altogether.

Also, all of the privacy we'd previously treasured and taken for granted had completely evaporated. Even with bungalows on either side of us on Ormes Road it seemed that there was isolation aplenty but, on Southall Avenue, our home was overseen from virtually every aspect by a whole host of others.

I acknowledge that it's perhaps a hackneyed phrase so I'll apologise in advance, but it really *was* like living in a goldfish bowl; no matter which way we looked, somebody always seemed to be staring back at us.

And, on Southall, they *were* a truly nosey bunch!

As for me, well, I remained in Rhydhir for the full five-year tariff, a noteworthy accomplishment considering my recurrent clashes with the powers-that-be there. I left in 1973 without having gained a single qualification but, given my ongoing wrangle with dyslexia, that probably didn't make a substantial amount of difference to me.

You see, even if I *had* passed a few exams and landed myself, say, an office job as a reward for that effort, then I surely would have been bounced out on my arse as soon as they'd given me a letter to write or a list of numbers to add up.

I had toyed with the idea of enrolling at college and doing one of their apprenticeships because I'd always worked more successfully and with considerably more enjoyment using my hands than I'd ever done while holding a pen. Ultimately, though, I knew that I'd be confronted with precisely the same dilemma; there would still be studying and tests and other horrors to be negotiated before I could even dare dream of waving a certificate in the air.

Nevertheless, finding a dependable source of income had become imperative so I had to secure something which satisfied my particular needs (in other words no reading, writing or sums to do), and that meant regular stop-offs at the Job Centre.

Fortunately, I didn't have to wait long before positive things started to happen.

My first exposure to working life was with Jenkins' Sweets, where I helped with delivering the big jars of goodies to Skewen's tuck shops. An extremely supportive guy by the name of Keith ferried me around in the van while I did all of the humping and carrying of the sweets, as well as the washing out of the empty jars and bottles at the end of each day.

I left there after three months and was subsequently employed as a labourer on a new housing development in Ammanford, but I didn't stay the course there either.

Next, I was taken on as an apprentice with *Tile, Roof & Floor*, which was based two-bus-rides away in Swansea. The pay didn't exactly rip up any trees but at least there was more job security plus, being as I was a trainee roofer, regular opportunities to muscle in on a few hours of coveted overtime.

Usually though, once I'd sorted Mum out with my 'keep' for the week, and invested a small amount in my new smoking hobby, there was never a great deal left over to start lavishing around.

Nonetheless I *did* manage to scrape together enough for the down-payment on my first motorbike, a twin-piston Suzuki-185 on-road machine procured from JT Morgan's in Neath, and for which I eventually forked out something approaching six hundred pounds.

That was an awful lot of money in the early 1970's!

But, I must put on my rose-tinted spectacles here and add candidly that, with its glistening bodywork and sleek curves which were pure skirt-bait, it *was* the definitive object of beauty. I'd ridden a motorbike before of course, thanks entirely to Stuart's albeit short-lived generosity, so I felt that, as a minimum, I'd conquered the fundamental art of balance. The bike that *I* was buying, however, was ever-so-slightly different to Stuart's in that it came supplied with an engine and, consequently, gears.

Now, my sixteenth birthday had passed some months before but, in the way I communicated with people that I didn't know or wasn't entirely sure of, I was no less timid or introverted as when I left Coedffranc. I retained an innate reluctance to ask questions for fear of bolstering everyone's conviction that I was a blithering idiot and so, reverting to type, I'd keep my mouth shut and hope my problem, whatever it may have been, would magically sort itself out.

Regrettably, when you're splashing out a load of money on your first motorbike, that strategy simply doesn't hold water.

Enough talk. Let's cut to the chase here.

Going on what I'd garnered from Stuart's old Bantam I knew that a motorbike's gear-shift was located near the foot peg on the left-hand side, and that the clutch was to be found in the left handlebar. What I *didn't* know at the time, purely because I lacked that crucial self-confidence to ask JT Morgan's elderly salesman about it, was that the Suzuki's gears were 'one-down-four-up', which meant that I needed to push the gear-shift *down* to obtain *first* gear, then bring it *up* to move successively through second, third and fourth.

So, after I'd mounted the bike and flicked the ignition switch I pulled away in first and, as I couldn't find second no matter how hard I rammed my foot onto the gear-shift, I remained in first as I jerked and jolted my way out of the showroom.

Believe me, the poor salesman's expression was an image to behold. If someone had given him a surprise enema I don't think he could have appeared any more distressed.
.Having said that, and given what I was doing to his precious bike, an enema was probably the one thing that he *didn't* need!

Anyway, as I screamed the thing through Neath, peaking at an near-respectable twenty-five miles per hour on the flat but still urgently trying to find second, I knew that something was seriously amiss. If I needed any confirmation of that fact then the perplexed open-mouthed gawps from pedestrians as I wailed past them would have told me everything.
By some minor miracle I'd arrived at Neath Abbey which is halfway between Neath itself and Skewen but realised that, to get the bike back to Southall Avenue, I then had to ride it up the hill.

Absolutely no chance, I thought, at which point the bike ground to an intractable halt outside the newsagent's.

It had locked solid.
I couldn't restart it, turn the wheel or do anything with it at all.

Yep, I'd welded it good and proper!

A couple of good-hearted riders, who I'd never seen before and haven't met since, did pull over to try and help a fellow two-wheeler, but they could do nothing with it either. However, they *did* describe the bike's condition as 'fucked', so at least I'd learned some new technical jargon.

I had a small amount of change in my pocket so I rang JT Morgan's from the call box near the newsagent's. Despite their undoubtedly having a damn good chuckle when they heard what I'd done (or *hadn't* done, as the case may be), they graciously came out, gave me a lift home and then took the bike away with them to be repaired.

I was separated from it for six whole weeks because the engine had to be completely rebuilt after its destruction on that sorry day, but when I *did* finally get the bike back I received the proper tuition from JT Morgan's regarding how to engage the gears and, thankfully, that mortifying debacle was never repeated.

Bloody hell though, did I keep that bike clean or what?

Maybe 'clean' is not the right word. 'Immaculate' possibly does my passion greater justice.

I was obsessive about maintaining it in absolutely pristine and beyond-showroom condition, right down to ensuring that there was no build-up of blue on the chrome on the exhaust ports. I'd regularly strip it down and lovingly reassemble it, but not before I'd polished, scrubbed and buffed up every component that I could wrap my doting fingers around.

The spokes gleamed, the mirrors sparkled and the saddle always shone as though it had never been sat upon.

All the while, *I'd* started to change.

My self-assuredness and masculine poise was maturing; girls would watch me at work on my pride-and-joy with a flirtatious flicker of their eyes, much to the infuriation of their boyfriends who, usually under their breath but sometimes more brashly, would call me all the pretentious arseholes under the sun.

 But I was ready. My moment had arrived.

I had a tidy job, a stunning motorbike, and a pair of underpants with fillings that were keen to start sampling the charms of the world!

As it transpired, they didn't have that long to wait.

"Anybody fancy tagging along to a disco?" my brother Michael asked one Friday night in the spring of 1974.

"Whereabouts is it?" I replied.

"It's up Ammanford way. I've been there before. It's not too bad I suppose, the beer can be a bit iffy, should be okay though as long as they've cleaned the lines out. My mate Tony's coming as well."

I didn't dare wait for Michael to change his mind. Within an hour I'd bathed, shaved and pulled on my flared trousers and flowery shirt with a collar nearly large enough to go camping in.
I then slapped on some *Brut 33* and, after entertaining my bedroom mirror with some hurriedly-practiced and none-too-convincing dance moves, I was raring to go.

Michael's Ford Cortina, the passenger seat of which I'd eagerly leapt into, had undeniably seen better days, months and years.

In fact, the only part of it which didn't make a bloody noise was the horn!

After we'd picked up Tony and some other lad who I didn't know (and I can't remember his name to this day, so I'll call him Paul), we finally rattled and misfired our way through Pontardawe and chugged on toward Ammanford.

Each of us said exactly four words when we parked up outside the disco building just before seven o'clock that night.

"Here we are then," said Michael.

"About sodding time too," Tony added from behind my seat.

"I need a slash," Paul grimaced.

"Jesus! What a shithole!" I grumbled.

Strictly speaking I suppose it *wasn't* a shithole but with a lick of paint, a few more roof tiles and the odd intact window it certainly would have been much closer to reaching that lofty standard. The interior was gloomy and smoky and it smelled as though a herd of camels had died in there but, in its defence, there *was* a bar, managed more-or-less ably by a big balding bloke with a Groucho Marx moustache.

We were all thirsty and in need of some refreshments shall we say, so it was to *him* that the three of us immediately gravitated (Paul, of course, had already popped to the Gents). We each supped our pints, found ourselves a table with a clear view of the whole room, then polarised our collective rubbernecking on what we were actually there for: women! There were about ten of them on the dance floor, all pirouetting around their handbags. There were some boys down there as well, strutting their stuff to Billy Preston's *Space Race*.

I'll admit to being a tad dejected when I saw the competition flaunting their hirsute chests and phoney medallions, but when two of them started showing more than a passing interest in each other rather than the ladies I started to feel quite a bit better.

The disc-jockey, unseen behind an impenetrable veil of cigarette smoke and his throbbing red and blue disco lights, garbled something through his uncalibrated microphone and clumsily switched songs from *Space Race* to *Keep On Truckin'* by Eddie Kendricks.

"Nice whoppers on that one there," Tony yelled above the blasting music while pointing at a girl dancing close by.

She couldn't have been more than fifteen years of age but she spoke with all the charisma of an overflowing cesspool and wore make-up which appeared for all the world as if it had been smeared on with a trowel.

And that's pretty much how it panned out for most of the night. We guzzled drink after drink and considered the merchandise parading before us as though we were in some kind of iniquitous cattle market.

Michael was the first to try his luck.

"*That* one will do for me!" he bragged, nodding toward a table around which sat three gigglers.

"What, the one with the braces?" Tony remarked, sniggering. "You'll have your gums torn to shreds if you try snogging with that!"

"I didn't mean *her*, you dickhead! I meant her friend! See her? The one with the dark hair!"

We all peered again.

"Not a prayer!" Tony rasped. "She'll bomb you out before you can even ask her name!"

"Bet you a pint she won't," my brother replied with a wink, standing up and stuffing his shirt into his flares.

"A pint? Okay butty, you're on! Shake on it? Right! Come on then, let's see it!"

"Watch and learn, sunshine! Watch and learn," Michael said before sauntering casually toward her table. "Just to let you know," he sneered over his shoulder, "Mine's a beer this time, not lager!"

On sidling up the dark-haired girl he crouched down so that his mouth was level with hers, then muttered something into her ear.

We gazed, and waited.
"Fuck off, you perv!" she eventually growled with all the finesse and subtlety of a flying manhole cover.

Perhaps we were all guilty of overplaying the juvenile taunts as the wounded and distinctly-unimpressed Michael re-joined the pack.

"Funnily enough, mate," chortled Tony, pointing toward the bar, "*mine's* a beer as well!"

Michael flicked us a defiant V-sign and, to evade the girls' ruthless heckling, walked the long way around to see Groucho who was vigorously wiping a filthy glass with an equally-filthy cloth.

During the course of the evening Tony also tried and failed more than once, as did Paul. However, despite only ever having left my chair to keep myself topped up with booze, I wondered whether I might have been faring a little better.

Near the padlocked fire exit a clique of four girls were cackling away, just as they had been for much of the night. One of them, who was vaguely curvaceous and pleasantly attractive with her long brown wavy hair, had clearly fathomed that I was glancing in their direction every now and again, and seemed quite content to return the occasional furtive glint.

This, I recall thinking to myself, was *very* promising.

The only snag was that, as far as talking to females was concerned, I was totally inexperienced and, hence, useless. But I knew I had to do something if I was genuine about wanting a slice of the action!

Time was rushing by, and I knew that Groucho would be calling last orders in less than half-an-hour.

I had to choose between 'now' and 'never'.

If I went with 'never' and just sat there playing it safe and slurping my pint, then I conceded to myself that it was highly unlikely I'd ever see her again.

On the other hand, if I plumped for 'now' then I calculated that one of two things would happen.
She could either blow me out of course, in which case that would be the end of that. I'd then just crawl inside my pint for what remained of the evening and forget the whole thing.

But, if she was a touch more amenable then I might just have a smidgeon of a chance.

So, I plumped for 'now'.

After waiting for Michael to clear off to the bar I took a large gulp for courage and ambled over to her table "Hiya," I somehow managed to warble once I'd reached there. "Anyone fancy a dance?"

To my amazement the one I'd been ogling stood up straight away, grabbed my hand and, just as the first unmistakable bars of *Tiger Feet* rumbled around the room, lugged me down to the floor.

I was very nervous, and I have to say that my dancing was truly appalling. My arms and legs were all over the place; it must have looked as though I was wrestling with an invisible octopus! She didn't seem too bothered though and, as soon as the song was done, we sat back at her table.

Once she'd kept her tongue out of my mouth for long enough to actually speak I learned that her name was Claire, and that she was hungry, and that there was a fish and chip shop around the corner.

That all sounded pretty good to me.
Besides, I'd had enough of the disco and the beer that tasted like dishwater so, on our way out, I told Michael to stick around and wait for me after the place closed as I wanted to get to know Claire ('Claire, this is my brother Michael. Michael, meet Claire') a little better.

Michael had a hesitant but unsavoury look on his face, as though he possessed some sensitive information that I wasn't privy to.

Claire's demeanour had also changed when she saw my brother. She fell very quiet and was obviously trying to avoid any inadvertent eye contact with him.

I'm sure that, *now*, you can better appreciate how raw I was in matters of the opposite sex. *You've* read the last few sentences and, in doing so, I'm sure that you've sussed what was going on. At the time I had the two of them standing in front of me and, even then, I still couldn't bloody work it out!

Naturally keen to expedite her escape Claire told her own friends to hang around for a while, and then the two of us made a hasty exit.

Not for chips, though. Oh no, no, no! We weren't going for chips!

She dragged me down some dingy side street or other until we came to a point beside a wall where a few of the bricks had lumps knocked out of them, leaving crevasses in the masonry each just deep enough to support a dainty toe or two.

She's been here before, I guessed.
She scaled the wall with well-practiced aplomb and I, like a bloodhound being teased with a rib eye steak, pursued her excitedly.

"Oh, hell!" I yelled as soon as my head had cleared the top of the wall. "It's a cemetery!"

Claire, leaning casually against one of the more imposing headstones as if it were a bus shelter, brought her finger up to her lips.

"Sssh! Come on!" she whispered.

What occurred next should require no supplementary narrative and, no, I'm *not* going to do any 'stiff' jokes either. Suffice it to say I felt about ten feet tall when I joined up again with Tony, Paul and a rather subdued Michael outside the chip shop, despite the seat and knees of my flares being plastered in mud, despite reeking of Claire's cheap perfume and despite seeing more stars before my eyes and having more wobbles in my legs than if I'd gone twelve rounds with Muhammad Ali.

The journey home was a bit prickly, as you might have expected.

Both Tony and Paul had fallen asleep because they were hopelessly drunk. Michael did the driving while I sat in the front seat pondering what that cemetery's groundskeeper would think when he discovered some discarded knickers and a tattered pair of tights on top of one of his graves.
After all, I had to keep my mind occupied with *something* because there was hardly a word spoken between us as we made our way back to Skewen. I'd learned Michael's idiosyncrasies over the years, and I understood perfectly well what his protracted silences usually signified.

What I didn't *realise*, certainly at the time, was that *I* was the cause of that latest one.

CHAPTER 9: MANY LESSONS LEARNED

So, my first relationship with a woman was underway.

You'll notice that I've used the word 'woman' there rather than 'girl' because Claire was older than myself by some four years and was, in consequence, considerably more worldly-wise in virtually every meaningful regard.

Not that *she* appeared too perturbed by that but, being so young, *I* might have been. She'd scribbled her telephone number on an empty cigarette packet following our liaison in the cemetery but I didn't have the mettle to ring her just in case I'd been cut adrift in the meantime.

Michael's adversarial attitude since the night of the disco wasn't doing my confidence any favours either.

As it so happened, when I *did* finally marshal sufficient nerve to make contact a couple of days later I was relieved to find that she was congenial and also excited about meeting up again. So, to get the ball rolling, she invited me up to her place in Brynamman, which is just outside Ammanford and fairly close to where I worked fleetingly as a labourer.
I anticipated a frosty reception from a protective mother and a distrustful father, a scenario which I recall made me exceptionally edgy, but the outing would at least offer the prospect of opening up the Suzuki on those narrow and largely-deserted mountaintop roads which lay between my home and hers.

Anyone familiar with the geography of the area will know exactly how uncannily bleak, but also how curiously beautiful, that secluded run 'over the top' can be.

When I arrived at Claire's, visibly apprehensive but still managing to look every inch the mutt's nuts straddling that spotless bike in my helmet and gear, two shocks awaited me.

Firstly, she had no father, certainly not one that I could see at any rate but she did have a brother who, like her mother Jenny, was very welcoming (for the sake of completeness, I later discovered that Claire's father was an abusive and violent brute who'd abandoned the family some years earlier).

Secondly, there was barely a piece of furniture or a fitment or a carpet or a pair of curtains to be seen anywhere.

And I'd believed for all those years that *we'd* had it tough in Ormes Road! Glancing around the house though I'd perhaps begun to appreciate what 'tough' *actually* meant.

After the brusquest of ice-breaking conversations with Jenny, during which I probably came across as some sort of hermit who until that day had never stepped beyond his own front door, Claire and I spent an hour or so walking the paths and country lanes surrounding the estate where she lived.

We returned to her home where I spent some more minutes speaking to Jenny as if I had a pair of socks stuffed in my mouth, and then I took my leave.

I desperately needed a pee while I was there but, being as I was way too diffident to ask if I could possibly use their toilet, I instead curtailed my homeward trip after around three hundred yards in order to relieve myself against someone's fence.

A few days later Claire journeyed over on the bus to see me but, given Michael's continuing vindictiveness which was always amplified whenever I dared to mention Claire's name, I thought it more prudent to show her some of Neath's delights rather than take her back to Southall.

Our first port of call whenever she travelled down was a cosy wine bar, located not too far from the train station. We'd then usually then head for the long-since-bulldozed 'One and Six', a sleazy little hovel of a cinema so christened because, in the old days, *that* was how much it would have cost you to get in.

Claire and I never went there to see a film, though.

Oh no, no, no! We *certainly* never went there to see a film!

We went there because it was dark and reasonably private, meaning that we were free to satisfy our carnal impulses.

The film was of no interest to us whatsoever.

By way of example, on one occasion the cinema was showing the children's masterpiece *Herbie Rides Again*, but even *that* couldn't deter us from fulfilling our urges.
So, if you were one of the kids in the 'One and Six' that day trying to work out why a Volkswagen Beetle seemed to be grunting and panting like a marathon runner crossing the finish line with a half-hundredweight of bricks strapped to his back, I can only apologise.

In all sincerity though, *that* was what my association with Claire appeared to be largely based upon: sex, and as frequently as possible if you please.

Despite not really having a tremendous amount in common we still sought to meet up as often as we could in order to, shall we say, further this association.

Michael did attempt to steer me away from Claire, but I was still too wet behind the ears and my brain far too scrambled by regular nookie to work out whether that dissent was for his benefit or for mine. What I *can* say for certain is that I flatly ignored him and so, within months of our first coupling after that disco in Ammanford, but *not* without Mum's and my father's blessing of course, I bade Claire to move in with us in Southall Avenue.

Even before she'd unpacked her suitcase there was nothing but friction and animosity between herself and Michael.

If he was in a room and Claire walked in then he would walk out, and vice versa.

If Claire said or did something that Michael didn't like then he would sneer indignantly or huffily shake his head, and vice versa.

They were rarely nasty or traded insults because they hardly ever spoke to one another but, in many ways, that latent acrimony only exacerbated the tension. The atmosphere had become horrendous, bordering on unbearable even, and yours truly had instigated it all by asking her to live there.

Nevertheless, like Claire I wanted to try and make things work out between us and so, over time, ceaseless intercourse had been cultivated into something of a brittle romance while the antagonism between her and Michael had disintegrated into nothing more spiteful than an obdurate silence.

Then, on one sunny afternoon in the spring of 1975, everything changed.

Claire and I were strolling through the centre of Neath when she stopped outside a jeweller's shop.

Her eye had been caught by some twinkly thing or other in the window, and she pointed at a small beige-coloured tray of rings.
Once I'd fathomed what she was staring at the beaming face of the shop's ageing proprietor had appeared, with near-telepathic timing, above the tray.

He and I exchanged glances.

Ah yes! he must have been ruminating. *Here comes another sucker who's ready to have his liberty and happiness pulverised into dust! Step into my office young man, why don't you?*

So I did, but not voluntarily. Claire hauled me into the shop by the wrist, and no less firmly than if I was being thrown into prison.

"Now then," muttered the jeweller after fetching the tray so that Claire could drool over the rings at closer quarters. "Which one would Madam like to try on?"

Now, I'm sure that you've been to such a jeweller's and so you'll be aware that these trays contain two things: rings and prices.
Depending on your gender you'll be mesmerised by one while flagrantly disregarding the other.

This was something I learned that very afternoon.

"Yes indeed, *that* is a most perceptive choice if I may be so bold, Madam. The stone is of the highest quality, point-two-five of a carat and slightly under four millimetres across. From one of the finest and most celebrated mines in South Africa, you know. It's serviced many of the royal residences from all over Europe for decades."

Before the jeweller could round up his cheesy sales banter Claire, having already slipped the ring on to her finger, was waving her hand around and gawping at the diamond from every conceivable angle.

"Do you like it?" she asked me.

I looked at the jeweller, then at the price on the tray, then at the jeweller again.

His expression suggested something like: '*That* was *not* a question. *That* was an *instruction* made to sound like a question. *She* wants it, *you're* paying for it and, if you don't, you'll never again see her ankles more than six inches apart!'

The canny bastard was even rubbing his hands and grinning at me!

I ached to say that I *didn't* like it, just to give her some breathing space to think about what she was doing and maybe cool off on the whole idea, but then I thought of those ankles…

"It's nice," I mumbled with as much conviction as somebody who's unwrapped a six-sizes-too-large hand-knitted reindeer sweater on Christmas morning.

Claire was still flourishing her left hand through the air as though she were conducting the Royal Philharmonic. "And it fits as well! Look!"
"Would Madam like to try on any of the other rings?"

"No!" she replied decisively. "I want *this* one!"

She'd answered the jeweller while glaring at me.

Strange, that!

"Okay, I'll take it," I said, thereby confirming what the jeweller had known all along.

"That's excellent, Sir. May I congratulate you both on your selection? Well now, that just leaves the small matter of the purchase itself. That'll be thirty-five pounds please."

Yes, I *knew* it was thirty-five pounds! I didn't need to have it bloody emphasized! After all, that's why he craftily kept the tray and the price tag in full view all the while!

I *really* wanted Claire to at least consider something a little cheaper, but then I thought of those ankles…

"That's fine," I lied with voice a-trembling.

From my pocket I then produced the cash, which was virtually my entire weekly pay with *Tile Roof & Floor*, and laid it tenderly on the counter.
I can confidently state that, throughout our short stay in the shop, I didn't see the jeweller's hands move as swiftly as they then did. Within seconds my money was gone for ever, snatched away and consigned to the deepest and darkest recesses of his till.

He and Claire then exchanged more pleasantries, a little paperwork and a small brown storage box in the unlikely event of her ever taking the ring off but, for me, everything had become a blur.

The shop seemed to be spinning before my eyes. Maybe, though, the shop was alright and it was *me* that doing the spinning.

Either way, I knew that I'd been duped.
We travelled back to Southall on the bus. Claire spent the entire ride flashing the ring around, clearly hankering for some daft old biddy to say 'Ooh, *that's* lovely dear! And is *this* your fiancée? Aren't *you* the lucky one?'

Meanwhile, I just stared numbly out the window and said a fond and silent farewell to the world I once knew.

Having somehow found sufficient willpower in my legs to lurch to our front door I wondered about what the hell I was going to say to Mum.

As it turned out, I needn't have bothered.

"Look, Violet!" Claire squealed on spotting my mother in the kitchen. "We're engaged!"

Mum said nothing, which was understandable seeing as her lower jaw had already plunged halfway to the floor.

My father called me a gormless prick, so at least he wasn't *too* annoyed with me.

Michael, after *he* found out later that day, didn't speak to me for a week.

In stark contrast Claire's mother, Jenny, was thrilled with the news.
I was furious with myself on two counts; firstly, for not having the strength of character to just walk out of the jeweller's instead of standing there like a numpty and, secondly, for not having the impudence to tell Claire that I had absolutely no intention of marrying her.

So, to save any upset and further aggravation I just went along with it all.

In the interim Claire, interpreting my lack of resistance as consent, got busy.

She wanted to get married in the June of that year, a mere two months after I'd been mugged and left for dead in the jeweller's, and she wasted no time at all in ploughing on with the arrangements. I helped where I could but my heart was cold, not because I didn't like Claire (I *did* like her, and very much), but because the speed and intensity of the whole thing terrified me.
Mum and Michael were completely against me getting hitched but the rest of the family, including my father, could hardly have cared less if they'd tried.

I knew I was making a big mistake. I just knew it.

My anxieties grew as the big date loomed but, having seen what it all meant to Claire, I simply didn't have the resilience to open my mouth and save myself from disaster. The long days and sleepless nights ticked by unerringly, and the window of opportunity for speaking up eventually shrivelled to the size of a dot.

The wedding day then arrived, and the dot duly vanished.

I'm just thankful that only a mere handful people were at the registry office that afternoon to witness the gargantuan balls-up that I'd set myself up to make.

The ceremony came and went, I remember murmuring 'I do' at some point and probably with as little certitude as it was possible to gather, and that was pretty much that.

There was no way that we could afford a reception, and it was unlikely that we'd have had more than a dozen turning up to gorge themselves even if we could have, so it was tea and biscuits and slices of wedding cake all round back at Southall.

If my face looked like a well-slapped arse in the wedding photos (as it did for months to come) then heaven only knows what it must have appeared like after Claire and I went to bed later that evening.
We consummated our marriage (in other words, we bonked just like we did every night), and then…

"Erm, Chris? There's something you need to know," she said.

I rolled over and stared at her.
She wore a smile, but it wasn't a relaxed 'I'm-so-glad-that-you're-finally-my-husband' smile. No, it was more of a skittish 'please-don't-be-mad-with-me-when-I-tell-you-this' smile.

"Need to know?" I replied charily. "What?"

"Well,' she resumed without meeting my eye, "you know the bad blood between me and your brother? I don't really know how to say this, but…well…it's all because we were seeing each other and having regular sex right up until I met you."

If any of you readers out there have an idea lodged in the back of your minds about compiling a tome entitled 'One-Hundred-and-One Ways To Completely Ruin A Wedding Night', then I bear good tidings for you: I've just given you one for free, so now you only have to find another one hundred.

I glowered at her for a while, but in truth I was just gobsmacked.

She didn't add anything more and, when she realised that I wasn't going to respond, primarily because my brain had stalled, she simply said: "Well, anyway, I just thought you ought to know."

She then turned over and pretended to go to sleep.

We spent the remainder of that night, and also the next night, separated by virtually the full width of the bed.

I confronted Michael some days afterward, but only after I'd plucked up sufficient courage to do so. He confirmed that what Claire had confessed to me was indeed a fact, but claimed he hadn't told me earlier because he wanted to spare my feelings.

That was bullshit, and I told him so.
To this day I'm convinced he didn't tell me because he supposed it would be a damn sight more hilarious if I found out *after* the wedding rather than before.

In all honesty it hardly mattered. Relations between Claire and Michael had subsequently deteriorated to such a low ebb that we had no alternative other than to pack our bags and somehow concoct a fresh start by living with Jenny in Brynamman.

The damage, though, had been done.
Despite never really wanting a marriage to Claire I still felt betrayed and, as the next few months dragged by, I found that any spare time I could have easily spent with her was being devoted to my precious Suzuki instead.

We were drifting apart and I couldn't see how that could be changed while those embroidered images of Claire with Michael remained etched in my mind.
Shortly after our first anniversary Claire had secured a new job as a seamstress in a local jeans factory. She'd settled in there very well and, I was quite contented to find, things between us had started to improve.

Then, and entirely out of the blue, there came the final straw.

She'd arrived home in tears late one night after attending a works' party. Quite naturally I asked her what the matter was, whereupon she admitted to secretly meeting an ex-boyfriend in a local pub about a week previously then having sex with him in the ladies' toilets.

All of my belongings were packed within the hour, and I was back on Southall Avenue within two.

Claire had pleaded for me to stay, but I couldn't.

It wasn't that her latest bombshell had flattened me like a steamroller. It hadn't, and that's the truth.
I think it all had to do with feeling hopelessly trapped in a bogus marriage which had, so far as I could make out at the time, no real chance of success.

Claire had creaked open my escape route after her party that night. Once I'd decided that I couldn't let it slam in my face again I was through it, revving my laden Suzuki, and gone.

I'm just so grateful that there were no children involved since that would have made the divorce proceedings so much messier than they were. As it transpired everything was settled out-of-court within the space of a few months.

Later in that year, and once the divorce had been confirmed, I bumped into Claire on Stanley Road in Skewen (as an aside, she would regularly visit Skewen following our separation to ask after me or to keep in close touch with Mum or my half-sister, presumably with the intention of ultimately patching things up between us).

Feeling unbelievably awkward I halted in my tracks like a rabbit spellbound by someone's headlights because I didn't really know what to say or do. Claire had stopped as well and, on realising it was me, started to cry but she still tried her best to look pleased to see me.
I had no idea what *my* face was doing, but it most certainly *wasn't* exuding any glee.

"Is that it, then?" she sobbed. "Is it all over?"

"Yes," I replied, quite sternly as I remember. "It's over."

She pleaded with me to consider starting things up again but at that moment I think I was more uncompromising and dogged then I'd ever previously been.

My answer was no, and it wasn't going to change.
I walked away from her shortly afterwards, and I never saw her again.

Around fifteen years ago I'd heard that Claire had passed away, from cancer as I understood it, at the age of forty-two.

Apparently she'd kept an appointment at her doctor's surgery and had collapsed and died in his room.

I've never held any grudges or bitterness toward her and, for all the other failings in our ill-fated relationship, I've never overlooked the fact that she did truly love me.

My one overriding regret, and I still hate myself for it, was that I couldn't grant the same affection in return.

After hearing the news of Claire's death I went to the cemetery where she's buried, simply to pay my last respects.

One of her friends told me where I could find her final resting place.

Her grave, tragically, was not marked with a headstone.
Instead, all that existed to confirm the spot was a flattened rectangular mound overgrown with freshly-cut grass.

I laid a small bunch of flowers upon it, and never returned there again.

CHAPTER 10: AT THE CROSSROADS

My marriage to Claire, and also those adulterous circumstances beneath the weight of which it finally buckled, certainly wrenched much of the wind from my still-youthful sails.

My Suzuki-185, however, was my closest friend, my agony aunt and my shoulder to cry on, all rolled into one.

Had I been as heedful of a husband's obligations as I'd been to keeping that motorbike in the best possible working order then maybe Claire and I would have remained together right through to the end of her pitiably short life.

But I wasn't and, whether for better or for worse, that's really all that I can say.

You may consider me callous but the simple nub of the matter was that I wasn't mentally prepared for either wedlock or the swathe of commitment that's packaged with it.

My physique revealed me to be a man, and my self-confidence had matured to the point where others could almost believe that I actually possessed some, but I suppose the susceptible child had never really gone away.
My bike, though, appeared far more forgiving of my fragilities than I think any woman could ever have been.

The atmosphere in Southall had barely improved from that which thoroughly poisoned the place when Claire was around.
In fact the rancour between myself and Michael had, if anything, *deepened* since my return from Brynamman and so, to release myself from his daily virulence, I started spending a couple of evenings a week at a pub called the Duke of Wellington in Neath.

It was there that I first encountered Sian, the next woman to crash-land on my world.
At the time she seemed so very different to Claire.

Claire was a solemn and very serious-minded girl who wanted to settle down and, with a perfect man, have perfect kids playing on a perfect front lawn with a perfectly-white picket fence for protection.

Sian, on the other hand, represented fun and freedom and exuberance.

She wasn't staid and, at the time at least, expressed no desire to get married.

As for children, she didn't seem in the slightest bit interested in them.

How prophetic *that* trifling observation would ultimately turn out to be.
I was understandably cautious at first about lurching into another relationship after all the goings on during my time with Claire so, for a spell, Sian and I remained little more than friends.

It wasn't long though before things (read: sexual relations) had escalated to the point where the necessity of meeting her folks had arrived.

Claire's mother Jenny, in spite of my coyness as you may recall, seemed to warm to me right from the off.

In stark contrast Sian's mother and father absolutely loathed me.

Well, no, maybe in retrospect that's a mite harsh.

They actually dubbed me a 'commoner' which, to my deferential mind, is merely a less distasteful way of expressing precisely the same sentiment.

In her near-sighted wisdom I strongly suspect Sian of hoodwinking them into believing that I drove a posh car, since that was probably the first box that needed to be ticked if one harboured any aspirations of being allowed to ring their doorbell.

So, when I screeched into her tree-lined road thrashing the living daylights out of my Suzuki, the pair of them must have shrunk behind their curtains with the stultifying disgrace of it all.
And I'd done my best to appear really dashing in my black polo neck jumper with jeans and denim jacket, my black leather boots, white helmet and riding gloves!
I was convinced that I looked no less suave than that guy from the *Milk Tray* adverts of old but, as I was soon to realise, her mother and father mulishly refused to see beyond the shame of their angelic daughter dating some subhuman Swansea gunge!

And, most importantly of all of course, what *would* the neighbours think when they saw me? (aside from maybe 'Go on, my son! Lock your back wheel up and screw that baby round their flower beds for a bit!')
Still, credit where it's due I guess.

After all, her parents *did* condescend to greet me, listless though that greeting was.

They even *spoke* to me, although I *was* made to feel like some kind of insanitary bog-dwelling amoeba.

Her father enquired as to whether I was into horses.

When he asked me that I initially thought he ran a little fetish club somewhere but, instead, I was relieved to learn that both he and his wife were enthusiastic riders with a strong interest in a local livery yard.

I would, of course, be exaggerating were I to suggest that they sneered down their noses at me so often that, in time, I was able to distinguish between them from the shape of their nostrils.

Nevertheless, I'm sure you've honed in on what I'm trying to get across here.

So, maybe my saying that they absolutely loathed me wasn't so far from the truth after all.

Now, to all you young people out there who have been similarly chastened by such a demeaning experience simply because you don't conform to someone else's parochial view of how the universe should work, I offer you this advice:

You have the right to become whatever *you* want to become, and to chase the dreams that *you* want to chase, without having to suffer any invidious or ill-informed persecution from others.

You *don't* have to have been born into a particular social class, or a certain stock, or inherited privilege, or money.

It's up to you.

It is *you* that decides what you choose to do with your life, and *not* them.

Think outside the box, and always be that much more determined today than you were yesterday.

Finally, don't allow the idiots who only *think* they know it all to bully you into submitting to their ideals because the two things that these people fear most, namely *your* tenacity to achieve your goals and their *own* crushing exposure as failures, will always hunt them down in the end.
Have faith in these words because they come from someone who's been there, seen it, done it *and* had a wardrobe in Southall Avenue stuffed with T-shirts.

At least, it *was* stuffed with T-shirts until I had to make room for Sian's clothes.

Yep, that's right!

I'd gone and done it again!
Despite her parents' audacious efforts to separate us, which included turning up at Southall late one night when Sian and I were (uh-hum) making the most of each other's company, I asked her to move in and she gamely accepted.

Everything started off really well between us.

We laughed and joked and kissed and cuddled, and Mum was really happy for me considering all that occurred during my two tumultuous years with Claire.

I just enjoyed being with Sian so, so much, and I was thrilled that she seemed so happy to be with me as well.

Once that first hour was over, though, things began to deteriorate quite markedly.

She used to love drawing me into arguments over the most insignificant and inconsequential rubbish.
Mind you, these weren't your common-all-garden barneys.

Oh, no.

These were all-out wars.

We'd often scream our heads off while standing nose-to-nose, and hurl things at one another with as much hatred as two hooligans pelting bricks through windows.

I'd always accepted that Sian had a tempestuous streak festering within her, but I hadn't really experienced it in all its redoubtable glory until she'd pitched up in Southall.

Yes, Claire and I had rows, many of them in fact, but definitely not like the monsters that Sian seemed so skilled in instigating.

In the early weeks I managed to hold my ground against her but, after that, whenever I spotted those subtle tell-tale shifts in her body language which hinted at an imminent eruption, I just wanted out of there and sharpish.

Unfortunately there *were* times when I *couldn't* pick up on them, for example whenever I'd committed the appalling sin of paying more attention to the polishing of my Suzuki than I did to her.

The element of surprise would then be with Sian and, boy, didn't she cash in big style! Through the vast majority of her outbursts I'd simply reconstruct the bike as rapidly and as calmly as I could, grab my helmet, flick the ignition switch and just bugger off somewhere, *anywhere,* as long as it was away from her.

On one particular life-defining day, though, I was a tad remiss in assembling everything with the appropriate care.

Whilst I sat on our driveway on that auspicious afternoon, blithely buffing up some component or other, she charged from the house ranting and raving about there being too many clouds in the sky for her liking, or something equally ridiculous.
Either way, she'd caught me on the wrong day; I was in much too cheery a mood to listen to any of her worthless crap.

As I put the Suzuki back together again, all the while pretending not to be shaken by yet another of her foul-mouthed tirades, I decided to just get on the bike and not return home until *very* late.

And so, after coolly donning my helmet I leapt onto the saddle and attempted to roar down Southall Avenue.

I could definitely feel, though, that something wasn't right with the bike.

Now, my Suzuki-185 had twin cylinder exhausts, which meant twin spark plugs, and a double feed to the engine coming from twin carburettors – boring stuff maybe, but crucial in understanding what happened next.

As I travelled along I was sensing a substantial reduction in the bike's normal power output.

More worryingly, I could smell petrol.

Even more worryingly I realised that this petrol, wherever it was and wherever it had come from, had ignited.

I glanced down and immediately saw wind-assisted flames fanning out between my legs.

To use a well-aired dysphemism, I absolutely shit myself.

I knew that the whole thing could explode at any moment, with me still on it!

By that time I'd somehow reached the junction with the main road, at the lower end of Southall Avenue.

I slammed on the back brake so hard that the bike skidded beneath me, splashing burning petrol onto my jeans.

As it slewed in one direction, I was thrown in the other.
The stricken Suzuki, by then on its side and spinning uncontrollably toward the crossroads with Pen-yr-Alley Avenue, had deposited a trail of blazing fuel in its wake.

My jeans had caught fire as well but, luckily, a sizeable number of frenetic swats with my gloves eventually extinguished any further danger from there.

The cars on the main road screeched and swerved around my bike as a plume of thick black smoke began billowing into the air.
I could tell straight away that the fuel tank itself was alight.

Then, WOOMF!

Up it went in a sheet of flames!
Hysterical and disoriented I immediately ran up the steps leading to one of the flats which overlooked the junction and begged the lady who lived there to dial 999 and get the fire brigade.

She didn't know me from Adam and I'd never seen her before either but, nonetheless, she *did* call them and I remain grateful to her for that.

The fire brigade in turn arrived promptly, but sadly not promptly enough.

My pride and joy had been totally incinerated.
The firemen showered the charred vestiges with foam, by which time the tank's remaining petrol had completely burnt out.

The police then turned up at the scene and took a snivel-strewn statement from me.

"You had a lucky escape there, son," the copper said afterwards.

Yes, I was well aware of that and I told him so, but my only wish at that moment was that my Suzuki could have had one as well.

As it was it was a goner, a burned-up write-off, torched beyond salvation.

Stupidly, but purely through my desperation to get away from Sian's venomous mouth on that fateful afternoon, I'd forgotten to reconnect one of the spark plugs, which meant that the chrome plate on top of the cylinder head was arcing against the connector which normally snapped on to that plug.

I'd also left off one of the feeds from the tank, which had caused raw fuel to spurt out all over the engine instead of going down to the carburettor.

So, that's a whole load of sparking going on and a shower of petrol, all within inches of my sweet hairy arse.

Not a good combination in anyone's book.
After waiting for the smouldering remains to cool down sufficiently to touch I heaved the bike upright and pushed it back up the hill to home.

With tears in my eyes I wheeled it around to the back garden and, ever the proud owner, rolled it back onto its stand.
Mum was totally shocked when I told her what had happened, but she was also very relieved that I was still in one piece.

She came out to look at the immolated Suzuki, and cried as much as I had done.

Sian's attitude was considerably less sympathetic.

"I've known it all along,' she growled. "You really are fucking useless, aren't you?"

At that, I went completely ballistic.

She and I then had another slanging match, except that *that* time I couldn't get away from it all by going to clean my precious Suzuki.

There was, after all, nothing left of it to bloody clean!

So, and without seeking acclaim for a rather poor pun, I just rode the whole thing out because I was too distraught to pay lip-service to any more of her garbage.
As far as I was concerned she could shout and scream as much as she liked and call me all the wankers under the sun if it made her feel better.

I could have been blown up but, quite obviously, she didn't give a two shakes about that.

Maybe she was just angry that I'd had the effrontery to still be alive.

Did I care? Not about her, *that's* for certain.

She could go forth and multiply in short jerky movements as far as I was concerned.

My only thoughts were for my once-magnificent Suzuki-185, which was then little more than a barbecued husk lying in state in our unkempt back garden.

Thankfully, and perhaps just a little miraculously, the insurance company paid out slightly under what they considered to be the depreciated value of the bike, prior to its cremation. That was all well and good, but I'd had the bike for nearly two years and so their reparation fell hopelessly short of what I needed to buy a replacement.

My nagging them about the immaculate condition in which I'd habitually kept it cut absolutely no ice with them whatsoever.

It seems that what the large print giveth, the small print taketh away!

Therefore, I'd been presented with a straightforward choice; do I plump for an affordable second-hand model and risk further expense in overhauling it to my own high standards, or do I spend some time in JT Morgan's seeing what I could get for the paltry amount of cash that I had in my pocket?

The second-hand option, in all honesty, was never one that I was earnest about taking up.

Aside from the aforementioned refurbishment costs I simply couldn't abide the thought of riding a bike that someone else had probably thrashed around for a couple of years without giving it so much as a cursory wipe with a duster, until it was time for them to sell.

So, down to JT Morgan's I went.

Despite them not having a Suzuki-185, which was what I *really* wanted of course, I still forced myself into a slightly downcast gander around their showroom.

Try as I might I couldn't imagine myself on any of the other road bikes that they had for sale.

Don't get me wrong, they were excellent machines in their own right, but they just weren't me.

I was about to call it a day and head home when my eye was drawn to a silver Suzuki TS-250 enduro bike, which had been tucked away in a corner.

I'd only once before seen a model which looked even remotely comparable, not in the flesh as it were but on television where, a year earlier, this similar bike had been used in a very impressive and brave attempt to jump thirteen single-decker buses at the old Wembley Stadium.

The unsuccessful rider crashed and broke his pelvis, but still managed to deliver a pre-comeback retirement speech to the watching world.

That bike was a Harley Davidson, and the rider's performing name was Evel Knievel.

Other than that I had no absolutely idea as to why my eye should have been drawn to that particular bike.

After all, I'd spent just over two blissful years with a Suzuki-185, which had been designed as an on-road model and nothing more.

The TS-250 could run on-road *and* off-road which meant that, as well as being designed for the smooth tarmac that the 185 was confined to, it was also comfortable working the softer and undulating topography of, for example, a motocross course.

As a result it was necessarily lighter in weight, smaller in size and, apart from perhaps a slick blue dash which ran along its entire length, I really didn't think it had anything that would immediately appeal to the opposite sex.
More importantly, I didn't have any idea of how it would handle or what it could do.
All I knew was that the more I leered at it, the more I wanted it.

I didn't have anywhere near enough money to ride it out of the showroom that particular day but, once my father had agreed to act as guarantor for the finance (yes, you *did* read that correctly!), I was able to ride home my shiny, brand new TS-250.

Sian raised no objections to me having this new bike.

Then again, maybe she did.

Trouble is, when you blank someone as much as I blanked her, it's often difficult to be sure.

So, what *could* the TS-250 do?

Well, the first trick I quickly mastered was the familiar 'wheelstand', or 'wheelie', achieved by opening the bike's throttle in first gear and, providing the engine has enough power, raising the front wheel into the air.

Not only could I pull a wheelie to order, but I'd also learned how to maintain one over a very respectable distance, such as the full extent of either Southall Avenue or Skewen's main road. The local girls were tickled pink by my playing to the gallery because only a few of them had seen any kind of stunt riding before, except perhaps in the movies or rare television clips.

Over time I'd started to build a reputation for being something of a showman, although some people (mostly the blokes, predictably enough) thought that I was more of a show-*off*!

Throughout that scorching summer of 1976 they barracked me from the pavements, directed obscene masturbation-related gestures toward me and called me things that even the most wayward of dogs wouldn't lick.

For the life of me I couldn't see what their problem was.

I'd reasoned that a musician would use a guitar or a keyboard to entertain, so why couldn't I use a motorbike?

Perhaps it was a jealousy thing.

Perhaps they felt threatened when their lady friends offered their appreciation to a local lad who was doing something a bit out of the ordinary.

Perhaps, though, I'm being just a little too gracious here and they were nothing but arseholes all along.

I wasn't too disconcerted by their taunts and catcalls, though.
To be brazenly truthful it simply felt good to finally merit some attention for something I'd accomplished, however uncultured that attention may have occasionally been.
I've always felt that two wheels and rain don't mix that well so, on one particularly wet Saturday afternoon, I kept the bike out of the elements and stayed at home in the dry.

My father was watching the horse racing on *World of Sport* which, for those of you that don't remember it, was ITV's cheap-and-cheerful answer to the BBC's *Grandstand*.

In between races the show's presenter, Dickie Davies, was asking viewers to send in any film footage of themselves taking part in unusual sports, or even doing stunts.

My memory wandered back to when I'd gazed with admiration and respect at that short clip of Evel Knievel at Wembley.

I then thought of my Suzuki TS-250 before reflecting on how high and how far Evel had coasted (in spite of the fact that he'd only just failed to jump those thirteen buses).

Finally, my mind began formulating a tentative plan of action.

I didn't have a Super-8 film recorder or projector (there were no camcorders or digital video in those days), but I knew where I could lay my hands on those in exchange for a few pennies.

Nor did I have any purpose-built ramps like the ones that Evel had but, located about a mile from Southall, there *was* an old World War II ammunition dump with lots of rough and rippling terrain due to its crumbling underground structures and network of buried passages.

So, that left only one question unanswered: could *I* actually do jumps on my Suzuki TS-250?

Well, there was really only one way to find out for sure.

CHAPTER 11: YOU HAVE TO START SOMEWHERE

The ammunition dump in Trallwn (pronounced 'Track-loon' for those who find that the Welsh letter 'll' doesn't roll off the tongue *quite* so readily) lay within Swansea's north-eastern suburbs, and around two miles or so from Southall Avenue.

As you've doubtless surmised it's no longer there, supplanted as it was in the early 1980's with a new road, a housing estate, some long-overdue landscaping and a superstore.

Yes, it may have slipped quietly out of existence but, with all due respect, it *had* been given license over the intervening decades to decay into little more than a ramshackle carcass of crumbling concrete. Nonetheless, I still remember it with great fondness as the location where my stunt-riding career genuinely began.

I'd known for some time that the site was being utilised by other bikers, and I was also aware that they'd established some natural ramps for their own modest feats, but it wasn't until *I* ventured there with my TS-250 in the late summer of 1976 that I truly grasped how absurdly acquisitive they were of the place.
Primitively gouged into the dump's earthy slopes, and in addition to the already-irregular and treeless backdrop, were three makeshift runs which the aforementioned bikers had prepared for their own 'exclusive' use.

I trialled each of those runs repeatedly but soon concentrated my energies on the one which was not only best suited my needs, but also that upon which my Suzuki was most responsive, namely the middle run. It was inclined at something approaching fifty degrees to the horizontal and, as such, it permitted me to attain not only height but a decent distance as well.

Jumping without any tangible goals or targets to beat wasn't likely to do me any favours at all, so I always sought to be competitive with myself by flying over 'cars'. Obviously there were no 'cars' parked there but I'd estimated that the width of such a vehicle would be five feet, were it to be present, so I'd mark off those intervals on the ground with stones or heel scrapes.

My most rewarding spell at Trallwn included a notable leap over 'nearly eight cars' (i.e. a distance of slightly under forty feet) which, considering I'd received no stunt-riding instruction whatsoever, I still judge to this day to have been a very respectable accomplishment.

Sometimes I even took my mother along to watch me!

She didn't understand that much about motorbikes but she realised full well that what I was doing with my life came with intrinsic dangers, so perhaps her outings may have been made as a result of deep-seated maternal concern rather than polite curiosity.
It should go without saying that I was apprehensive when I first started off at the dump but, by ensuring that I took no unnecessary risks and by being patient enough to build up my expertise and knowledge in a gradual way, my self-assurance and poise became more robust with each passing week.

Naturally enough, I spent as much time making a pigs-arse of things as I did in getting them spot-on but, with each frustrating failure, both my motivation and determination to improve would harden that much more.

However, the local bikers weren't at all impressed and they were always resentful of me using what *they* perceived to be *their* private runs. Their indignant opinion, from what I could only infer because they never came close enough to actually speak to me, was that the entire area was *theirs* and that, as an undesirable outsider from Skewen, I had absolutely no business being there.

At its worst their attitude was one of unwarranted belligerence; at its most foolhardy, it was consciously obstructive.

Allow me to elaborate.

On one particular scorcher of a day three of them (two lads and a girl) had taken it upon themselves to stand quite deliberately at the highest point of my preferred run, just after I'd prepared myself for a routine practice jump.

What *really* pissed me off though was that, because they'd undoubtedly fathomed that it afforded me both lift and length, they *knew* damn well it was my preferred run.

I glowered at them through my helmet's visor; they smirked back.

I waved angrily, so naively crediting them with some small degree of common sense, but they didn't shift.

I revved my engine to the max; still, they wouldn't budge.

You want to be clever bastards then, do you? I thought. *Well, that's just fine by me!*

I engaged first gear, screwed the bike as hard as I could and, after an unimpeded blast over fifty or so yards, launched myself sweetly off the rough ramp and flew over their heads to a height of about twenty feet.

I'll freely admit that I had major reservations about what I was doing, and anyone who tells you that they haven't before committing to that kind of exploit is lying.

But I was angry. *Very* angry in fact, and I needed to make my point.
So, I soared cleanly over the top of those three cretins and came down on the other side with one heck of a crunch because, when all is said and done, my TS-250 was an enduro bike and *not* a motocross bike, meaning that it simply wasn't designed for such an outrageous stunt. After disturbing a cloud of dirt and dust on landing I locked the brakes, threw the bike around with no less bravado than the great Steve McQueen in his pomp (thereby throwing up even more muck), and just stared at them.

If it's indeed true that a picture is worth a thousand words, then the frozen expressions of horror and astonishment etched across their weedy little faces could have been traded in for the complete works of Shakespeare.

They probably thought I was totally insane but, at the same time, they *weren't* stupid and so I'm sure they also reasoned once and for all that I wasn't going to be toyed with.

Suffice it to say, they didn't dare block me again.

I persevered for a while at Trallwn with my self-styled training regime but the Dickie-Davies-thing, which I desperately wanted to have a crack at, had always remained uppermost in my thoughts.

Alas, I realised that if I wanted to be taken seriously as a stunt rider, and therefore have maybe half a chance of being seen on *World of Sport*, then I *had* to be that much more polished in how I presented myself and my work. Besides, by that stage I suspected that I'd outgrown all of the possibilities that the ammunition dump had to offer and recognised that it was perhaps the right time to move on anyway.

My first step after taking the decision to leave Trallwn was to manufacture a proper ramp. I'd never yet constructed anything on that scale, but my understanding of how the TS-250 behaved during each phase of a jump taught me much of what I had to know, in so far as the design aspect was concerned at least.

So, I commandeered two scaffolding planks and fixed them firmly onto an improvised 'A'-frame.

I accept that, by itself, that sounds like an extremely crude prototype but I was more than satisfied with what I'd knocked together, not least because I also had the insight to incorporate cross-branching which prevented the contraption from collapsing forward when my bike slammed onto it at speed.

Finally, on a cloudy Sunday afternoon and with the help of some mates, I transported the completed assembly down to a disused back road close to the ruins of Neath Abbey.

Sian and her friend divided the filming duties between them, and captured my every move while trying their very best (bless them) to appear almost interested.
I took the time to reassure them that, since they were still familiarising themselves with what I'd asked them to do, they should treat the whole thing as a rehearsal and concentrate only on becoming acquainted with the camera's controls.

Shrewdly, of course, that also served to remove some of the pressure from myself.

After setting up the ramp in a quiet spot I kicked off the entertainment with a number of well-practiced wheelstand routines. Those might have worked marginally better had I not been wearing flared jeans, which acted like windbreaks whenever I surged forward. Still, we managed to get a couple of maintained wheelies on film and so, with my self-belief on a jittery high, it was time to unbridle the main attraction.
I didn't have anything to jump over as such, apart from scattered potholes and a few desiccated dog turds, but I had my tried-and-trusted 'cars-and-markers' system from the ammunition dump and so, by adapting that, I had the means of reliably calculating just how far I'd gone.

On my maiden attempt I hit the ramp with one hell of a shunt at something like thirty miles per hour but thankfully the 'A'-frame held firm and a wobbly but otherwise unspectacular jump was safely tucked away under my belt.

The second effort passed off similarly to the first, although I was a smidgeon more adventurous in opening up the bike.

I managed to keep good control through both of those jumps by maintaining a perfectly-straight trajectory and without nose-diving or drawing the bike up toward the vertical - all essential techniques for any aspiring stunt-rider.

On the third go (if we regard the first two to be mere range-finders) I covered forty-one feet, which at the time represented my personal best by about a yard.
I did lose it slightly, however; just over halfway through the airborne stage my Suzuki started to tip forward. I didn't have a second ramp to absorb the force of my landing and so it was the front wheel which took the brunt of the bike's impact upon the tarmac. The spokes immediately sheared off the hub and the wheel's rim was compressed into an oval shape but, luckily, it didn't disintegrate completely. Had it done so then the front forks would have been thrust onto the hard ground, thereby causing the bike to go arse-over-tit, and I'd have been catapulted head-first through the air to meet what might well have been a messy death.
But it hadn't, which meant that I'd successfully executed a jump of forty-one glorious feet, as I'd previously boasted.

Now, during that Wembley performance of one year previously Evel Knievel cleared a distance of over one hundred and thirty feet.

So, you'd be forgiven for asking yourself, what's the big deal with one of only forty-one?

Well, firstly, let's not forget that Evel had been stunt riding since the early 1960's and could call on the accumulated experience of hundreds of faultless and not-so-faultless jumps, within which I suppose that failed 1975 attempt would have to be included.

Secondly, he benefitted from professionally-assembled and state-of-the-art ramps which incorporated materials designed to take the fullest advantage of his bike's qualities, rather than having to make do with two rotting scaffolding planks nailed onto an 'A'-frame.

Thirdly, he rode a Harley Davidson which was well suited for stunts akin to the jumping of thirteen single-decker buses; I owned a Suzuki TS-250, which most definitely wasn't. Yes, okay, I *know* he crashed on that day at Wembley, but he *still* covered the distance and *that*, for me, was the most significant benchmark.

As far as I was concerned that forty-one-foot jump in 1976 entitled me to view myself as Wales' first and *only* motorcycle stunt man.

The Land of Song had always enjoyed a tradition for producing great sporting heroes but, to me, and without wanting to sound ill-mannered or disrespectful toward those men and women who were all phenomenal talents in their own right, they all seemed to be rugby players or footballers or boxers or track-and-field athletes.

I reckoned that I was doing something 'new', something that 'stood out', and in consequence I deemed that I had every justification in considering myself to be somewhat special.

Moreover, I really believed that I'd found a calling which properly defined me – the Valleys' answer to Evel Knievel no less, and the grainy but priceless footage that Sian and her friend had secured on that memorable day had done nothing to crush that belief.

Having said all of that it should be remembered that, no matter how prodigious I then thought myself to be, I wasn't quite superhuman enough to straighten out my own front wheel! Fortunately though, I was well acquainted with an outstanding Morriston-based mechanic who, over the coming years, would re-rim and re-shape the many wheels that I so nearly destroyed, thereby without my incurring the expense of buying from new.
He used to charge me thirty pounds to repair a wheel; to put that into some sort of perspective, I was earning just forty-five pounds per week in the supermarket.

After some minor film-making issues had been dealt with, and also once the bike's front wheel had been reincarnated and I'd made a number of teensy adjustments to the 'A'-frame, I was ready to do the show for *World of Sport*.

Sian was then the sole cameraperson, and was perhaps more eager than she'd previously been because I think some glittery pound signs had started to flutter before her eyes.

Anyway, I recall performing a couple of impressive wheelies before completing a short series of jumps using my 'A'-frame ramp, and then finished off in true-daredevil fashion by springing the local canal from bank to bank.

Sian, to be very fair to her, had recorded everything successfully.

We got the footage developed and, after watching it over and over to make sure everything was as perfect as it could have been, we dispatched the reel to London Weekend Television, the producers of *World of Sport*.

On each and every Saturday for the next few weeks we'd sit anxiously in our living room in Southall, waiting for the fruits of our combined labours to be screened between horse races but, and I apologise for the cheap joke, we saw not a Dickie-bird of our precious film.

Undeterred, I therefore resolved that the mountain must go to Muhammad!
And so, after booking three days off work I headed to London on the train with the cheerless Sian in tow and, armed with our projector and a small selection of my treasured films, we set about fulfilling the seemingly-crazy intention of dropping in unannounced on every stunt agency that we could find.

We managed to gate-crash nine such companies.

Each of them showed us the door, with the majority barely decorous enough to give us the time of day.

I guessed at first that my riding was somehow not what they were looking for but, with the benefit of hindsight and some later experience of working in television, I'm now much more inclined to think that my shyness and the consequent inability to string two words together were the most debilitating factors contributing to those rebuffs.

If that's indeed the case then, in all likelihood, my riding *was* what those agencies wanted to see but, self-evidently, my meekness wasn't going to be tolerated by any of them for long enough for me to even turn my projector on.

On the last of our miserable and mostly unrewarding days in London we went shopping in *Lewis' Leathers*, where something possessed me to splash out on an all-in-one motorcycling jumpsuit.

I sketched the design that I wanted on the suit for the benefit of the store's tailors. They then took my measurements and told me that the fully-adorned vestment would be delivered to our address in Southall Avenue within a fortnight.

At the time it seemed a meagre consolation when set against three dismal mornings and afternoons of unremitting rejections but, as well as providing me a slither of solace, I thought it might give me something to look forward to.

En route to Paddington railway station we walked by the premises of *Stunts Unlimited*, an agency which, until that moment, we didn't even realise existed.

Feeling as though we had nothing further to lose we shuffled inside and, for the only occasion during those seemingly-endless hours traipsing around the rain-soaked capital in search of just one morsel of appreciation, we were met at last by some welcoming faces.

Whilst *Stunts Unlimited* couldn't provide me with any work they did offer much encouragement and also gave me the telephone number of another up-and-coming but more established rider called Eddie Kidd who, they felt, might be willing to pass on some valuable guidance. Eddie's name was already familiar to me, and I'm certain it is to you as well; he'd started jumping at around the same time as myself (he is, though, over two years younger) but he was the first to make it into the limelight.

We thanked those at *Stunts Unlimited* for their time before hurrying excitedly to Paddington. There I found a payphone and I dialled the number that they'd given to me.
Eddie wasn't at home at the time so I instead spoke to his father (who, coincidentally, was also named Eddie), and he generously imparted some of the most important advice that I've ever had. He recommended that I put together a promotional pack containing photographs, a brief introduction to myself and my achievements, a selection of letterheads and a handful of business cards. He also gave me the contact details of several agents who, he said, were always on the lookout for new talent to showcase at outdoor galas and festivals.

Sadly, Eddie Kidd Senior is no longer with us but I'll always be indebted to him for his bigheartedness that day because, without it, the opportunity to get my first critical foot onto the stunt-riding ladder would have surely remained elusive.

After we'd returned home I wasted no time in getting myself sorted out. I visited a printing firm in Neath later that week, armed with photos and a hand-written profile, and requested an affordable number of the packs of the type that Eddie Senior had described.

Once that work had been signed off I immediately sent each of the packs, which I have to say looked fantastic, to the various agencies in whose directions he pointed me.

I also felt that it was time to move on from the Co-op supermarket and look for a job that was just a little more 'me'.

In the meantime it seemed that my name and endeavours had come to the attention of a local newspaper, which sent a journalist and a photographer along to my homemade practice arena at Neath Abbey. That exposure in turn led to an unexpected communication from the Neath Round Table, who wrote to me enquiring as to whether if I'd be interested in jumping over ten cars at the town's upcoming carnival.

Yes, I quickly replied, I most certainly would, especially as I'd just taken possession of my one-piece riding get-up from Lewis' (although I didn't tell them that bit!).

There was a lot of publicity in and around Neath for myself and for what I'd been booked to do, and the planning even got as far as a meeting with the company which had been earmarked to erect my ramps but, unfortunately, the Round Table then claimed that they couldn't raise the funds for the necessary scaffolding, and so that was the end of that.

I was totally gutted, and I began to feel like a mouse trapped in a maze with no scraps of food and no exits.

I also found myself on the receiving end of a good deal of criticism for that stunt's abandonment because the widely-held perception at the time was that I'd somehow 'chickened out' of the gig.

Nothing, though, could have been further from the truth.

For the record I'll state here and now that I badly wanted to go for that jump because I realised it would have given my fledgling career the impetus it so desperately needed.

Unhappily it wasn't to be, but it wasn't all doom-and-gloom.
The positive media coverage that I *had* received led to a sponsorship package with a Port-Talbot-based company *Kickstart Motorcycles*, and that enabled me to part-exchange my long-suffering but beloved TS-250 in favour of a beautiful Suzuki RM-400.

I still had to pay the balance on that new machine, however; the deal I signed with *Kickstart Motorcycles* obliged them to shell out only for its upkeep and maintenance.

And so, at long last, I owned the kind of professional motocross bike which could bash down the door to the kind of extravagant jumps that I'd dreamed of taking on since those first tentative forays at the ammunition dump, while the financial support from *Kickstart Motorcycles* would help with the many day-to-day expenses borne while stunt riding.

That, of course, would have included the cost of making my squished front wheels round again!

So, as you can see, everything was finally starting to fall into place for me.

But then, and totally out of the blue, Sian angrily announced that she was pregnant.

CHAPTER 12: BECOMING SOMEBODY ELSE

Our son, Shane, was born in Neath General Hospital on the twenty-eighth of July, 1977, and I love him no less now than I did when I first held him on that incredible and emotional day.

For Sian, as is often the case with first-time mothers, the pregnancy was beset with a number of psychological challenges. Given a little reassurance she seemed to cope with many of those challenges admirably well but, regrettably, not quite so the others. Following Shane's birth her resentment of me burgeoned exponentially and, sensing that she and I were drifting apart with our priceless and vulnerable child caught in-between, I knew that I had to do something to lessen the festering tensions for everyone's sake.

So, as Sian became neither more agreeable nor overly maternal as the weeks passed, and after presuming that maybe our leaving Southall Avenue might be beneficial to all concerned, I added my name to the waiting list for a council house.

Also, and after spending an afternoon in the depressing and dingy Job Centre, I submitted myself for a position as a trainee operative with the National Coal Board.

In other words, I'd applied to become a miner.
I waited patiently for *any* telephone call that would give things a push in the right direction but, just like the local buses, two then came along pretty much at once.

"I've got a job in a colliery," I half-heartedly revealed to my family, and also the increasingly-choleric Sian, after the first of those long-awaited calls.
I should really have been passably excited about reaching the end of my days in the Co-op, especially as I was moving on to something with a better wage and more sociable hours, but Sian's antipathy toward me didn't wane anywhere near as much as I'd hoped it would so that really took all of the gloss off the change.

With trademark composure Mum did her best to play the unenviable role of devil's advocate, but Sian wasn't having any of it.

Of my request for a council house, there was still no word at all.

All of that it itself was stressful enough but there'd also been no acknowledgement of receipt of my promotional packs from any of the agencies that I'd sent them to, so *Kickstart Motorcycles* were becoming restless. With hindsight their concerns were understandable as they'd generously agreed to cover the costs of the Suzuki RM-400's maintenance as part of my sponsorship deal. As you would expect, they wanted some exposure for their company in return and they wanted it quickly.

However, I'd realised from an early age that life is not about bemoaning the storms; instead, it's about straining to sing in the rain while holding your head up high.

At the time though my father, who'd bequeathed many long years of graft and sweat to the National Coal Board, seemed almost elated that I'd finally found what he termed 'a proper job'. To him, 'a proper job' was where *somebody else* told you where to go, *somebody else* showed you what to do, *somebody else* needed to give their permission before you could visit the toilet, *somebody else* told you whether or not you could have a holiday and where *somebody else* paid you one quarter of what you were actually worth to them.

Very often, or so it appeared from my *own* denigrating experiences, you'd be inciting ridicule and contempt in a working class bastion like Skewen if you wanted to fight your way up the ladder in order to be that *somebody else*.

"So, who was it that you spoke to on the phone then?" my father asked me afterwards.

I told him the name of the bloke who'd offered me the job, but he didn't recognise it. As far as he was concerned, it was probably just 'somebody else'.

Little did I realise then that my spell at the mines would turn out to be not only life-altering, but also so very nearly life-ending.

I'll divulge all of the details regarding *that* little saga later.

"Brilliant! I've been booked to do some jumps in Devon!" I yelled gleefully after I'd finished with the second telephone call which came just days after that from the NCB.

I have absolutely no idea what 'Brilliant! I've been booked to do some jumps in Devon!' translates as in Swahili, but I may as well have found out and told everyone *that* way for all the positive reaction I received.

The call came from the *Daubney Variety and Gala Agency* who, as well as securing my agreement to do the Devon gig, expressed their regret for not getting in touch sooner as their events schedule for that year was already choc-a-bloc.

Aha! I realised, with some relief. *That's possibly why the other agencies I contacted haven't been in touch yet!*

Kickstart Motorcycles were justifiably delighted that I'd secured some paid stunt work but my mother's response was perfunctory at best, while Sian was totally disinterested and my father was nowhere near so highly enthused. Still, that event in the tiny but remarkably picturesque village of Clovelly, which lies about twelve miles west of Bideford, wasn't taking place until the June of 1978 so I figured that *that* was plenty of time for Sian's demeanour to change, even if no-one else's did.

With the target for all of her ceaseless loathing (that's me, if you hadn't already guessed) down in the South West for a weekend, she might have some freedom to get used to the idea of being a mother, and hopefully even embrace it.

Now, what was it that Robert Burns told us about the best laid schemes o' mice an' men?

Anyway, I digress.
My brief career as a mine worker began at six o'clock in the morning on a bitterly cold and soaking wet Monday in the early February of 1978.

The first training I was required to undertake was at Ammanford's Abernant colliery.

Going down the pit's vertical lift shaft was always going to be scary for newbies like myself and the other recruits who were shivering their knackers off alongside me. I wasn't looking forward to it one iota, and I don't think they were either.
Joe, the experienced hand who simply couldn't wait to get us underground, tried to chill us out as we descended by cheerfully relating a story of an old miner of yore who'd accidentally fallen down the open shaft and, as rumour had it, when the bits of his body were eventually recovered his hair had actually turned white.

Gee, thanks for that Joe!

We also learned that, sadly, a poor pit pony had plummeted down there as well.

When we reached the bottom of the shaft Joe released the gates and there I stood with my legs trembling and staring fearfully, for the first ever time, into the murky depths of the floor of a coal mine. It was cold and airless, and it felt as though no-one had ventured down there for ages. That wasn't so far from the truth since what we were being shown was a disused seam; Joe informed us, and in no uncertain terms, that we wouldn't be allowed into the working mine until we'd stopped 'crapping our wears about being downstairs'.
Once my eyes had adjusted to the light from my helmet's head lamp I could see that a number of the seam's wooden braces had either collapsed or snapped.

I remember thinking to myself: *Should we really be down here? It doesn't look safe to me!*

"Sandwich anyone?" Joe chirped after we'd negotiated a couple of hours of his instruction. "If you've brought your own then feel free to get stuck in. I've got some cheese-and-tomato ones here if anyone's peckish. I can't stand cheese or bloody tomatoes, so you boys just help yourselves."

And there we sat, heaven knows how many hundreds of feet underground, at an abandoned and dusty coal face which had little or no load-bearing support and nibbling anxiously on our lunch like petrified hamsters while listening to more of Edgar Allan Joe's disconcerting tales.

When I *did* begin down the active mine I quickly found that, because everyone was so approachable and cordial, Abernant was actually a more-than-decent place to work. My shifts at the colliery started, as you now know, at six o'clock in the morning and ended at twelve which meant that, even after I'd returned to Southall and had a long soapy bath, I was still able to dedicate a couple of hours each weekday to my Suzuki.

On my reaching the surface following one particular shift the colliery's managers told me that they'd received a telephone call from the BBC, who asked whether I'd be prepared to give an impromptu interview on a radio show fronted by Nicola Heywood Thomas.

"When did they say they'd ring back?" I worriedly asked the 'somebody else' who'd relayed the disturbing message.

He glanced at his watch and raised his eyebrows. "Ooh, let's see now. Ten minutes?"

What?! Was *that* all the time I had to prepare myself before addressing the nation? Ten minutes?

I'd never before spoken to a group of more than three people but, in just ten minutes (make that nine), my quivering words might be heard by as many as three million!

That is, if I decided to go ahead with it…

Then I realised I *had* to do it, because if *Kickstart Motorcycles* ever got wind of the fact that I'd bottled out of that golden opportunity to give them a free plug on the radio then that would be the end of the sponsorship deal, my RM-400, the jumps down in Clovelly, everything.

If there was one occasion in my life when it truly did feel as though I was being squeezed between a rock and a hard place, then *that* was it.

My gut churned over and over as I followed 'somebody else' into the colliery's admin block, scrutinised inquisitively by a whole host of individuals who I'd never clapped eyes on before, and would never see again.
I was invited to sit on a plastic chair beside a small square table. Upon that table there was a telephone.

"When the BBC call," I was advised by a very professional-looking lady, most probably a secretary of some description, "it'll come through on *that* line. It's all yours then. Good luck!"

Her encouragement fell on deaf ears; my heart was thumping no more vigorously than if I was spending my last moments on Death Row before walking the green mile but, in all seriousness, I needn't have been so alarmed. When the BBC rang the colliery, and they did so precisely when they said they would, they were very reassuring and, being sympathetically aware that speaking on radio was entirely new to me, talked me through all that they wanted me to do.

Before and during my interview Nicola Heywood Thomas did everything that she conceivably could do to try and put me at my ease. When we were live on air she asked about what first got me into stunt-riding, my plans for the year, what I'd been booked to do at the show in Clovelly (not that I knew too much about it myself at that early stage), and my job down the mine. She was completely professional from first to last and perhaps that's why, at the time of writing, she remains one of Wales' most popular broadcasters.

No-one at home heard the show although one or two people around Skewen *had* caught it and wished me all the very best for the future, sentiments which gave my stuttering confidence and capricious self-esteem a tremendous and timely boost. To this day, though, I've *still* not had the opportunity to listen to that interview in full.

My training at Abernant ended just weeks later and I was shifted on to another mine.

I have no longing whatsoever to mention the name of that place and it's no longer operational anyway so, for the sake of keeping the narrative ticking along and for no other reason, I'll call it Llacuff.

After all, if the mighty Dylan Thomas can call a fictional town Llareggub by writing something backwards then I think I'm well within my rights to re-christen my colliery Llacuff since *that* name, providing you accept that there is no 'k' in the Welsh language, would be fully in keeping with what the other miners there thought of me.

That said I should state that, at the outset, they behaved no differently towards me than they did to each other. Their collective attitude altered sharply though following something which I imagined would have been viewed more with amusement than anything else.

Shortly after I started in Llacuff I received a request for a short interview and photo session for 'Coal News', which was the NCB's equivalent of a tabloid.

Like the BBC they wanted to know more about my stunt-riding.

I could only guess that they'd learned of my passion from 'somebody else'.

I was intrigued nonetheless, and invited their reporting team down to the Neath Abbey ruins where I still practiced my jumping, not with my faithful 'A'-frame any more but with new and more practical ramps designed for both launch and landing.

They took a few snaps of me in 'airborne' mode, asked some questions, wrested some sound bites from me and then went away again.

I'd seen copies of 'Coal News' floating around the canteen at Abernant when I was there – it was most definitely a periodical for those whose world began and ended at the front gates of

their colliery so I really didn't think that I'd get more than a couple of well-buried column inches somewhere deep in the paper, and only *then* providing they'd run out of coal-related articles with which to titillate their readership.
I couldn't have been more wrong if I'd tried.

As I held in my hands a copy of 'my' issue I simply couldn't credit what I was looking at. There I was and on the front page no less, next to and just above a photograph of Arthur Scargill.

The way the editors had laid it out was comical because, having used an image of me pretending to leap over something-or-other, they made it look (completely by accident, I hasten to add!) as though I was about to come crunching down on dear Arthur's head!

They'd even given me a clever little headline: 'Flying Pitman Fears No Evel!'

I remember grinning from ear to ear with the humour of it all, but there weren't too many smiles to be had from anyone else.

From that moment my so-called colleagues could be divided into two distinct categories; those that were unfriendly, rude and borderline vile, and those that I'd never met.

It seemed that if, as a Llacuff miner, you had any misplaced designs on being someone of ambition (as I did, of course, in my own humble way), then there was every likelihood you'd be singled out for some very unpleasant treatment.

They utterly despised the notion of anyone they were forced to rub shoulders with following a dream, unless of course that dream kept them shackled to the pit.

There's a well-known Welsh chant which claims: 'We'll keep a welcome in the hillsides'. It's inconvenient that the lyrics of that song don't actually make it clear in *which* hillsides said welcome is to be found but, if such a list *were* to exist, the hillsides flanking Llacuff colliery would be highly unlikely to feature therein.

In short, during all of my fifty-seven years of life, those miners were the most abhorrent and repulsive clique of narrow-minded individuals that it's ever been my misfortune to encounter.

When I started in Llacuff I was informed that I'd be taking over Max Boyce's old locker. I've no idea how they regarded Max when *he* was mining there during the day and out making his name on the club circuit in the evenings, but I sincerely hope it was nothing like the appalling way they behaved toward me.

I was made to feel no more tolerable than a leper and their ignorantly switching from speaking in English to Welsh whenever I appeared served merely to reinforce my segregation.

That, of course, was what they'd wanted all along.

They'd presumed, rightly as it so happened, that I had no devotion to either the colliery or mining and, therefore, that I didn't court any aspirations to follow in my father's footsteps (while *he* never actually worked at Llacuff he was well-known and regarded positively by many there).

So, on a 'good' shift, I would turn up, clock in, spend seven hours being totally ostracised, clock out and then go home to my bike. On a 'bad' shift I might be ridiculed or humiliated or both, or maybe an attempt would be made on my life.
Yes, you *did* read that correctly.

I couldn't prove anything of course, but a fleeting look of disappointment from one of your 'fellow men' can sometimes reveal an awful lot.

Before I clarify the essential aspects it's important to realise that my duties at Llacuff were based entirely on the surface, and the three-man 'team' of which I was a part, albeit an extremely unpopular part, functioned roughly as follows:

Coupled rail wagons bringing their full loads of coal would emerge from the mine. Those wagons would then be uncoupled one at a time.

The first wagon in the line, with a combined weight of perhaps three to four tons, would roll down a short slope with phenomenal momentum and power onto a level bridge. There it would be brought to a halt, and a lever would be pulled which released its coal onto the back of a lorry which was waiting below the bridge. It would finally be pushed out of the way by the next laden wagon to be released, and so the process would continue.

My job was to recouple the empty wagons ready for the locomotive to shunt them all back into the mine.

The wagons were ageing, and the mechanisms which enabled them to rattle freely along the tracks were prone to frequent seizing; one of my more perilous chores included the releasing of those mechanisms whenever they so jammed.

On this one haunting day I was told by the detestable character working the stage behind me to liberate one such gismo. As I toiled at doing so a *full* wagon was 'inexplicably' released. It trundled down the slope, picking up speed all the while, before reaching the bridge where I was still struggling feverishly with the *empty* one.

I was left with just seconds to dive out of the way; had I not escaped as swiftly as I did then, almost certainly, I'd have been crushed to death.

Badly traumatised I immediately went to see the colliery's managers about the incident, but I couldn't believe how completely indifferent they were both to me and to what I'd told them. Basically, I was instructed to forget it ever happened and also warned that, if I didn't or I made any attempt to go public and besmirch the fine name of the colliery, I'd be replaced immediately by someone who'd be more grateful of the chance to work.

So, in summary, I believed that I'd been the victim of attempted murder and, because I had the cheek and the audacity to kick up a fuss about it, they threatened me with the sack!

After that I naturally became extremely apprehensive and vigilant and, without exception, trusted no-one.

Not only were the people I shared my shift with trying to bump me off, but I realised that the colliery's management would turn a blind eye if they succeeded and would conveniently shrug off my slaying as 'just one of those tragic things that occurs every so often in coal mining'.

I should have confided in my instincts and left Llacuff there and then. *No* wage, I concluded, could sensibly be weighed against the real risk of being assassinated.

Then I thought of little Shane, and of what Sian might do to my genitalia if I walked out.

So, and undoubtedly against my better judgement, I stayed there.

If my existence in Llacuff was a misery after the 'Coal News' thing then as a consequence my futile whistle-blowing it became nothing less than insufferable.

Having everyone ignore you is one thing, but being treated like you're a snitch and, consequently, no better than vermin is something else altogether. It was as if, after I'd voiced my grievance, I'd become *persona non grata*.

I couldn't understand why they disliked me so much and, to this day, I still can't.

My philosophy, as it's always been, is that if someone seeks to do something unusual with their life then, as long as it brings no harm to others, give them a lift and encourage them.

Is it really necessary to be so vicious to those people that yearn to get on and improve themselves? After all, what possible purpose can such discrimination serve, other than to mask the perpetrators own deficiencies and patent lack of respect?

I've always regarded myself as an open book; I don't think I have, or have *ever* had, any airs and graces. With me, what you see is what you get and to have to work in an entirely spiteful environment like Llacuff was something I soon found to be almost impossible.

I wanted only to enjoy trying to excel at something that was a bit out of the ordinary and, if I was lucky, see something of the big wide world while I was doing it.

Was *that* really so wrong?

Did *that* truly warrant such a display of animosity and hatefulness?

Well, *they* obviously thought so and, being so hopelessly outnumbered by miners and management alike, there didn't seem to be a great deal that I could do about it while the option to quit Llacuff remained out of the question.

On that soul-destroying basis alone the early summer of 1978 was no better than horrendous, but there was a silver lining to all of this.

Some additional information regarding the event in Devon, which I'd gathered was to be held in the grounds of the majestically-titled Clovelly Court, had begun to trickle through.

I'd previously assumed, not unreasonably, that it was going to be a motor sport weekend of sorts, with plenty of action on both two wheels and four, with me doing my thing, loads of others doing theirs and thousands applauding and cheering from behind the ropes.

Erm, no. Not quite.

It was actually an arts festival ('arts', as in painting, sculpture and dancing) hosted by Lady Henrietta Rous, and I was the only stunt-rider, or indeed rider of *any* kind, that had been booked to appear there.

The event was scheduled to run from Saturday the twenty-fourth to Monday the twenty-sixth of June; I'd be jumping, according to the organiser's provisional schedule, on the Sunday. We were also told that the entire weekend would be covered by Westward Television which, at the time, held the region's ITV franchise.

The organisers requested that I travel to Clovelly Court a few days prior to the event, in order to meet with the firm that had been contracted to put up my ramps, and to inspect the work that they'd done for me.

It was, as it turned out, a good thing that that request was made because, after heading down there with the boss of *Kickstart Motorcycles* for company, I just couldn't believe how astonishingly brainless the scaffolders had been.

CHAPTER 13: ADRENALIN VERSUS INCHES

If one has any aspirations of using a motorbike to jump over things then one should use a ramp of some description in order to get oneself off the ground.

In addition to that most obvious of benefits a *well-designed* ramp, as soon as one rides onto it, should act to compress the bike's suspension system, thereby giving one an additional but critical 'spring' on take-off.

That's why a ramp shouldn't be overly long when compared to the jump that one seeks to execute. As one rides up a ramp any compression of the suspension will gradually diminish; if the ramp is *too* long then *all* of the compression will most likely be lost by the time one reaches its apex and the bike will tend to dip toward the ground as soon as it tastes fresh air – not good.

Furthermore, as the angle between ramp and horizontal *increases* then the momentum which can be carried from one's run-up and onto that ramp will subsequently *decrease*. Likewise, one's *speed* will decrease which, self-evidently, is also undesirable.
If the ramp becomes *excessively* steep then it ceases to become a ramp in the conventional sense and begins to assume all of the impact characteristics of a brick wall which, if one is hammering toward it head-on at seventy miles per hour, doesn't bode well.

Hence, finding a ramp inclination and length with which one is comfortable necessitates a compromise; those attributes must suit not only the rider and the particular stunt in question, but also the mechanical features of the bike upon which he or she wants to accomplish it.
For me, an angle of ten degrees seemed to work best. Eddie Kidd's ramps were, I believe, a degree or two steeper but certainly no more than that.

So, you might imagine how loudly my warning bells jangled when I arrived at Clovelly Court for the first time and saw that the scaffolders had fabricated *my* take-off ramp with a slope of appreciably more than forty-five degrees to the horizontal.

Sixty feet or so away from it (i.e., the width of ten vans, which was what I'd been booked to jump), and inclined at much the same ridiculous angle, was my landing ramp. That, though, was totally redundant because if I'd ridden on to my take-off ramp as it had been constructed then I'd never have bridged that gap in a million years.

"I can't use that!" I remember complaining to the senior scaffolder.

He looked at me, then at the ramp, then at me again. "Not steep enough?" he suggested and without sarcasm, alarmingly.

"No! It's *too* steep! That thing will either kill me or launch me into orbit! I'm not putting a single tyre on it until you drop the angle!"

I then gave him much the same monologue on the essentials of ramp design that you've now sat through.

He'd clearly sponged up everything I tolerantly imparted to him because, when I went back to Clovelly Court on the Saturday (I wasn't jumping until the Sunday, you'll recall), everything looked as it should've done to begin with.
I determined the angle of the remodelled take-off ramp with a spirit level; eleven degrees, so that was fine.

I checked that there was no give in the planks forming both the take-off and landing ramps but, mercifully, there were no concerns on that score either.

I also examined the safety ramp, which was a horizontal platform covering the last two vans, and there simply a precaution against a 'short' jump; again, no problems.

I carefully scrutinised all of the scaffolding to make sure it was secured in place and had no loose or incomplete sections, but everything seemed hale and hearty.

Thoroughly satisfied I thanked the scaffolding guy for the extra work that I'd made him and his team do, and at such fleeting notice.

"My pleasure," he said, although I knew full well that it wasn't.

Before Sian and I left for our bed-and-breakfast I thought it might be an idea to have a wander around the festival, just to get a feel for the thing and maybe meet a few people.

Before very long I found myself being introduced to Lady Rous, the event's host, who was totally charming and never less than an absolute joy to speak to. She said that she was looking forward to seeing me jump, and asked if everything was as I needed it to be.

Thinking much the better of highlighting the scaffolders' previous daftness while also remembering how grateful I was that they'd sorted everything out, I replied that it was.

The festival itself was very cultured and quite high-brow here and there with its poetry readings and oil painting workshops but, being as it was such a gorgeous day, everyone appeared to be in terrific humour and delighting in whatever it was they were doing. I was just a little agitated that there didn't seem to be huge numbers of motorsport aficionados there.

Sadly, there weren't many around on the Sunday either; my first attempt at jumping the ten vans on that afternoon, having rounded off a few practice runs to gauge the level of traction between my bike's tyres and the lumpy terrain, would be watched by the proverbial three-old-blokes-and-a-dachshund.

I glowered at my now-modified take-off ramp, which lay in wait for me about a hundred yards in the distance.
"Come on! This is just like Neath Abbey or the ammunition dump!" I remember whispering to myself. "No different! No different at all!"

With that surge of self-motivation I opened the throttle, screamed forward with almost everything that the bike could give and hit the ramp at sixty-five miles per hour, but I realised straight away that I hadn't given it enough welly and that I was going to land short.

Sure enough, my Suzuki came down on the safety ramp and with such force that the plank I landed on promptly snapped into two. My rear wheel went straight through, such was my energy on contact, and it left an ugly dent in the roof of some poor farmer's van which had been parked underneath and which, presumably, he'd happily volunteered for my use.

The bike bounced up again and eventually touched down halfway along the landing ramp. After that I retained full control all the way through to the run-off.

Right! I thought, after completing some manoeuvres to confirm my RM-400 was not damaged. *I've got this bad boy sussed now! No way am I fucking up the next jump!*

After a couple of minutes of psyching myself up I sat in my saddle glaring pensively at that ramp again like a cheetah staring down its quarry.

I'd reasoned that a speed of sixty-five miles per hour, while normally comfortable for me, wasn't sufficient there because not only did I have to clear the ten vans but I also needed to overcome the pseudo-drag effect caused by the chewed-up field.
To improve my chances I also sneaked an additional twenty yards or so of run-up and, with a wide open throttle, I powered toward the ramp yet again while keeping the bike as steady as I could over the rutted topsoil.

A split-second after I roared onto the planks I knew that all would be well; the initial contact was crisper and, since I'd maintained a steady speed of seventy miles per hour over the ground, the bike had the necessary oomph.

I think that a whiff of complacency and perhaps too much adrenalin may have kicked in at that stage because I pulled the bike right up when in flight meaning that, if I didn't make a nimble correction then my front wheel would be directly above the rear one on landing and, in consequence, there was a danger I'd be coming down underneath the Suzuki rather than on top of it. Instinctively I made that vital adjustment and, after effecting a safe touchdown and keeping good lines through to the run-off, was greeted at that farthest end of the field by Lady Rous who was eager to congratulate me on what I'd achieved.

I thanked her for her very generous compliment of course but I wished, just as she probably did, that more people could have seen me in action.
Then again, what did I expect?

It *was* an arts festival after all.

Was I egoistical enough to believe that everyone would just 'down tools' with their drawing and folk dancing and magic shows just to come and see me and my testosterone sail over ten vans on a motorbike?

Well, yes I was as it goes, but I'd learned an important tenet nonetheless, and it can be expressed something like this: it's not necessary to be *watched* in order to be *seen*.

That three-day event at Clovelly Court, which I admit to thoroughly enjoying despite the meagre turnout for my own slightly out-of-place contribution, had been extensively covered by a local newspaper. That exposure led to a telephone call from Trevor Redmond, the New Zealand-born former speedway champion who'd become a respected manager and a dynamic promoter of niche sports like stock car and American hot rod racing at, amongst other places, Newton Abbot Racecourse.

He wondered whether I'd be interested in appearing in a contest called 'World of Wheels' that he was presenting at the aforementioned venue on Sunday 6 August. He mentioned that Eddie Kidd had topped the bill at a similar event in a previous year and had successfully jumped over ten cars using a restricted run-up; *that*, as you've doubtless surmised, is where the rider strives to achieve the optimum approach speed over a shorter distance than usual.

I hadn't experimented much with restricted run-ups and wasn't sure about how well I'd do, so I told Trevor I'd think about it and get back to him.

He then said that I'd be paid five hundred pounds to do the show, plus he'd throw in my travelling expenses and accommodation.
I said yes, I'd be thrilled to do it.

Hey, come on! Don't start wagging your finger at me now just because I'd started chasing the money around!

Yes, I loved motorbikes and everything that went with them, but I was also trying hard to manufacture a living out of it all as well!

For the Clovelly Court gig I'd earned three hundred pounds (minus the thirty-odd pounds booking charge for the Daubney Variety and Gala agency), and now Trevor Redmond wanted to offer me five hundred pounds to smash one of Eddie's lesser-known records!
Putting the two together that's eight hundred pounds, less the agent's fees.

To dress that up in a 1970's context for you I was earning one hundred and eighty pounds *per month* with the National Coal Board. So, my combined pay for appearing at Clovelly and then Trevor's event (i.e., just two days of work discounting travelling time) represented *eighteen weeks* of abuse at Llacuff colliery.

You know that I've never been a genius at maths, but I assure you I didn't make any mistakes with *that* calculation!

It wasn't all fluffy rabbits and rainbows though. On returning to Southall Avenue from Clovelly I learned that *Kickstart Motorcycles*, and for reasons I could never fathom, had decided to withdraw my sponsorship package.
So, as far as my transportation to and from shows was concerned, and also the essential maintenance of my RM-400, I really thought I'd been drop-kicked all the way back to square one.

Happily, after hearing I'd accepted Trevor's invitation to appear at his 'World of Wheels', *Celtic Trailers Ltd* of Neath came dashing to my rescue. They kindly offered to provide me with a purpose-built motorcycle carrier in return for prominent coverage of their company on my promotional material, plus some signage on the RM-400 and also our car (after *Kickstart Motorcycles* had pulled the plug Sian agreed to ferry me around in her new Rover while Shane would stay in Southall with my mother).

So, during the early hours of Saturday August 5th we travelled down to Newton Abbot Racecourse and arrived in glorious sunshine for our pre-arranged appointment with Trevor.

On meeting him, and on witnessing first-hand the proof of his tremendous work ethic and vision, the sentiments which kept recurring in my head were: *This guy is good, and I need him in my corner if I'm serious about being something!*

He'd obviously toiled incredibly hard to put the 'World of Wheels' together; there were little racing tracks and karting circuits and displays and all sorts scattered around the Racecourse's periphery but, I'm sure all you followers of the sport of kings will be relieved to know, nothing upon the sacred turf itself!

He'd also procured a professional ramp for me to use which, I gathered, had previously belonged to another stunt-rider who'd tragically died while attempting to jump eighteen cars. It had been erected in front of the main grandstand and appeared, at first glance at least, to tick all the boxes on my mental wish list.

However, in spite of Trevor's thoroughness I still insisted on performing my usual inspection.

I made sure that inclination of the ramp was my preferred ten degrees (which it was, roughly), I verified that the ramp's individual sections had been properly fastened together (they had been, and meticulously so) and, finally, I checked that the ground forming my run-up and run-off was as flat and as dry as it could have been (again, full marks to the man!).

While you're mentally assembling an image of all of this I should state that there was no landing ramp; Trevor had already informed me that my first task would be to *equal* Eddie Kidd's ten-car record and, if I achieved *that*, extra cars would be added on my next jump to give me the opportunity of breaking it outright.

If I *did* claim Eddie's record then, depending on how I felt, even *more* cars would be brought in for subsequent attempts until I decided that enough was enough. So, instead of a ramp I'd be landing on a narrow strip of gravel beyond the last car, wherever that might have been positioned.

He wished me luck for the following day before we said our farewells (by that time lots of others had arrived at the place coveting his attention) and made our way to the hotel that he'd generously pre-booked for us.

The following morning, and after scoffing as robust a full-English breakfast as I think I've ever done, Sian chauffeured me and my Suzuki back to the Racecourse.

As far as my own itinerary was concerned I couldn't have bid for better weather; the day was beautifully warm, which I hoped would encourage plenty to come and watch, and there was scarcely a cloud in the sky which meant no rain and so no build-up of hazardous moisture on my ramp.

I dearly wanted a legion of motorsport devotees to turn up and, wow!

Didn't I just get one!
Without any exaggeration there must have been six thousand there on that day. The grandstand was jam-packed to capacity but hundreds more spectators were eagerly squeezing themselves into the areas flanking my run-up.

I'd seen hordes like that many times on television of course, but being right in the midst of one gives you a very different perspective altogether, not to mention the most exhilarating buzz.

I've never forgotten that experience to this day, and I don't believe I ever will.

Having already watched some kart races I had one final briefing off Trevor before that all-important first jump.
While I was with him he asked me how I was feeling. I replied that I was excited about what I was there to do, and also that I was eager to trump Eddie Kidd's achievement.

He looked pleased by that, and added that there was someone else there who wanted to meet me.

"Chris?" he announced with all the loftiness of a court usher. "I'd like you to meet Dave Taylor. Dave, this is Chris Bromham."

I don't think my jaw could have dropped any lower if Trevor had introduced the guy as Clark Kent!

After all, *that* was Dave Taylor!
The Dave Taylor no less, the deified 'wheelie king' of his day who, in said fashion, had ridden around the Isle of Man TT course in its entirety!

Anyone who'd ever leapt onto a motorbike in that era would have heard of Dave Taylor, and they would have regarded him with the same veneration as anyone who'd sat at a piano would have bestowed upon Liberace.

I spoke to Dave with no less reverence than any apprentice might when in the company of the master of his chosen craft. He wished me the best of luck (as did Trevor) and said he was looking forward to seeing what I could do.

Great! No pressure then!

It must be said that Trevor Redmond's crowd-working skills were extraordinary. With his microphone in hand his voice reverberated through the grandstand's many loudspeakers, building everyone (including myself as I sat with my bike at the end of my run-up) into a frenzy of anticipation.

Nevertheless I tried to block all of that out and focus solely on that first jump but it wasn't easy, especially as I knew that the 'wheelie king' was out there somewhere earnestly observing every move I made (or *didn't* make, as the case may have been!).

Between the hundreds of pairs of eyes ogling me from both sides I could see my ramp just forty yards ahead.
Behind that ramp ten stock cars had been crammed snugly together; a successful leap over *those*, as Trevor was passionately relaying to my captivated audience, would be sufficient to match Eddie Kidd's record.

"Come on Chris!" Trevor yelled into his microphone. "You can do it!"

That, as he'd explained during his briefing, was my cue.

I took a deep breath, revved the engine a few times (Trevor told me that they'd lap that up, and they did), engaged first gear and, after opening the throttle, I was away.

My tyres kissed the ramp in no time; I mounted it cleanly, kept the bike on a perfectly straight line through the air, cleared the tenth stock car with clearance aplenty and crunched down onto the gravel without so much as a shudder.
Everyone was in raptures!

Revelling in their ovation and giving myself the 'Yes! Yes! Yes!' inside my helmet I could just make out Trevor's muffled tones telling the multitude that they'd just witnessed a wonderful jump and that they'd be hearing from me shortly. That type of padding was essential at such events; if I'd rattled through my jumps one straight after the other then the whole thing would be finished in no time and any sense of spectacle would be lost.

"So then, Chris," Trevor screamed into his microphone after I'd joined him in front of the grandstand. "You've *equalled* Eddie's record, but are you ready to *beat* Eddie's record?"

"Definitely!" I shouted, buying in to what was expected of me. "Bring it on!"

The crowd cheered again, Dave Taylor gave me a double thumbs-up from his vantage point and, eager to savour that remarkable day for all it was worth, I again donned my helmet and returned triumphantly but unhurriedly to the run-up.

As before, my ramp stood forty yards ahead. Beyond it, although I couldn't actually see them, a further two cars had been parked alongside the original ten.
My audience had grown significantly and appeared much more zealous than before. I pondered whether they yearned to see me prevail as an all-conquering hero or fail calamitously within the chaotic carnage of busted bodywork and broken bones.

Those that craved the latter, I resolved, were going to be very disappointed.
"Go on Chris!" Trevor screeched. "Take your place in the 'World of Wheels' Hall of Fame!"

I will, I vowed to myself over and over. *I WILL!*

My engine snarled; I'd only let it devour the first of those forty yards when I was good and ready (and when I'd finished teasing the crowd of course), and not a moment before.

All I could hear was shouting and slow hand-clapping; even Trevor's increasingly-animated spiel was drowned out by the vocal encouragement of the spellbound thousands.

It was time.
Clutch down, into first, brakes off, gone.

Within seconds I was soaring off the top of the ramp.

I'd opened the bike up as much as I possibly dared on that reduced run-up and, at the very instant I took flight, I sensed I was going to make it.

Everything felt right. It was as though the bike knew *exactly* what it needed to do.
Then, and after what seemed like an age, I touched down cleanly onto the gravel having just (but *only* just) missed the twelfth car.

But, *only just* was good enough!

As the near-riotous cheering confirmed I'd broken Eddie Kidd's record!

After all the phenomenal hard graft and countless hours of practice I'd put in just to get to *that* point in my career, and in spite of the hatefulness of the Llacuff miners and the complete apathy of my family, I realised that I'd finally arrived as professional stunt-rider.

I pulled a celebratory wheelie as I rode through the gravel but, in truth, I felt so fantastic that I could have done one on a unicycle if there'd been one lying around.

"Congratulations, Chris!" enthused Trevor who was wearing the joyous smile of a promoter who knows he's dropped the jackpot. "The record's all yours! But what about jumping fourteen cars? Do you think you can do *that*?"

"Yes!" I cried through my own self-indulgent grin after he'd thrust his microphone under my nose. "Of course I can do it!"

The crowd's reaction to *that* should need no further chronicling and neither should Trevor's for that matter.
As I jostled my way back to my bike it felt as though all of the other sideshows had stopped and that every one of the six thousand pairs of eyes packed into the Newton Abbot Racecourse that day belonged to me, and to me alone.

So there I stood, astride my trusty RM-400, leering at the ramp ahead and picturing in my mind's eye the fourteen stock cars on the other side.

I knew that, to get over them, I had to screw that bike with absolutely everything it could give me. I'd barely cleared the twelve cars so I understood all too well that my margin of error had all but vanished.

I simply had to nail it!

Seconds later I was thrashing down the narrow run-up with as much power as the bike could have put out.

I slammed onto the ramp, but then…

No! I realised with horror before I was soaring over the seventh car. *This isn't right! I haven't got enough! Oh, SHIT!*

It was going to be tight. *Very* tight.

Stunt riding is a sport where destinies are often determined by inches.
If you're a few of those inches over then you'll clear the last obstacle and be hailed as a superman.

If you're just one of those inches under you could be seriously injured or even, in everyone's nightmare scenario, killed.

I was perhaps half a second away from my first significant meeting with one or other of those inches.

My fate was completely out of my hands.

The dice had been rolled and, feeling utterly helpless, all I could do was pray that someone up there was watching over me.

CHAPTER 14: RIDING HIGH

If someone *was* up there observing that catastrophe as it unfolded then, regrettably, they were rather lethargic in assuming a more proactive role.

In their absence my *rear* wheel clipped the roof of the fourteenth car which, in turn, caused my *front* wheel to instantly plunge towards the ground. That abrupt shift in direction wrenched my grip from the handlebars and, hurled from the bike's saddle like a cowboy who's been flung off a bronco, I began somersaulting along that slender track of chippings.

Again and again I glimpsed the blue sky as it flashed past, then the grey gravel, a cloud of dust, and then the sky once more.

Flip-flopping in my wake was the Suzuki which, at one point, slammed into my chest before one of its still-warm tyres chafed my neck.

Then, there was nothing. I wasn't tumbling anymore, and everything had gone dark.

I could hear screaming, lots of muffled yells and the ever-sharpening crunch of anxious footsteps stampeding towards me through the gravel, but the cheering had ceased.
My eyes started to refocus but my nose could smell only stone. I'd come to rest face down but, either by some miracle or sheer blind luck, I wasn't in significant pain.

I could sense which parts of my body had clouted the chippings but there was no acute or piercing agony, often the tell-tale indicator of a shattered bone or two.
One person crouched beside me, followed by another and then a third. Cool fingertips groped my neck and wrist, presumably in search of a pulse, and my name was called repeatedly; I later discovered that those hands *and* that frantic voice both belonged to Dave Taylor.

My faculties were returning, and in sufficient measure to appreciate, at least blearily, the fretful activity all around.

Aside from the occasional dull throb and tender spot beneath my leathers I realised that I was more or less okay but *they* didn't know that and I wasn't in any hurry to let on either, thinking instead it might be more fun to cheekily milk that singular moment for all it was worth.

After all, receiving such compassion and in that abundance was very new to me.

I prolonged my Oscar-worthy enactment of a corpse for a spell but then, not wanting to overplay the part and risk endangering my credibility, I prudently brought down the curtain on my puckish performance. So, while allowing my limbs to gently 'jolt', I 'groaned' a couple of times and then 'struggled' to my 'wobbly' feet.

On 'raising' myself upright I removed my helmet and, in the style of the last gladiator standing, thrust it aloft.

Deafening cheers of approval, and probably some of relief as well, resounded all around the grandstand. Sian gave me an all-too-rare hug, Dave Taylor shook my hand as vigorously as if he were churning a bottle of tomato ketchup while Trevor, a few yards distant having arrived on the scene a little later than everyone else, applauded wildly and pumped his fists into the air.

I looked back in the direction from which I'd come; about ten feet away two stewards were pulling my Suzuki upright and, thirty-odd feet beyond *them*, I could see the red livery of that fourteenth car (which belonged to a guy called Jan the Man – more on him later) blinking between the wandering spectators.

That was how far I'd cartwheeled - forty-something feet.

Soon afterwards Sian and I were shepherded into the rear of a St John Ambulance by a small team of paramedics, but I still managed to wave nobly to my lauding public and also to a handful of insatiable press photographers before its doors were sealed.

With the circus well and truly over I was driven, and with some haste, to a hospital in Torquay.

After being examined in the emergency department I was whisked into a tiny cubicle where a grumpy and not-to-be-messed-with doctor removed several slithers of embedded rubber from my neck. He also gave me a tetanus injection in my *gluteus maximus* (or, colloquially, the cheeks of my arse!).

I was discharged an hour later and soon afterwards I bumped into Trevor, who was waiting for me in the hospital's reception area. Seemingly thrilled to see and hear that I'd suffered no lasting damage he congratulated me on delivering a fantastic day's entertainment and mentioned that he would like to become my manager in the near future.

I told him that would be brilliant, and that I was very grateful to him for all that he'd done for me.

I then asked about my Suzuki; he said that, aside from a twisted clutch lever and some unsightly scratching of the paintwork, it was in good nick. He also confirmed that, since it was getting late, he'd taken the liberty of re-booking our hotel room for that night.

Both Sian and I were tired and emotionally drained and Trevor had already recognised, as had I, that having her drive from Newton Abbot to Skewen through the wee small hours was a non-starter.

He commended me again on all I'd done and then, wholly reassured that I was in decent spirits, he left.

We arrived back in Southall late on Monday afternoon but there was no fatted calf to be seen or any sincere interest from anyone with regard to how my weekend went, nor was there any genuine concern about my injuries (slight though they were) or any excitement about my breaking Eddie Kidd's restricted-run-up record.

Even Trevor's offer to manage me got the tumbleweed treatment.

All hail the valiant return of the prodigal non-person!
That said, the chance to make a clean break from those sapping surroundings *had* come; after waiting the best part of a year for them to contact me the council had finally written and with the option for us to take up a council house.

I was over the moon, as were Sian and my mother, while my father rejoiced at getting 'that little bastard' out of his hair once and for all.

We (that's Sian, Shane and myself) moved into our new home during the first week of September.

Having sampled the high life at Trevor's 'World of Wheels' I was chomping at the bit to leave Llacuff and the coal industry full stop but, with Shane to provide for and a whole new set of responsibilities to somehow juggle, I couldn't yet contemplate taking that chance.

Besides, the event season for the calendar year was all but over; I'd have been fortunate indeed to get a booking for any show between November and March but *that*, sadly, was the period when the extra cash would have been most welcome.
As it transpired, and due entirely to Trevor's tireless efforts, I appeared at four more shows up to the end of October.

The money I earned for doing them wasn't huge as the big summer events had all been staged and so promoters' budgets had effectively dried up, but it did help to pay for a little furniture, some new clothes for Shane and a decent Christmas.

However, as the weeks passed I wondered whether the council had given us that house because nobody else was mindless enough to take it. Our miniature coal fire barely warmed the living room and the central heating system was so old, noisy and knackered that it may as well have not been there for all the good that it did. The place was hellish draughty; the rotting window frames were overrun with fungus and damp while our tiled roof also craved some serious attention (and some new tiles!), but I just didn't have enough money to put all of that right straight away.

There were other issues that needed sorting as well, including the papering over of the cracks in my faltering relationship with Sian, but during that bitter winter my only priority was keeping Shane warm and if that meant covering him with overcoats while he lay in his cot because we couldn't afford blankets then, fine, that was the way it had to be.

For me, 1979 couldn't have come soon enough.

I'd already resolved that *that* was the year I'd be saying bye-bye to Llacuff and taking more purposeful bounds toward the big time. After all, I already had everything I needed to get myself there. I owned an excellent and reliable bike, two strong ramps, the continuing support of *Celtic Trailers Ltd*, the persuasive and ubiquitous Trevor Redmond as my manager-sort-of and a blossoming reputation for high-quality stunt-riding and the showmanship that went with it.

I had precious little in my wallet admittedly but I didn't *owe* anything, at least not in any unnerving quantities.

And so, with the evenings drawing out at last, I started training harder for that event season than I think I'd ever done.

In addition to practicing and polishing my jumping techniques I'd spend hour upon hour fine tuning *this*, experimenting with *that*, altering *this* and scrapping *that*.

In the meantime Trevor was brandishing his magic wand and getting down to some scrupulous work on my behalf.

My first engagement of the season was at Doncaster Racecourse, where I'd been booked to jump eight cars first of all, then ten, then twelve; a mellow start, just to ease me back into the swing of things.

I might then find myself plying my trade at a disused aerodrome near Bristol, or at a brownfield site in the Midlands, or in the glorious wide-open spaces of the grounds of a Shropshire manor house; every weekend I was somewhere different, and becoming that much more accomplished with each successive show.
All of the pieces were slotting into place because Trevor, it seemed, knew exactly what the jigsaw was supposed to look like.

For the first time I had more going *into* my bank account than was haemorrhaging *out* which meant that Sian and I, having called a ceasefire in our increasingly-fractious association, could give Shane a wonderful second birthday.

Planning ahead to the following winter I replaced our old central heating system with a brand new all-singing-all-dancing contrivance with radiators that actually worked. We also modernised some of the kitchen and swapped the worst of those window frames as well. All I then hungered for was a one-way ticket out of the abominable Llacuff colliery, but I didn't have to wait long for that thankfully and, when it *did* arrive, it was courtesy of somebody I'd never even met.

Peter Brayham was, and posthumously remains, one of the most respected stunt coordinators in the long history of British film and television. His list of credits, which becomes more impressive with each successive reading, includes the classic movie 'The Guns of Navarone', some of the earlier James Bond pictures (he actually appeared in 'From Russia with Love'), 'The Sweeney' with Dennis Waterman and the late John Thaw, 'The Bill', 'Cracker', 'Life on Mars' and the updated 'Dr Who' to name but a few.

He even doubled for John Wayne in the film 'Brannigan', in a scene where the aforementioned luminary's title character was meant to fly across the opening Tower Bridge in a car!

If you've ever enjoyed any of these and found yourself immersed in a high-speed chase, a fight, an alien ambush or some other nail-biting action scene then there's a strong chance you'll have been lapping up some of Peter's extraordinary work.

I first learned of his name in a telegram (which I still have) from Trevor, dated September 14th, 1979. The message read as follows: *Peter Brayham wants you to jump in the Eddie Kidd film. You had better tell him I'm your manager.*
I simply couldn't believe what I was looking at!

Me! In a *film*!

I was happier than I'd been for many a long month when I read that telegram, I can tell you!

So was Sian for that matter and, for a while, our mutual acrimony was put on hold.

Suitably excited I rang Peter that very afternoon (Trevor had included his telephone number in the telegram), and my first impressions of him were of somebody who was warm, refreshingly easy to talk to and thoroughly professional.

After I'd clarified Trevor's position in the grand order of things Peter started telling me about the film which, I learned, was to be called 'Riding High'.

He explained that I'd be doubling for two actors who were playing stunt-riding characters, and that I could expect to be working on and around the Isle of Sheppey in Kent for two to three weeks, depending on the weather and a number of more complicated movie-making factors. He said that I'd be paid one thousand pounds per week while on set which rendered his final question, namely 'Are you interested?', totally superfluous.

On October 13th I received a second telegram, from Peter himself; I was told to phone him immediately.

My initial fear was that the whole thing was off but, no, it was anything but.

He told me to make my plans to travel to London on November the twelfth and visit *Highwayman Leathers*, where I'd be fitted for the two outfits I'd need for the film. Then, after staying in a hotel overnight at the film company's expense, I was to take a train from Victoria to Sheerness, on the Isle of Sheppey, first thing the next morning.

I was advised not to burden myself with any onerous baggage, which worked out just fine because Sian was more than happy to stay at home anyway.

So, with all of the arrangements confirmed I could at last tell Llacuff colliery where they could shove their bullshit job and, to the day it finally closed its gates, I never went back there.

After heading to London and *Highwayman Leathers*, where I was measured up for the costumes of the colourfully-named 'Judas S. Chariot' and 'The Halifax Hellcat', I made my way the following morning to the Isle of Sheppey and met Peter Brayham, Ross Cramer (the film's co-writer and director) and Eddie Kidd.

Peter issued me with a watching brief for that day but, in all truthfulness, there wasn't a great deal to watch.

Film-making is a fascinating process I suppose but, for the uninitiated like me, it's also pretty soporific.

The shooting for that particular section of the movie took place not far from Sheerness, and on an expanse of bleak, flat terrain about half a mile inland from the beach.

Everyone else had clearly been there for some weeks, including Eddie, so I felt completely out of place and not at all comfortable, but I was relieved to find that I wasn't the only one there who had far too much time on his hands.

"Alright, boyo?" came the hammed-up call from the passenger seat of an old truck parked nearby.

Zoot Money, a star of the 1960's music scene, had made his name performing with, amongst others, the Animals. His proficiency with keyboards is nothing short of legendary; his skill at mimicking the Welsh accent, perhaps not quite so.

Still, at least he'd made the effort to acknowledge I was there.

"So, who the hell are you then, boyo?"

I introduced myself, and told him what I was meant to be doing.

After we shook hands he told me who *he* was, and he talked about the teddy-boy character ('Dorking') that he was playing.

At last, I had someone to talk to!

Despite the difference in our ages and the disparity in our show-business experience Zoot and I became big friends during my two weeks on the Isle of Sheppey.

Every morning at breakfast (the entire cast and crew stayed at the Westcliff Hotel in Southend-on-Sea) he'd play a few songs on the white piano in the dining room, which helped everyone to chill out before another hectic day of filming.

Bill Mitchell, who played 'Judas S. Chariot', would grab my face and give me a kiss after we'd eaten each morning and say, in his eminently husky voice: "This is the guy that makes me look real good!", and strung out the word 'real' as though it contained twenty 'e's.

I wouldn't have been able to make him look real good though had I not challenged Peter over the bikes which had originally been brought in for me.

Perhaps mesmerised by the name 'Harley Davidson' and its inextricable link with Evel Knievel, the film company procured two such machines for my use.

Unfortunately, there were many models which carried the name 'Harley Davidson', and the two I gasped at in horror that morning certainly *weren't* designed for doing jumps. In fact, they were so flimsy that I didn't think they'd even be able to support an impact with a take-off ramp.

Don't get me wrong here, the bikes looked great with their slick curves and with the stars and stripes plastered all over them, but they were perilously unsuitable for the type of work I was expected to do.

"But *you're* a stuntman," Peter growled after I'd shared my concerns with him. "*You're* supposed to be able to jump over anything!"
It was no use. I had to give him a demo.

Taking on the sixty-foot-jump which had only that day been assembled as part of the film's set inside Southend's greyhound stadium, I opened up the Harley on the approach, suffered a massive decrease in speed when I mounted the ramp and, after nearly being slung off the bike, landed somewhat awkwardly a laughable ten feet away.

When Peter saw the Harley's response to all the distress I'd put it through he knew I was telling the truth and, acting on my recommendations and after barking at some people down the phone, demanded two Yamaha-YZ400's instead. Those new bikes arrived the next morning, and that meant that we could finally get down to what I was actually there for – jumping!

I think Eddie was pleased about that as well. For over a fortnight he'd been riding around the Isle of Sheppey's sand dunes and flatlands and the streets of Sheerness and Sittingbourne, being filmed from just about every conceivable angle over and over and over again.

I'd only known him for a couple of days but we were getting along really well.

I could tell that he was restless though.

It should go without saying that stunt-riding was as much his obsession as it was my own but now *his* time, *and* mine of course thanks to those Yamahas, had arrived.

For the next week the film crew's efforts were concentrated on that greyhound stadium, and nothing else.

Professional ramps had been set up at its heart, and the place had been decked out to look like a proper biking amphitheatre.

We'd be jumping over foam and, with the aid of a large number of gas burners, fire.

I was constantly made to switch between the 'rival' characters of 'Judas S. Chariot' (that was Bill Mitchell's part) and 'The Halifax Hellcat', played by Ken Kitson, so between jumps I'd be hurriedly switching costumes as well.

Peter even asked if I could crash a motorbike deliberately.
When I said that I could he got me to ride at speed into some bales of straw into which special powder had been added to give the impression of an explosion on impact, but without any flames.

Of course, Eddie and I were necessarily competitive with our jumps and I think that, in terms of projecting some realism onto the silver screen, both Peter and the film's director, Ross Cramer, encouraged that and squeezed onto celluloid every last hint of it that they could possibly get.

I really felt as though I belonged there.

I was a 'somebody' on that set, and I was respected for the hard-earned expertise that I was able to contribute.

There was only one person there that didn't like me and, instead of facing up to me and airing his grievances as any honourable man would, he oh-so-bravely smeared some shit, and human shit no less, on the rims of my 'Hellcat' boots.

I know who did it, and he knows that I know, but I can't prove it, and he knows that as well, so I'm just going to leave it there (but it's no-one that I've already mentioned).

One afternoon an ITN (Independent Television News) team appeared on set and interviewed both me and Eddie about the film.
Eddie was the bigger name though, especially so close to his London roots, so it hardly came as a surprise when I dashed back to the Westcliff Hotel at the end of the day to catch the broadcast and saw with much disappointment that ITN only aired *his* piece.

Am I hearing you cry: "That's not fair!"?

Well, maybe you're right, but let's not forget here that Eddie was actually the star of the film (playing the dispatch rider 'Dave Munday') as well as being one of the principal stuntmen, whereas I'm not even mentioned in the end credits!

But, hats off to him because, as I only found out when my involvement in 'Riding High' was drawing to a close, without his say-so there was no way I would have been invited there to begin with.
You see, over dinner one night he revealed that he'd collected all of my press cuttings and, when Peter Brayham asked him who'd be a valuable support rider, he replied with my name.

So, thank you for that Eddie, it has always been very much appreciated.

It seems though that he did have some reservations about doing the movie's climactic jump, over an eighty-four-foot-wide gap in a ruined viaduct in Essex, and sensibly so because any rider attempting that stunt and getting it wrong would have undoubtedly been killed.

Peter rang me about a week after I'd returned to Southall and asked whether I'd be prepared to step in for Eddie in that final scene.
Naturally I said yes but, on hearing that I'd subsequently agreed to do it, Eddie quickly changed his mind.

I've watched the film many times since and, I have to say, he nailed that stunt pretty well, although I did hear that he apparently cut his leg apparently on a protruding branch of all things when he landed on the other side of the gap.

Other than that, though, all I can say is well done to him.

Sadly, 'Riding High' bombed when it was released; I travelled to a cinema in Llanelli to see it when it came out, but I had the place virtually to myself; even the poor usherette looked embarrassed!

You'd have to be a biker and a lover of motorbikes to know about the film which has, through the intervening years, grown into something of a cult classic within that fraternity.

I would strongly suspect that for the vast majority of the people who worked on it, it's been forgotten and consigned to the mental scrapheap.

For me though, it's something that will forever have a place in my heart.

Peter Brayham passed away on December 7th, 2006.

Working with him on 'Riding High' was an absolute joy, and I will always be indebted to him for that opportunity he entrusted to me all those years ago.
Eddie Kidd's personal difficulties in recent times have, sadly, been very well documented and I've no desire to highlight them again here.

Instead, I'd prefer to remember him as the outstanding rider he was, and as the incredible motivation for my career that he became.

Nevertheless, I would like to dedicate this chapter's penultimate paragraph to those whose favourite word is 'can't'.

On Sunday April 17th 2011, and after taking his place alongside all of the other competitors, Eddie started the London Marathon using a specially-adapted walking frame rather than his wheelchair. His only objective was to complete the course; he achieved that objective on Monday June 6th, a full seven weeks and one day later.
The very best of luck to you Eddie - I really hope you find the happiness that your continuing courage and determination deserve.

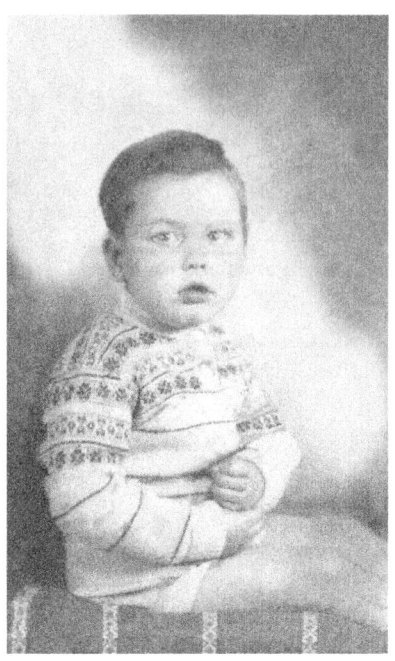
Me at about three years old

Me at about six years old

Donna age about six. Photo was taken in Auckland, New Zealand.

My first bike, a Suzuki 185. She burst into flames. Had this event not happened, I probably would not have found my career.

Swansea Airport 1981. Just before by 28 car jump. Photograph courtesy of South Wales Evening Post.

Practice jump before the start of the New Zealand tour 1982.

20 Lorry jump 1986. Photograph courtesy of Vanguard Engineering.

My Time Machine replica. It took me eight years to build. This helped with my bereavement.

Me as Judas S Chariot on set of Riding High   Donna and I celebrating the success of 1986.

Donna's passport photo to come to Britain 1982   Taken two weeks before Donna's death.

Donna with Natalie (left) and Natasha 1991

Family photo taken two weeks before accident. Back row is my son Shane and my Dad and Mum

Donna pregnant with Natasha 1991   Donna at the American Adventure 1989

Me with Donna's brother Gene and his wife Joanne 2007

My wife Anna-Marie when I first met her in 1994

Anna-Marie and I 1995

Us with our good friend Chris Barry

My beautiful girls, Natalie left and Natasha right. Taken in Crete 2009

At home with Natalie

Natasha and I in the Lake District. One of my favourite places.

Anna-Marie and I with Matthew Kelly. On the set of Stars In Their Eyes

CHAPTER 15: DREAMS

After *Riding High* I amassed a back-catalogue of more than five hundred cameo appearances in big-budget action films and television series and, in the process, earned more money than I scarcely believed was possible.

I toured the world in my private jet, rubbing shoulders with the rich and famous and considerably more than mere shoulders with the busty and the beautiful.

My name was eulogised by everybody, from the schoolchildren of Stockholm to the cabbies of Cape Town, and from the furniture makers of Faisalabad to the high-and-mighty of Hollywood.

The United Nations even advocated that July 20th (my birthday) should be observed internationally as 'Chris Bromham Day' with altars constructed in any location with a human population greater than zero so that lesser mortals could offer deference at the feet of the idol.

Naturally, such fame and veneration comes at a price and, in my case, my pockets were metaphorically ransacked each morning when I woke and recognised all over again that the abyss separating Technicolor-tinted dreams from sepia-stained reality is sometimes dishearteningly wide.

It *is* true that I held great aspirations for my career following that first enticing nibble of the showbiz cake but, frustratingly, after *Riding High* that was all I ever seemed to get – nibbles. I *would* appear in several productions admittedly and gain positive mentions in dispatches along the way, but nowhere near as many as my self-indulgent imagination would regularly deem plausible.

And so, instead of waking in my Pasadena penthouse suite and planning for another day's hard graft doubling for Stallone or Redford I'd instead find myself in, say, a three-star hotel in Perth (that's the one in Scotland, *not* Australia) and stewing over whether the show I'd travelled there to do would turn over enough money for me to be paid.

Having said that, the weather which titivated the one show I *did* do in Perth was magnificent, and so much so that even sun-drenched Pasadena would have surely conceded defeat with dignity.

It took place, if I remember rightly, in the late spring of 1980.

My 'relationship' with Sian had become remarkable only for its capacity to plummet to new lows and so, with it probably having succeeded in unearthing yet another around that time, she was more than happy to stop at home while I journeyed north.

Our staying together was of no mutual value but we wanted Shane to have the benefit of some exposure to 'family life' before what we perceived as the inevitable split, and in a last-ditch effort to achieve that we agreed to invest one thousand pounds of the two thousand I earned from *Riding High* in a stall in Porthcawl market.

The remaining one thousand was spent, as you'd expect, on supplementary improvements to our home, including a new bed for Shane, but that first speculative foray into commerce was an exasperating and unalloyed disaster.

We paid upfront for a one-month hire of the stall then enthusiastically filled it with bric-a-brac like watches, ornaments, jewellery, lighters, pens, and so on, but within a fortnight it was plain that we'd committed a colossal blunder in taking it on because we were barely grossing enough to cover our daily fuel costs.

Once the month was done so were we; we closed the stall, wrote off the existing stock and I never did anything as daft as that again.

Anyway, let's get back to my appearance in Perth.

In spite of Sian's disinterest with both myself and what I regarded as my *proper* work I didn't venture there alone because, only weeks before, I'd established my own four-man support team - the 'Black Barons'. Their role was to entertain a crowd with jumps, wheelies and other tricks whilst I prepared for my own performances, but they'd also be on hand to do other jobs as required.
Thankfully the superb conditions that day attracted a healthily-large horde to the showground.

Alas, it was a shame that, due to my own folly at forgetting that if I wanted something done properly then I should always do it myself, they didn't stick around for long.

The 'Tunnel of Fire', with which I'd agreed to regale the good people of Perth, is a highly hazardous stunt requiring meticulous organisation and extraordinary care in its execution.

The 'tunnel' aspect consisted of a skeleton of iron tubing fashioned into an elongated frame, and through which I would ultimately ride. That tubing was enveloped in chicken wire which, in turn, was stuffed with dry straw and doused with petrol.

All being well a single strike of a match would generate the 'fire' component.

As show-time approached I realised that the promoter, in his not-so-infinite wisdom, hadn't arranged for my petrol to be delivered to the showground. So, with my agitation mounting, and with all of the Black Barons otherwise engaged with their various crowd-pleasing tasks, I sent a young steward to a nearby filling station to purchase a couple of jerry cans.

When he returned with the goods his senior colleagues saturated the straw and, with yours truly poised astride my RM-400 and anxious to enthral the expectant audience, the tunnel was set ablaze.

Now, we all know that petrol gives off fumes when it burns but, provided there's sufficient ventilation, as any completely open venue by definition would have, there's little danger or risk of discomfort to any suitably-distanced by-standers.

On the other hand, when *diesel* is ignited it releases thick, black and acrid smoke which, if a sufficient volume is burning merrily, will clear even the most exposed site of people in a proverbial jiffy.

You've fathomed what I'm going to tell you next, haven't you?

Yes, well, maybe it was my fault for expecting too much of that steward.

When I told him to go and buy me 'some petrol' I somehow had it fixed it in my mind that he might actually contemplate returning with 'some petrol', rather than two containers of 'some diesel'.

As a consequence of my own stupidity the hiatus between the first flames appearing to the last spectator disappearing was no more than five minutes.

Of course, the promoter completely freaked.

Once he'd angrily summoned the fire marshals to extinguish the tunnel he came over and called me lots of things that male cats wouldn't lick, as well as something that a female cat licks quite often, before storming off his then-deserted showground.
Given the choice I would have packed our stuff up there and then and absconded from Perth post-haste, but in order to get myself and the Black Barons home I needed to be paid and that meant going cap-in-had to that same pissed-off promoter and penitently requesting the four hundred pounds that we'd been booked for.

If you're wondering, *that's* why I didn't moan to him about my non-existent petrol.

I've seen four hundred pounds being counted out many times both before and since, but never have I seen it done so deliberately, so silently and with such hostility.
Anyway, with my cash secreted away and with the Black Barons in tow I departed nippily in case he'd changed his mind and chased me with his heavies to retrieve it but, mercifully, that didn't come to pass.

Even so, after urgently vacating our hotel rooms we loaded the vans and bike trailers and wasted not a second in fleeing south to the safety of the English border.

Three weeks and several extremely nasty arguments later I'd finally accepted that Sian had moved from being 'my partner' to simply 'Shane's mother' and that's how I still refer to her today.

I'll utter her name only when pressed into do so, and that which I've used to identify her in this book is false.

I apologise for misleading you in that way but I hope now you'll understand.
A weekend away from her interminable grouchiness was a blessing, although being apart from my son became more of a wrench as the months dawdled by.

Not only did I miss Shane enormously while I performed at one noteworthy two-dayer in Chichester in the early summer of 1980 but the exasperation of being denied any amenable female company was also biting hard.

That particular show ticked along smoothly enough I suppose but it's difficult to concentrate on riding a motorcycle when one's testicles, which under such carnal deprivation will appear to weigh a ton, are scraping along the ground behind one and sniffing frantically for somewhere to check in for the night.

Thankfully a Good Samaritan was at hand, and in the guise of a pretty blonde lady who'd spent that entire first day wiggling her shapely backside around, poking everyone's eyes out with her chest and giving *me* the full-sized come-on.

She was still hanging around the place long after the Black Barons had helped me lock all of the gear away.

Aye aye, my brain was cogitating. *This looks promising*.

My gonads, on the other hand, were bouncing around inside my undies like two kangaroos in a mail sack.

But what could I do?
I couldn't take her to the hotel because each of the Black Barons knew Shane's mother, and God only knows what would have happened if *that* little nugget of information had trickled into her ear.

My van was a non-starter, stuffed as it was from floor to roof with biking kit and, besides, it reeked of engine oil, sweat and coffee.

Sitting on top of my horizontal safety ramp and meditating about how easy it would be to snuggle down on top of it all night long and not be spotted by anyone, especially in the dark, I simply couldn't find a solution.

If I may I'll shunt the story forward by fifteen minutes.

"Ooh, it's alright up 'ere innit?" Alison said (that, I'd taken the trouble of finding out after I'd removed her blouse and skirt, was her name) as she lay nine-tenths-naked on top of my safety ramp.

Within another five minutes my pelvis was hammering away like a woodpecker's forehead.

It's probably not that easy to initiate a conversation whilst being subjected to such a buffeting but, seemingly, Alison was much-practiced.

"Someone's down there," she whispered.

In that situation the phrase 'someone's down there' can have one of two meanings, depending on your rationality of thought at the time.

My own testosterone-stimulated interpretation caused me to look toward my groin.

Nope, I satisfied myself silently. *No intruders 'down there'.*

"*No!*" she tried growled impatiently while gesturing towards the ground. "I mean *down there!*"

I glanced to my right and caught sight of a torch beam swinging almost randomly around our ramp.

I clenched both my pairs of cheeks and tried, in defiance of every masculine urge in my body, to stay as motionless as possible. I could hear creepy footfalls all around, and the light from that torch was being thrown onto everything; at one point it missed my backside by inches!

Whoever was waving it around had only to walk up my landing ramp and that would have been that – game over!

But it didn't happen.

After ten nerve-wracking minutes of grasping what it must have been like to escape from a prisoner-of-war camp the footsteps became fainter and the glow from the torch dimmed.

"He's gone," Alison said.

In that situation the phrase 'he's gone' can have one of two meanings, depending on your rationality of thought at the time.

I suspect she was talking about the torch-wielder.
Instinctively though, I again glanced down to my old boy; self-evidently she was quite correct on both counts.

For whatever reason she wasn't at the showground the following day which was a pity because, putting our alfresco sex to one side for a moment, she was friendlier and more pleasant to me in our half-hour together than Shane's mother had been at any time during the previous three months.

I never saw her again but, Alison, if you're out there somewhere then thank you for a wonderful night, rudely interrupted though it was, and I really hope you're well.

An event nearer to home was always prized from the point of view of saving on travelling expenses, so I could really profit from shows like that staged at Aberdare's Michael Sobell Centre later in that year.

In addition to the enhanced financial incentive for appearing there I'd also been booked to break the world record for jumping over a curtain (or line) of fire which, at the time, stood at a fraction under one hundred feet.
There were no dramas on that occasion; everything passed off swimmingly.

Not only would I match that distance on my first warm-up jump but I surpassed it by some twenty feet on the next attempt, thereby creating a new record which still stands at the time of writing (January 2014).

Having claimed one recognised record I yearned, if I could, to sweep the board.
While it's all well and good having that ambition, staging such displays remains expensive and, in 1980, few promoters were willing to take the gamble of relying so heavily on fine weather and a good turnout.

Therefore, I realised that if I wanted more records then I had no alternative but to organise and publicise those events myself.

Shane's mother was surprisingly supportive.

I can only speculate that the pound signs were flashing before her eyes again but I can't really berate her for that, not when I also had them in front of my own. After all, I desperately wanted Shane's childhood to be more comfortable than mine ever was and here, I gauged, was the perfect means of achieving it.

The amount of hard work and commitment required to make it materialise though caught both of us totally unawares.

Nonetheless, and after much negotiation with the relevant authorities and unnecessarily long-winded consultations with the council, it was finally confirmed that I would jump thirty-five MG cars at Swansea Airport on May 25th, 1981.

Having advertised the event we contacted local celebrities in the hope they might have felt sufficiently philanthropic to dig deep, simply to get our ball rolling if nothing else, but we were to be disappointed.

That left us with no option but to use our *own* money to hire the airport, meaning that the project was one thousand pounds in the red before we'd even drawn breath.

However, our widespread appeals for sponsorship led to some welcome media attention; the local radio station, Swansea Sound, plugged the event ever more regularly and in peak-time slots as May 25th approached, and both HTV and the BBC confirmed that they would be sending film crews to the airport on the day.

Reading all of this you're possibly reflecting that everything was slotting nicely into place, but we had a problem; as first-time promoters we didn't have the slightest clue about what we were doing so, if anything, that media attention essentially compounded the pressure and generated more difficulties rather than alleviating the ones we already had.

Our inexperience proved to be even more ruinous on the day of the jump.

We'd budgeted to accommodate five thousand at Swansea Airport but, in reality, more like thirty thousand turned up. People were quite literally arriving by the coachload and, while I watched dumb-struck from the airport's watchtower, a friend informed me that I'd be a wealthy man once the day was over.

Sadly, that wasn't how it transpired.

The crowd was six times larger than what we'd catered for, which meant that there were insufficient marshals to collect and safeguard my money. Consequently, members of the public were actually *pretending* to be marshals and pocketing whatever cash came their way. If that wasn't enough I'd been let down at the last minute with the thirty-five MG's so I had to put my trust in that self-same public to provide twenty-eight of their own cars for me to jump over.

If that doesn't constitute the most ludicrous of ironies them I'm afraid I don't know what does.

As for the show itself the repercussions of a lack of effective crowd control were becoming all too apparent. Approaching my take-off ramp for the first time at something approaching ninety miles per hour I was aware that the spectators were not only swarming like ants in my wake but, more disturbingly, they were also encroaching from either side before I'd even passed them by.

In my landing area they applied a little more common sense and kept their distance, but I was still left with a much thinner and shorter run-off than was comfortable.
For the second jump I had the Black Barons riding up and down in a futile bid to keep everyone back. Their sterling efforts brought me more space temporarily but, in a contest of wills between four on one side and thirty thousand on the other, there can really only be one winner.

With my safety fears mounting I'd already determined my third jump would be the last.

For that final attempt I opened up my Suzuki with more than it had ever given and I had no real excuse for failure because while the width of my run-up had shrunk discernibly as the afternoon had gone on, its length was effectively unlimited.
I launched myself from the take-off ramp and, with a mixture of elation and relief, grounded the bike halfway down the landing ramp having comfortably cleared the twenty-eight cars and the safety platform.

The Guinness Book of Records had declined our invitation to send representatives to Swansea Airport that day, but that wasn't a problem since one spectator, who patently considered himself to be Norris McWhirter's understudy, strolled nonchalantly from the crowd and, with a black felt pen, marked me using the tyre print from one of my earlier jumps.

I knew where I'd just landed; I'd cleared one hundred and seventy-six feet.

By that doughnut's reckoning though, my third jump was a paltry one hundred and fifty-one feet.
I was absolutely incensed, and was even more enraged when I learned that the assembled press and media had collectively mistaken *his* mark to be the valid one!

When I later saw the relevant photographs in the newspaper which covered the event I could clearly see that my suspension was compressed on landing. I then knew I was right; *that* was where I'd grounded the bike, and one hundred and seventy-six feet from where I'd taken off.

Despite my curtailing that dreadful day at Swansea Airport some nasty stings in the tail still awaited us.

Firstly, and thanks mainly to the diabolical dishonesty and pitiable pilfering of a minority who came along, instead of the fifteen thousand pounds I'd estimated I'd earn I left the place with marginally under two thousand.

Secondly, the unexpectedly-large attendance meant that the airport's grounds and perimeter fencing required extensive repairs. The bill for said damage, when I received it about a week later, was for slightly over seventeen hundred pounds.

So, instead of the cool fifteen grand that we'd projected we'd earn from the event, we actually sulked away from it all with less than three hundred quid.
To say I was upset would be a gargantuan understatement; without question that was, and remains, one of the direst moments of my life.
A well-organised and lucrative show would have set me up for a couple of years, even after we'd re-carpeted our house, bought a new car, taken Shane on holiday and done all of the other things I wanted to do.

As it was I'd ended up with an absolute pittance, a jump which should have been a world record but wasn't because that plonker had marked it twenty-five feet short and, besides, the Guinness Book of Records couldn't be bothered to show up anyway, and a day which had the potential to be wonderful and memorable but which, in reality, was a total shambles.

Many people have the preconception that stunt-riding is glamorous, and that those who do it earn a mountain of cash.

Well, with a good wind behind you that may well happen but it certainly didn't for me on *that* day, that's for sure.

Hence, with my dreams for a comfortable life for Shane crushed all over again I was back on the road on weekends, but at least someone else was then doing the promoting and burdening the responsibilities rather than me.

For example, I spent Shane's fourth birthday, on July 27th 1981, at a three-day weekend gig in Newcastle-upon-Tyne although, as was becoming normal, he and his mother stopped at home.

We were all bundling everything away on that Monday when, for disconnected reasons known only to myself, I decided to try out one of the ramps that the Black Barons employed in their firewall stunt. Carelessly I'd forgotten that the Suzuki's handlebars were wider that those on their enduro models so, after I'd roared up the incline, my RM-400 clipped the (unlit) wooden frame mounted its top.

I was thrown from the bike and, apparently, landed in a crouched posture about fifteen feet away.

I say 'apparently' because I was wearing a heavy bell-helmet at the time which caused me to jar my neck, so I was knocked senseless as well.

I was rushed to hospital where, from what I was told afterwards, the jibberish I was spouting was becoming vaguer and more irrational with each passing minute. People I once knew were becoming strangers as I prattled away to them and, by the time I reached the hospital, I didn't know where I was, who I was, what day it was or even what planet I was on.

After being hurried into the emergency unit I was sedated and, almost immediately, collapsed into a deep sleep.
When I woke the first things I clapped eyes on was a penis and its attendant genitalia dangling smugly beside my bed.

I slowly cast my drowsy gaze upward so that I might see the individual to whom they belonged.
The luckless bloke's head, I noticed when my focus had returned, was sunken on one side because sizeable proportions of his skull and brain had been removed. I'm certain he was trying to stare at me but, being as he was so severely walleyed, it was hard to tell for sure.

I recall feeling genuine pity for the man, but that didn't stop me from wishing he would remove his 'meat and two veg' from my face!

Eventually the poor nurse, who probably had more trouble from me than she ever did from that tragic guy, ushered him back to where he should have been.

Four strange men then turned up.

They sat around my bed and started asking how I was feeling. They said they were the 'Black Barons' or something like that, but I had absolutely no idea who they were. They kept calling me 'Chris' strangely enough so I groggily presumed that that was my name.

After they left I asked the nurse what time it was.

She answered, and I asked her again.

She again replied, but I wondered what time it was so I thought I'd ask the nurse.

My memory, as you've probably guessed, had been completely erased, and only after a couple of days had passed did fuzzy details start to return.
Having said that I *can* remember being wheeled into the ward's sitting area to watch somebody called Prince Charles get married to somebody else called Lady Diana Spencer, but I still had no real idea of who or where I was, or why I was there.

After being discharged a day or two later I was kidnapped by those Black Barons, put into a van which reeked of engine oil, sweat and coffee, and then driven hundreds of miles to South Wales of all places.

At the time I was surprised by how well my abductors were treating me; at one point they even bought me a drink and a packet of sandwiches from a motorway service station.

Needless to say I slept well that night, and for some nights afterward.

And now, here's the moral.

The three important assets to possess in any job where circumstances frequently appear to work against you are: keeping calm, working hard and being patient while waiting for the inevitable rewards.

This chapter highlighted the first and second of those virtues; the next is all about the third.

CHAPTER 16: TO PARADISE…

John Waterhouse was one of that era's eminent promoters and I'd heard from the grapevine that, during the summer of 1981, he'd be bringing his latest extravaganza to Aberavon Beach (that's about a mile from Port Talbot).

Keen to discover if I could muster a living without rambling up and down the country every weekend at my own expense I collated my profile information and, when he and his travelling circus pitched up in town, headed over there to meet him.

He'd organised plenty for the fervent spectators to revel in; I was already aware that he had a penchant for car stunts and the lion's share of the acts that day were indeed on four wheels but, notwithstanding, I gravitated towards the sole motorcyclist who was doing some flicks and tricks on the fringes.

This guy had also set up a rudimentary ramp and was jumping over a handful of cars. He seemed to be doing reasonably well, maybe a little shaky here and there, but on his final attempt he pulled the bike right over and slammed onto his back and with one heck of a thud onto the gravel bed but, thankfully, without any serious injury.
Yes, okay, he was clearly inexperienced, as I was at one time, but I've frequently said that the best way to learn my trade is the painful way and so I did have genuine sympathy for my fellow artiste.

Nevertheless, and without wanting to sound conceited, I knew that I was the more competent rider so I introduced myself to Mr Waterhouse once his show had finished.
He knew who I was so I was thrilled about that and he also appeared impressed with everything I'd done to that point; that, at least, was an encouraging opening gambit.

He also admitted that he hadn't yet sorted out the two-wheeled aspect of his programme so, fortuitously, I didn't need to give myself the hard sell either.

He then revealed that he had a show going to New Zealand in the upcoming months, and asked whether I'd be interested in tagging along. After replying that I most definitely *would* be interested he pocketed one of my flyers and pledged to contact me soon.

I find myself wishing sometimes that everyone else's definition of 'soon' read something like my own.

I went through agonies waiting for that call but, true to his word, he eventually phoned around mid-October with news that my return ticket to New Zealand had been reserved and that I'd be flying to Auckland from Heathrow on November 19th.

Hearing him tell me that was an absolutely incredible feeling, and second only perhaps to an orgasm.

With that excitement though came some apprehension; I'd not flown anywhere in my life before, and the only time I'd stepped on a plane was when I accidentally trod on my brother's *Airfix* kit, yet in four weeks I'd be travelling at someone else's expense to one of the farthest countries that it's possible to go!

I asked him for how long I should expect to be away from home, to which he stated that the tour would end in mid-February, 1982.

Three months, then.

The thought of being separated from Shane for so long wasn't appealing, but I was considerably less reluctant to be saying cheerio to everything else, including his mother. That said, the tour had blessed me with the perfect opportunity to extricate myself from her headlock once and for all, and when I hinted that that was indeed my intention she was almost exultant.

So, the grand plan shaped up something like this; while I was romping around New Zealand, Shane would stay with my mother in Southall while *his* mother would finally move out of our home and then, as far as I was concerned, she could do whatever she bloody well wanted.

She did still drive me to Heathrow though, probably to make sure that I didn't ruin her life by having a change of heart about going on the tour. My mother came along as well, so there was *some* civilised conversation in the car on the way up at least, while Shane stayed with his mother's parents because I judged that a four-hundred-mile round trip would be unduly stressful for one so young.

Besides, I needed all the luggage space I could get.

So, after sharing terse goodbyes with Shane's mother for what I sincerely hoped would be the final time I negotiated Heathrow's hectic check-in desk and then, like an utterly disoriented new-born duckling, looked around feverishly for someone to latch on to.

There were many people catching the same flight and I gathered, from eavesdropping on their chit-chat, that most were flying out for the same reason, but I could also tell that those guys were seasoned campaigners and obviously well-known to one another so I kept myself tucked into the background until a bloke with the deepest Scottish accent I've ever heard sauntered up to me and introduced himself.

"Douglas Earth," he announced cheerfully, and almost clearly. "Pleased t'meet ye!"

"Chris Bromham," I replied, shaking his hand. "I'm a stunt motorcyclist."

"Chris Bromham, ye say? Erm…ach yes, I've heard of ye! Yer the wee bairn that jumped at that airport, aren't ye? Well done, laddie! Ye done a good'un there!"
And that was that; I'd made a friend!
I was grateful for it as well because a flight from Heathrow to Auckland, especially with a refuelling stop thrown in, is incredibly long and monotonous, and I'm sorry to say that once you've seen the top of one cloud you've seen them all.

Douglas, however, was an accomplished stunt-car driver who'd worked with numerous promotions around the world so he became an absolute goldmine of guidance on what I could expect and how I should be around certain people whose names I shan't divulge here.
He was understandably more clued-up with regard to the New Zealand tour than me, and it definitely sounded as though my two-wheeled displays would be vastly outnumbered by the four-wheeled ones but, being as it was one of John Waterhouse's promotions, I'd already resigned myself to that.

On arriving in Auckland's gorgeously-green and spacious suburban sprawl some thirty-five hours after leaving cold, overcast and drizzle-drenched London we were shepherded onto a luxurious coach and driven the eighteen kilometres to the Remuera Motor Lodge, situated (as it still is) in a picturesque residential area and about an hour's brisk walk from downtown.

The Remuera's accommodation consisted entirely of chalets.

I was able to have my own chalet, as were the majority of those on the tour such was the size of the place. The lodge had an outdoor swimming pool, two exquisite restaurants and more bars than I could count, all surrounded by thick subtropical woodland, Auckland's fabulous skyline and panoramic views over the Pacific Ocean.
When besieged by such splendorous scenery it's tough to accept that, somewhere far over that unblemished horizon, there could possibly exist a place called Skewen.

After spending that first day sleeping off jet lag, which isn't easily accomplished in the humidity of a Southern Hemisphere summer, we journeyed *en masse* to the nearby Avondale Racecourse for the filming of the promotional television commercial and also the photo shoot for the tour's glossy brochure.

The commercial, which was recorded in blinding sunshine and beneath the bluest sky I'd ever known, turned out to be tremendous fun.

Everyone, including myself, zealously paraded their talents for the many cameras, and the resulting thirty seconds or so of action-packed motoring mayhem would ultimately be broadcast on New Zealand's national network every few hours.

My first significant disappointment though came with the arrival of the brochures two days later.

My picture was in there, as was everyone else's, but while *their* profiles had been included *mine* was conspicuous by its absence.
I'd been cited as a 'top motorcycle stuntman', which was agreeable enough I suppose, but the brochure said nothing more about me; my name wasn't there, nor was there any biography or list of achievements or any mention of my record attempts, successful or otherwise.

Make no mistake about it, *that* was a let-down and, at the time, it did niggle me.

After my grumblings had circulated the lodge a compassionate roadie reminded me that, while I was unquestionably the star of the tour's motorcycle stunts, those same motorcycle stunts were *not* the stars of the tour.

To pile insult onto humiliation I was later informed by another stuntman that I'd have to build my own ramps.
Was he being serious? Me? Building my own ramps?

I thought at first that this was one of those practical jokes played on a typical newbie, akin perhaps to asking me to fetch a tub of elbow grease or a left-handed screwdriver but, no, what I'd been told was correct.

I *would* have to assemble my ramps although I soon learned that everyone else would be constructing *their* specialised props too and that, in a nutshell, encapsulated the tour's ethos; everyone was expected to chip in with the donkey work and pull their weight to help make the whole thing a hit with the fans.

All in all I guess that my ego did take a couple to the chin during those first unsettling days, but at no stage did I regret my decision to go there. Besides, my list of friends was steadily growing, and I was absorbing more from them than I'd ever done during six troublesome years of straining to conquer my craft alone.
Every weeknight we'd be taking our show to a new venue; one evening we might be in Wellington performing before ten-thousand people, the next we might be flying to South Island to pander to the stunt addicts of Christchurch. Everyone was extraordinarily competitive, and we each wanted to fulfil that show-stealing turn that would make the crowd go crazy so, before each event, we'd be dreaming up increasingly innovative ways of making our acts even more sensational.

Such an intense and demanding itinerary meant that living out of suitcases became par for the course so a 'local' event was always welcome as we could then return to the familiarity of the motor lodge that same evening.
An afternoon free from any work commitments was unusual, but highly valued when it came along.

On one such afternoon I spotted the beautiful and dark-haired lady who gave my Brut-infused chalet its daily spruce bouncing up and down on the Remuera's poolside trampoline.

She recognised me and smiled warmly.
"Would you like a jump?" she asked.

There are a number of gentlemen's clubs in Swansea where you'd have to pay damn good money for an invitation like that.

"Ooh, yes please!" I slobbered, with playful enthusiasm.
New Zealanders, like the British, have innumerable gaudy synonyms for 'sex', but 'jump' isn't one of them.

How was *I* supposed to know *that*, though?

She was a smart girl in every sense of the word, and I think she promptly twigged that what *she* intended from her question and what *I'd* imprudently inferred from it could hardly have been more disparate. Nevertheless, and in spite of that distinctly prickly moment our rapport, along with the respect I held for her, became more robust with each passing day.

Her name was Donna.
While vacuuming my chalet one lunchtime she told me that she'd recently returned to New Zealand after a spell working in Australia and, as her mother still lived in Auckland, she'd taken a job in the Remeura until something better came along.

She was always so charming to talk to and so alluring to be with that I sometimes toyed with the idea of trashing my chalet in the evening so that she'd have to stay longer in the morning.

I didn't need to though, because she seemed more than happy to prolong her visits anyway.

I should state at the outset that I thought more deferentially of Donna than I had of any of the other women who'd wafted in and out of my life.

Here, for a change, was someone who was polite, amiable, interested in me and in what I had to say, and stunningly gorgeous to boot.

Yes, I recall resolving to myself. *I want to be with this woman.* Not for one night of passion and a cheap notch on the bedpost you'll understand, but as a devoted and trusted companion for the coming years.

So, you might imagine what a wallop it was to my *solar plexus* when she casually divulged that she was married to some Italian guy.

While surprisingly repentant after dropping that bombshell she did admit that their relationship was passing through an extremely fraught phase but, at the end of the day, 'married' means 'unavailable' whatever the circumstances and there was nothing I could have done about it.

She would regularly meet up with her brothers of an evening time in one of the Remuera's bars, and even *they* could detect the chemistry crackling between us.

And so, to veer me off the scent of their inaccessible sister they fixed me up with an otherwise-lovely Red Indian woman named Lisa.

She wasn't who I wanted to be with obviously but, accepting quite rightly that there was no prospect of a future with Donna, we spent a pleasant night together all the same.
The following morning the bikini-clad Lisa and I were having a spirited splash-about in the pool. Once we'd finished we began drying ourselves off, but then who should be charging towards me from the lodge's main building but Donna.

She looked annoyed but, at first, I didn't understand why.

"So, what about us?" she yelled in my face and with her hands pressed firmly into her hips.

Somewhat bemused I glanced at Lisa, then back at Donna. "Well, there can be no 'us'," I shrugged. "You're brothers have made that clear, and so have you. You're married, after all!"

Two seconds later I found myself back in the pool, having been consigned there by a startlingly-potent two-handed shove.

Aha! I mused after surfacing in time to see Donna storming back toward the main building. *Maybe, then, there could be an 'us'*!

From that moment I vowed to do everything in my power to make her my own.

I understood perfectly where her brothers were coming from with their efforts to steer me away, and I don't think they ever liked me anyway, but after that farcical incident by the pool I was as confident as I dared to be that we would one day become a couple.

For her part, Donna empathised with her brothers' motives and, after forgiving me for my transgression with Lisa, confided that she also longed for us to be together. That couldn't have sounded any sweeter to my ear but Donna, being as she was so upstanding and dignified, wouldn't allow our relationship to develop any further, not even to a brief kiss or holding hands, until she'd properly concluded everything with her husband.

I stood beside her when she telephoned him (they'd already been living apart for some time), if only to provide her with some moral support.

She asked him for a decisive separation and, although I wasn't party to his response, it was evident that he was exceptionally laid-back about granting Donna a divorce.

To her, *that* was sufficient; even though the official *decree nisi* would take some weeks to be issued, she was satisfied that her marriage was finally over.

Appropriately enough there was a party at the Remuera that evening, not for us but to mark the birthday of one of the stuntmen.

I sat next to Lisa because Donna's brothers had yet to hear of the latest momentous developments, while Donna herself sat quietly opposite.

She believed that she was playing footsies with me under the table when, in fact, she was tickling Lisa's instep instead!

Lisa kicked out, and Donna hacked back.

It was becoming awkward and tense, not least because they didn't really get along anyway. As heartless as it may sound I wanted nothing more to do with Lisa, and I certainly didn't want to ruin my opportunity with Donna by being seen too often with her. Still, the night wore on, the party slumbered toward a semi-drunken close and Lisa, having realised the situation that she'd unwittingly been thrown into the midst of, toddled home with her friends.

Donna and I consummated our relationship that night in my chalet and I have to say that I'd never been more content with life or with myself.

She became a regular on the tour after that, and later declared that she'd seen more of New Zealand while with me that she'd ever done during her previous twenty-odd years of living there.

One of our first shows as a recognised item was in Napier, located around two hundred and fifty miles south-east of Auckland.

My schedule for that evening included a jump over twelve cars.

Nothing unusual about that you might say, but the venue was completely open with no markers to work from, and I didn't have a speedometer on the Suzuki RM-250 I'd been sponsored to use (I'd actually been given two bikes; one I rode, the other I stripped replacement parts from).

Therefore, I was effectively 'speed blind'.

Forced to change gears according to engine noise alone I approached the ramp way too fast and ended up clearing not only the twelve cars but a further eighty feet of ground beyond them. My impact upon the tarmac, when it finally arrived, was so severe that the bike's belly smashed down and left an unsightly groove on the landing strip, while the violent reaction between bike and ground propelled my legs aloft.
Had I not been gripping the handlebars as tightly as I had been then my voyage back to Auckland might have started there and then.

As it was, and after reclaiming control of the bike like a gymnast cosseting a pommel horse, I deliberately locked up the back wheel and threw it back and forth at high speed, thereby whipping up a haze of smoke which made the crowd howl with delight.

Even the roadies were amazed with my jump, and wasted no time in measuring my distance. By their reckoning I was airborne for one hundred and fifty feet, and all off a piddling sixteen-foot-long ramp!

While everyone on the tour was suitably spellbound with my proficiency with my riding prowess they apparently weren't overly enamoured with my expertise with wheelstands. Indeed, if truth be told, the overwhelming consensus was that every other stunt rider they cared to name could execute them with greater skill.

Good-humoured effrontery though it was I'd had more than enough of their ribbing by the time we did a gig in Queenstown, so that night I decided to show them once and for all who the wheelie-daddy wheelie was!
Now, my Suzuki RM-250 was a so-called 'two-stroke' bike and was, as such, not particularly suited to such brazen showboating.

Wheelies, in my opinion at least, could be sustained more effectively on a 'four-stroke' bike, an example of which would be a Honda XR of the type that I subsequently borrowed from a member of the audience.

Disinclined as I was to demonstrate my worth with a tame bog-standard wheelie I decided to present one 'off the seat', with one of my legs on the bike and the other off it.

Sometimes such stunts can be spectacularly botched, but when they go right they are an absolute wonder to behold, with the power to enthral even the most hardened of audiences and to stun legions of doubters into shameful submission.
Sadly, mine wasn't one of those.

Within seconds of roaring off and drawing up the front wheel I flipped the Honda through one hundred and eighty degrees.

The bike wrenched itself from my control and, as I was wearing no protective leathers or gloves, it stripped away the skin from my fingertips and palms in the process. The subsequent strain on my left forearm had tugged a vein, which was still draining blood, clean through my skin. I also grazed my kneecaps almost to the bone, and suffered goodness knows how many other cuts and bruises before I'd ceased tumbling.

The bike fared no better; the handlebars all but shattered when it clattered onto the ground some yards away, while the side plastics were buckled far beyond any hope of repair.

I spent that night being stitched back up and convalescing in a Queenstown hospital, and wishing instead that I was back in Auckland with Donna, but at the time the gashes in my dinted pride pained me far more than any of my physical wounds.

I could barely walk or sleep for a week, and seeing everyone else having a ball at the shows while I had to look on from the periphery really cheesed me off.

The tour's organisers weren't too pleased either because not only were they without their star motorcyclist for a number of events but they also had to fork out for a new Honda XR.

Being at any venue without Donna was hard, but thankfully I wasn't the only one who had love waiting in Auckland and yearning to dash back there after a performance.

Jan the Man (Remember him? I clipped his stock car at Newton Abbot Racecourse in 1978) was one of the tour's more eye-catching stunt-drivers, and had been accompanied to New Zealand by his wife. Naturally she'd seen Jan doing his stuff at shows for years, and most likely knew that she'd be following him for years to come as well, so the thought of trekking all over the country for more of the same probably held no appeal for her.

As a result she usually stayed behind in the Remuera, happy no doubt to catch up on some peace and quiet while the place was three-quarters empty.

Jan, though, was probably on a promise so, after this one particular event, he and I shared a car back to Auckland so he could see his own good lady and I could spend some quality time with Donna.

At this point I have some charitable advice for you; *never* accept a lift off a stunt car driver when he or she is in a hurry to get somewhere!

Rarely have I been so terrified.

We hurtled through New Zealand's outback for goodness knows how many miles, through fields and over gravel roads and taking U-bends *sideways* above drops of hundreds of feet down steep mountainsides!

I'm not exaggerating when I say I was gripping the passenger door's handle so tightly that, by the time we came within sight of Auckland, I'd lost the circulation in my hands!

During performances the New Zealand public had probably never seen anything like Jan, other than on the *Dukes of Hazzard* or something similar.

It must be said though that he was a phenomenal driver; completely insane, but phenomenal nonetheless.

The tour ended in the middle of February, 1982, but I remained in New Zealand for one further month while Donna did everything that she had to do and saw everyone that she wanted to see prior to leaving New Zealand for her new life in South Wales.
Her entire family was so shocked and disappointed that she'd decided to emigrate, and I sympathised fully with their reaction.

Donna was upset as well because that was the only family, and New Zealand was the only country, that she'd really ever known.

In addition to the emotional issues I quickly realised that the cash I'd managed to save from my one-hundred-and-fifty-pounds-per-week for doing the tour wasn't sufficient to bring her back to the United Kingdom.

My ticket home was already sorted of course, but Donna's wasn't.

So, we held a garage sale, where she shifted her wedding outfits and I parted with all of my camera equipment amongst other bits and bobs.

It was almost like being back in Porthcawl market although, unlike *that* fiasco, we didn't have to wait long before we'd raised a decent amount of cash.

So, Donna purchased her one-way ticket to Heathrow at Auckland airport and after many tearful farewells I could finally jet back to the United Kingdom with the new love of my life sleeping serenely by my side.

CHAPTER 17: ...AND THEN TO BROMLEY

I'm sure you'll recall the final scenes of that perennial festive favourite *The Wizard of Oz*, in which Dorothy passes from a breath-taking and magical realm teeming with sumptuous and vibrant colour to a pallid and all-too-familiar panorama sewn together with threads of drab, insipid greyscale.

One pair of ruby slippers aside, taking a flight from Auckland to London is actually surprisingly similar.

Heaven only knows what thoughts were filling Donna's mind as we sluggishly descended the stack of planes queuing to splash down on Heathrow's sodden tarmac, going round and around as though trapped within some slowly-gyrating Kansan tornado.

England's green and pleasant land was down there somewhere, obscured beneath a featureless quilt of low cloud and a mattress of depressing wintry drizzle, and I strove to assure her of that several occasions but she appeared less than convinced and understandably so.

My God, I despaired while she stared through her window with the merest suggestions of sadness and resignation. *What have I done?*

After finally landing and shuffling our weary way through the overcrowded Customs hall I found a payphone and rang Southall to let everyone know that I'd arrived back safe and sound (but I mentioned nothing about Donna). My mother (who answered) was delighted to learn that I was home, and added that there was someone there who wanted to have a word with me.

Oh no! I quailed with due dread. *Not Shane's mother! Please don't let it be Shane's mother! I can't cope with any of her brainless bullshit now! I'm too knackered!*

But, no. It *wasn't* Shane's mother.

It was Shane himself, and when I heard that boy's wonderfully innocent voice my legs almost gave way beneath me.

Then the tears *really* started to flow and Donna, who I imagine knew full well who was on the other end of the line, offered a supportive hug. In fact, I was blubbing so much Shane must have thought he was talking to someone half his age!

The technology of the early eighties, though, was no less cold or heartless that its descendants of the modern day; a minute or so after I'd rammed my last two-pence-piece into the slot the line went dead.
Never before had I wanted to get home with such urgency, and never before had that home felt so far away.

With renewed resolve we pushed and jostled our wobbly column of luggage onto the Underground, and changed trains at Earl's Court for Paddington Station where we hurriedly scrambled on board the next Inter City train to Swansea.

I'd hoped that the weather would perk up as we rumbled westward through Berkshire and Wiltshire, to give Donna something of her new world to look if nothing else, but apart from infrequent flashes of blue sky and the sun-soaked lustre of a distant field between showers she enjoyed no such good fortune.

Suitably underwhelmed, she succumbed to another catnap.

Shane's virtuous tones were still teasing their way through my mind while I sluiced down my revolting British Rail sandwich with a carton of their blandest so-called coffee, and so there I sat, counting the seconds, clocking up the miles and picking crumbs of stale bread from between my teeth as the dreary countryside streaked past unheeded.

By the time we'd tugged our suitcases across the pitted concrete of Neath railway station's shadowy platform we were both totally exhausted and hopelessly in need of a week of sleep.

Dragging the dead-beat Donna to Southall and torturing her with the strain of meeting my parents wasn't a savoury proposition, at least not at that moment, and Shane's mother was still shacked up in our council house which meant that going there was also a non-starter, so with virtually all of my remaining cash I booked us in to the nearby Castle Hotel.

I simply had to see Shane though before we collapsed into bed; Donna, being Donna, was completely sympathetic and didn't utter a single word of complaint.

I then asked her if she'd like to meet him.

I fully expected her to say no because in all honesty she could hardly keep her eyes open but, being Donna, she said yes.

So, I rang Southall once again, that time from the Castle's lobby.

Thankfully Shane was still there but, better even than that, his mother wasn't.

After some hurried closing words I dashed to the town's taxi rank, leaving Donna behind in the hotel to snatch a few precious minutes of rest, and instructed the bewildered cabbie to drive to Southall Avenue as quickly as he dared go.

We were there within minutes and, after the briefest of greetings to all concerned during which I remember mumbling to my startled audience something or other about bringing a woman back from New Zealand, to which my father replied "What? A *real* one?", we settled the increasingly-agitated Shane into the taxi's rear seat and raced back to the Castle Hotel. After running through a multitude of different heart-warming but tear-jerking scenarios in my mind, each of which ended with an affectionate embrace between the two, I was finally able about five minutes later to take Shane to our room and introduce him to Donna.

Donna certainly did her bit; she was affable and open and anyone watching might have been convinced that she'd known Shane all of her life. Shane, on the other hand, was considerably less forthcoming, and so much so that had he been just a few years older I would have admonished him for being rude.

As it was he was wary and shy and very young of course, and clearly not at all at ease with the deeply confusing situation into which I'd unthinkingly dropped him.

Donna fought hard to break the ice but, after only the briefest of awkward silences, I could see that not even a small nuclear explosion would have punched a hole through it.

Enough's enough, I decided. *It's time to take him back to Southall.*

Soon afterwards the three of us took the stairs to the lobby where, before Shane and I headed off, Donna sought once more to rupture his dogged defences. She bade him goodnight and ruffled his hair, to which playful civility he mischievously responded by pushing her backwards over someone else's suitcase.

Yet, and in spite of that bluntest of affronts to her dignity Donna, being Donna, merely lifted herself back to her feet, dusted herself down, and smiled.
Two days later, and after a situation precipitated by my blowing the last of my cash on our temporary lodgings in the Castle Hotel, I felt it was time to take Donna around to Southall to meet my parents and, surreptitiously if necessary, to reclaim my old room as our own.

I'd already briefed them over the telephone and in considerably more detail since Shane's fleeting stopover at the hotel, believing that that would have afforded sufficient time for any shock value to wane.

Clearly, I hadn't given them long enough.

My mother seemed largely indifferent to Donna and greeted her accordingly, while my father was distinctly pensive, said next to nothing and didn't stick around for too long.

Donna must have felt so awkward but, to her eternal credit, if she was upset then it certainly didn't show.

Still, they did at least consent to us assuming residence of my bedroom, but without the enthusiasm or elation that I'd foolishly banked upon.

I don't think I was asking for much, apart from a little understanding maybe and some slight suggestion of a genuine welcome seeing as Donna had given up her home and family and travelled God knows how many thousands of miles to be there, but there we go.

I suppose there's none so naïve as those that never learn.
There was marginally more cordiality on show as the days and weeks passed, but without any real lessening of the tangible unease in the place. Both my mother and father must surely have guessed that it was my intention to marry Donna so I/we confirmed it for them, to put any lingering doubts out of their minds if nothing else.

After all, one doesn't bring someone halfway around the world just for a dirty weekend!

Unfortunately, and due to some uncharacteristic carelessness on Donna's part, the sound of wedding bells were quickly to become as faint as they'd been at any time since our arrival in Southall.

For some time previous to this calamitous howler plenty of official-looking letters relating to Donna's divorce had flown between Southall Avenue and New Zealand.

My parents paid little attention to any such correspondence which landed on our doormat, surmising in all probability that it was all legal or citizenship documentation concerning her move to Wales.

She was extremely meticulous about keeping the aforementioned literature out of sight and did so successfully with each letter she received, except one - the one which my father happened to stumble upon.

Your memories of the earlier chapters of this book might still be fresh in your mind.

If they are, then there should be no necessity for me to recount his reaction to discovering that his son had brought home a spoken-for woman from a four-month jolly in New Zealand.

Donna, with admirable resolve and unshakable courtesy, tried so hard to explain that her marriage had, to the eye of any impartial observer, been over for a year or more but he wasn't having any of it and, to make matters worse, my mother was affording him a supportive ear.

Predictably enough relations deteriorated quickly, and that was pretty much that; Donna and I were left with no option but to leave.

After letting it be known that we sought somewhere to live either in or around Skewen a local girl, who lived with her young son but luckily had a bedroom to spare, agreed to put us up until we could secure something more permanent.

For me it was the ideal arrangement as Shane lived nearby with his mother which meant I could see him more often than I might have done if we'd remained in Southall.

However, had we been aware of the tragic history of that house before moving in then we might have looked elsewhere, and I think any sensitive person would have acted similarly if they'd known that an entire family, including a baby, had perished there in a horrendous fire.

I'll make no bones about it – it *was* a spooky place.

Hardly a night would go by without its little raps and knocks and shuffling noises and, no matter which room one happened to be in, one always felt as though someone else were there, lurking unseen somewhere in the shadows and watching one's every move.

Donna's brother, Richard, came over from New Zealand to stay with us for a week (his girlfriend at the time lived in London) and, being as he was completely freaked out by the house, insisted that she return with him to Auckland.

Richard didn't approve of the situation between me and Donna anyway; the house merely provided a convenient reason for him to voice what he clearly felt was a legitimate protest.

During the closing days of Richard's progressively-rancorous stay I became aware that Donna herself was starting to buckle under the weight of his obstinate coercion, and for the first time since setting foot in Wales she hinted darkly at a desire to return home.

I was consumed with anger, not with her but with myself.

I'd begun to question whether I indeed had the right to uproot Donna from everything she'd held so dear but, after bidding a particularly tearful farewell to Richard at Neath railway station, she reassured me that she *was* happy after all and that she wouldn't have changed her decision to leave New Zealand for a life with me should she have had her time all over again.

My parents, it seems, had also been wrestling with a change of heart, and invited us back around to stay in Southall if that was indeed what we wanted. It was and very much so because that creepy abode, comfortable and cosy though it superficially appeared, was simply too much for us to cope with on an emotional level.

It was oppressive and unnerving and ominous and – yes, okay, I'll use the word even though I'll probably be inviting ridicule from some quarters - haunted.

The only spirits I had any interest in were the distilled kind; my mother knew that, and offered us each a glass on our return as a sort of 'house-warming'. My father, who'd elected not to be sociable for reasons best known to himself but which I reasoned would surely be made clear to all in due course, had gone out.

Still, at least with everything a little more settled for the time being, I could refocus my attention to getting myself back on the UK event circuit.

I was no longer interested in messing about with minor weekend shows where I couldn't express myself in the way that I craved to do.

I wanted to break world records and, since one of my greatest ambitions was to claim as my own that for jumping over double decker buses, that's what I decided I'd go for first off.

And who was that record holder of the time? It was Eddie Kidd, quite naturally, with a leap over fourteen of them.

I determined that I would attempt a jump over twenty.
Donna, who'd seen me perform many times in New Zealand and understood my passion while having complete faith in my competence, said that she would support me every step of the way.

I then only needed two things; a motorbike on which to break the record, and a show to ride it at.

Getting hold of a bike, I thought, was the lesser of those two concerns as I still had plenty of contacts in the trade despite my four-month sabbatical in New Zealand and, if all else failed, I could always borrow a suitable machine rather than try and negotiate terms of purchase with money that I didn't have.

Finding a promoter willing to pay the money needed to market and present such an attempt was always going to be harder.

I had no manager at that point, and none of the agents with whom I'd previously had good relations had been in touch with bookings, so I was left with no option but to thumb through the directory of outdoor fates and galas for the summer seasons of 1982 and 1983 to try and find that ever-elusive pot of gold.

Virtually every call I made was rebuffed as soon as I'd made my intentions clear, and those that weren't involved a long-winded and ultimately broken promise to get back to me.

The phone bill must have been enormous and, since I wasn't bringing any money in and Donna wasn't able to as she still wasn't technically a UK citizen at that point and wasn't allowed to work, I had no option but to leave it to my parents to sort out (although I did reimburse them as soon as I was able).

Donna then said that she had a weirdly good feeling about an advert for Bromley Carnival which had been tucked away near the back of the directory. I was sceptical because I saw nothing there which made it stand out, but with little left to lose, I bought into her optimism.

As soon as I dialled the number for Bromley Carnival Committee (the organisers, simply the 'Committee' hereafter) and started speaking to them, everything began falling beautifully into place.

Some way into that positive conversation they asked if I'd like to do the jump for charity. Of course, I said yes!

I've always been a supporter of such causes and so I was delighted that my efforts would also benefit others but, in that particular case, there was the added bonus that none of the sponsors who might agree to put up a share of the cost for staging the show would ask for a monetary return on their investment.

That was just as well, since I'd calculated that staging a world record attempt of the kind that I was planning would swallow up the thick end of twenty thousand pounds.

I mentioned that fact to the Committee, but they wouldn't be discouraged. They remained very much up for what I had in mind having reassured me that the money would be raised from local concerns, and confidently invited us up there for a meeting and a tour of the venue.

You can imagine my excitement when, being as I was a huge fan of science-fiction stories, I learned that Bromley was the birthplace of the incomparable H.G. Wells and also that Norman Park, where I was scheduled to jump on August 29th 1983, was one of his preferred sanctuaries from the rigours of perfecting the written word.

Perhaps more importantly from a practical point of view, Norman Park couldn't have been more perfectly laid out for what I wanted to achieve.

The Committee explained that, providing I was happy, they'd make some rearrangements to the Carnival's ground plan in order that I could utilise the park's natural but gentle four-hundred-foot long slope.

I told them that, yes, that would be fantastic.

I also specified that I would need a fifty-foot-long take-off ramp inclined at ten degrees to the ground it rested upon and, averse as I always had been to taking unnecessary risks, I requested a horizontal safety platform covering the last four of the twenty buses.
They said that nothing I was asking for would be a problem.

Great!
That meant I could finally turn my attention to the small matter of getting my hands on a bike.

I contacted *KTM-Sportmotorcycle AG*, an Austrian manufacturer which had based its United Kingdom operation in Yeovil. I explained to them what I was doing, and that I would need the largest available 'cc' in order to do it.

After taking up their invitation to visit Somerset to discuss the finer points of my record attempt they agreed to loan me a KTM-495 (hence, a model with 495 cc's of horse power), easily the tallest bike I'd ever ridden!

KTM also supplied a mechanic whose job it was to service the bike and to make sure that everything was as right as it could possibly be for my appearance at Bromley Carnival.

What more could I have asked for?

Well, I suppose twenty identical buses would have been nice, but I was later told by the Committee that there were some issues with getting sufficient numbers of my preferred variety, so I ended up with a mixed bag of all sorts of sizes..

So, instead of jumping twenty of the buses I requested I'd actually be flying over a mixture of eighteen multi-sized ones, with unsightly gaps in between.

A local public relations company had been contracted to cover the event and I have to say that, one lapse of professional judgement excepted, they did a magnificent job. They'd secured the attendance of all of the UK-based television stations, as well as strong delegations from networks based in the United States, Canada, Australia and a number of other countries as well.

As with the fiasco at Swansea Airport there was no representation from the Guinness Book of Records. Thankfully, that didn't matter too much because, in their absence, all that was required to verify a record was the signed testimony of two officials, and so the Mayor of Bromley and one of the town's policemen were drafted in to do the honours.

Strangely enough my memory of the jump itself is somewhat cloudy, which is a real shame because I bagged two records with my first 'live' attempt.
Firstly, I roundly eclipsed Eddie's fourteen-bus obstacle record by clearing the eighteen that had been driven into place for me, *and* leaving a bit to spare.

Quite a bit to spare as it so happens, because I also smashed the distance record. I lost that record a couple of years later to another jumper, however my obstacle record still remains today, thirty one years later.

Andy Warhol promised me fifteen minutes in the limelight, and I certainly revelled in my ration after Bromley Carnival.

My achievement must have been picked up by every news agency in the world and, no, before you start shouting at me, I don't think that's too much of an exaggeration.
I even featured in an episode of *Ripley's Believe It Or Not* which was hosted in those days by Jack Palance, a giant of the movies in every sense of that word.

Obviously such exposure was very welcome but I really didn't think that my jump was going to be as big as it was (you'll have to excuse the double-meaning there).

My only real regret was that I didn't have the management to exploit that coverage to its fullest so that my career might then have moved up to the next level.

Nevertheless, I was invited on to Russell Harty's chat show but then the PR company messed up big style by asking the BBC for a five-thousand-pound appearance fee, and sadly that was the end of that.

Mercifully, thanks to our technological world which the internet has effectively reduced to the size of a keyboard, I can still enjoy that Bromley accomplishment courtesy of YouTube.

Many of that website's followers have voted it the Number One motorcycle jump of all time, although in my humble opinion there are a number of jumpers out there who are far more worthy of this title than me.

I genuinely thought that my records would only have stood for a couple of years and no longer but, as a close friend recently informed me, I was cited on a recent national radio programme as the holder of some manner of *new* record for having held *that* record for a record length of time!
Nowadays, whenever I hear Bromley being mentioned in connection with H.G. Wells, or maybe even Enid Blyton or Charles Darwin, my mind is immediately thrust back to that monumental August day in 1983.

The memories that I still possess of the event are powerful and heartfelt, and even now they fill me with immovable pride.

But I remember Bromley for another reason, a reason which I have yet to share with you but will do so now.

Bromley may not be Auckland or Frank L. Baum's Emerald City, but is the place where Donna and I had a belated but wonderful honeymoon, interrupted though it was by my appearance at the Carnival!

Those memories I would prefer not to share because they are obviously very personal but they are also exceedingly precious and poignant, and for self-evident reasons which will soon be disclosed to you.

CHAPTER 18: THE HAZY EIGHTIES

My recollections of the 1980's are certainly not as distinct or well-defined as perhaps one might expect them to be.

Personal reminiscences from that decade, which are typically nebulous at best, can abruptly appear without warning at the forefront of my mind and usually without any perceptible stimulus, but can then once again drift frustratingly from my despairing grasp and leave me groping in the dark for what should rightfully be mine.

Those memories may be cherished, inconsequential or throwaway; my faculties, which don't discriminate, will gleefully whisk them around in a foggy cerebral soup and then randomly trawl out one or two of them to ruthlessly dangle before me.

It's propitious indeed that I compiled scrapbooks of as many articles relating to my work as I could gather because, without them, my exploits during those years would surely have vanished forever. The value of such a loss would be untold, because not only was that section of my timeline the most productive and busiest in terms of the sheer quantity of stunt-riding I was undertaking but they must also rank amongst my most joyous, shared as they were with the love of my life, Donna.
Is there a connection between my unusual profession and my bouts of selective amnesia, I wonder?

After all, it's been well documented that some career boxers have encountered some mental difficulties later in life, and it's been speculated that the countless blows that they've taken to the head whilst plying their trade might have played a significant role in accelerating an otherwise natural process.

Also, in more recent times, suppositions regarding the possible detrimental effect of repeatedly heading one of those heavy old-style footballs have enriched that debate.

So what about spending a lifetime repeatedly returning to earth from a height of somewhere between twenty and thirty feet astride a motorcycle? Might such impacts have a cumulatively negative effect on the central nervous system and, therefore, the machinations of the brain itself?

Well, given a well-executed and cushioned landing on a suitably-configured bike then a single descent is highly unlikely to be harmful by itself, but what about the collective toll of maybe thousands?

Do you remember me telling you about my accident in Newcastle, after which I spent a few days in hospital but where I might have well as been on a different world? You probably won't be surprised to learn that that wasn't the only sudden jolt my head suffered during my active years.

Yes, I was always meticulous regarding the many safety-related aspects of my riding, but the simple truth of the matter is that merely striving to avoid a *serious* accident is considerably easier than seeking to effect a perfect, stress-free, landing each and every time.

In that futile quest for excellence the odds will begin to stack up against you, the statistics ultimately gain the upper hand and, consequently, with each apparently 'successful' jump the memories begin to fade.

For example, in the previous chapter did you notice that I explained that Donna and I spent our honeymoon in Bromley, and yet I'd failed to mention anything about our wedding itself?

Is that down to carelessness, or simply one rough landing too many?

Either way, I have a responsibility to put the record straight for you.

Donna and I were married at Neath's registry office on 8th August 1983.

She looked absolutely magnificent, dressed as she was in her finest jeans, T-shirt and brand new trainers.

You'll be glad to hear that I made much more of an effort because, in addition to my own jeans-shirt-trainers combo, I had sufficient pride in my appearance to throw on my denim jacket as well.

Time, you should understand, was against us.
The preparations for Bromley Carnival were in full swing, and we'd only dashed back to South Wales to tie the knot in a hasty ceremony witnessed somewhat impatiently by my mother and father before we headed straight back up to Kent that very same day.

If ever there was the definitive drive-thru wedding then, surely, that was it!

We *did* have a reception of sorts when we returned home, where the small and close-knit circle in attendance congratulated me not only on becoming a husband but also on my achievement at the Carnival and the global exposure which followed on behind it. Even so, for 'reception' you should *really* be reading 'night in the local pub'.

Soon after the dust settled on all of that I was invited over to the United States by an American television network who (if I'm remembering this correctly, and it's a big 'if' of course) had dispatched a crew to Bromley Carnival.

Regrettably, this is where things start to become increasingly vague.

What I *do* know beyond all doubt is that, on my return to Wales, I spent a considerable amount of time restoring one of the fifteen motorbikes used in the popular *Street Hawk* television series before passing it on to the now-closed *Cars of the Stars* Motor Museum in Keswick.

I'm often asked about what might be my favourite bike out of all the ones that I've owned down the years. Typically I would respond with some variant of 'horses for courses' but that *Street Hawk* bike, though often challenging to manoeuvre, is always up there.
Yes, it looked superb fitted as it was with all the flashy mod-cons that would qualify it to be reduced to a scale model and packaged as a money-spinning Christmas toy, but it also came with something which appealed to my sense of nostalgia on a far more personal level; a jet-black superhero-standard outfit for its rider.
I admit that I probably looked more like a muppet than a master of his craft whenever I dressed myself up in it but, hey, what grown man wouldn't wear a costume like that to feel like a champion, just for a little while at least?

Am I the only one with my hand up?

Okay, that's fair enough. I'll take the hint. Time to move on I think!

One of my first significant engagements after returning from the States took place at Peterborough's enormous and impressive East of England showground during the balmy summer of 1984.

I'd been booked to make an attempt at another obstacle record (please keep the word 'attempt' in mind as it'll assume greater importance later) by jumping thirty-one cars, for which I was to be paid eight thousand pounds for my trouble. In 1984 that *was* a sizeable amount of cash but please remember that I always needed to pay a lot of people for their help in making any given show happen and, once that was done, I was never left with a lot for myself.
I'd been forced to part with my old bike (not the *Street Hawk* one, but a proper stunt one) to cover the cost of some transatlantic travelling expenses, and so I was left with no option but to sift through my list of contacts and try and borrow a machine to take up to Peterborough.

Through doing so I asked one particular motocross rider if he had a suitable model available. He said that he did, which was great news of course, but what he actually loaned me was nothing short of a wholesome wreck. It had been thrashed to within a millimetre of its life and, as I had no time for any meaningful testing before leaving South Wales, it had to be left until my practice jumps at the showground before I realised there was no conceivable way that the thing could provide me with the lift, and therefore the distance, that I so desperately required.

Donna was also concerned, and persuaded me to extend the safety platform to cover an additional eight cars.

Spookily enough, but thoroughly in keeping with the sixth and seventh senses that she seemed to possess, she insisted on that precaution before I'd even mounted the bike for the first time.

And, boy! Was I grateful for her intervention because I *did* fall short in practice and, without that safety extension, there can be little question that I would have lost my life there and then. Naturally enough I was relieved to have cheated *that* fate, but I did so at the cost of grasping that the record I'd travelled there to claim was hopelessly beyond my reach.

Sure enough, come the event itself, that was precisely where it stayed.
I bore considerable remorse because I was being paid eight grand but I'd failed to get the organisers the record, and hence the publicity, that they craved and probably budgeted around.

They must have recognised that my professional pride was dented, so they offered to lighten my burden and clear my conscience completely by not paying me at all.
I'm sorry but, guilt trip or no guilt trip, *that* definitely wasn't happening.
Their argument was that, in their eyes, I'd bombed miserably with what I'd been booked to accomplish, and hence I'd forfeited the right to any earnings.

I remained admirably calm after inviting myself into their boardroom about an hour afterward because I'd fathomed many years before that the pen is mightier than the sword, especially when that pen is used to sign a contract.

I countered their contention by drawing their half-baked notice to said contract, within which it was clearly stated that I was to be paid eight thousand pounds for making an *attempt* (remember the word?) at the record.

I had, therefore, fulfilled my side of the agreement; I'd made an attempt.

The teensy little detail that I'd not succeeded was utterly irrelevant, as was the fact that I'd gone to Peterborough with machinery that was barely fit for the knacker's yard.
I'd made an attempt, just as the contract required me to do and, as far as I was concerned, that was all that mattered.

The intimidating atmosphere which sizzled around that conference table could only have been cut with a razor-sharp knife, perhaps not too dissimilar to one that each of the blokes in there thirsted to plunge into my back. There sat those twelve-or-so snooty so-called gentlemen, all suited and booted, all leering at me as though I were no better than some worthless and insignificant Taffy turd, and each and every one of them, through defending the indefensible, was in the wrong.

Money goes to money, or so they say, but getting it to travel in the other direction can be nay on impossible sometimes.
Unless, of course, there exists a signed and binding commitment to make it do so.

They paid up grudgingly, but I think the gnashing of their teeth when they handed over the cash could have been heard back in Skewen.

They held back a few hundred for themselves, but I could live with that. They had dissatisfied people to pay off after all, just as I did, so as soon as I'd made safe my wages I bid them all a frosty farewell and beat a hasty retreat back onto the A1.

Bob Jeffries.
 I'm sorry if that seems something of a random name to appear immediately after an account in which that particular person played no part, but I wanted to get it down on the page before I forgot it again.

It's a name that filled everyone that knew it with genuine warmth and, during one near-catastrophic gig in Carmarthen, perhaps there was a little more warmth flying around than his colleagues might have wished for.

You see, Bob was something of a loner, and was also a tad scatter-brained. He had no other life other than touring the country as a self-proclaimed 'roadie' with me and my stunt team (the 'Black Barons' had morphed into the 'Sky Riders' by that time) and, as a result, his head was usually bouncing with so much enthusiasm that, occasionally, his common sense would have to pack its two suitcases and get the hell out of there.

All of which was a shame because, putting his all-too-regular episodes of inattetion aside for a moment, he really was a decent enough guy.

Do you recall the diesel-doused 'Tunnel of Fire' from that show in Perth? Yes, I know it turned out to be a total shambles on *that* day, but I kept my faith in it and, in time, it became a much-requested and dramatic cornerstone of my performances.

That day in Carmarthen, and thanks entirely to Mr Jeffries, it became considerably more dramatic than anyone could have bargained for.
Everything was going so well too; my team were gleefully stuffing the tunnel with straw and soaking it with the petrol, although quite a few splashes of fuel were naturally ending up on the bone-dry grass.

The *same* grass, incidentally, where Bob had laid the torch in readiness to light it.

This, I should tell you, all happened during that scorching summer of 1984, when fields like that one in Carmarthen were like parched tinderboxes and in need of no encouragement from someone like Bob to go up in flames.

But, as soon as Bob put a lit match to the grounded and unlit torch, up in flames it went. The Tunnel of Fire went the same way of course, *while the roadies were still working inside it.*

I'm sure he would have recognised his error straight away. If he hadn't, then the other roadies dashing past him and yelling with their clothes ablaze would have provided him with a most useful *aide-mémoire*.

Thankfully, and pretty miraculously now that I'm giving it sober consideration some thirty years later, those guys weren't seriously burned. They were badly singed maybe, and hot under the collar in every conceivable sense of that phrase, but not seriously burned.

Poor old Bob.
He wasn't with me for too long after that but, despite what happened that day in Carmarthen, informing him that his services were no longer required wasn't easy.

No, I *didn't* sack him, and you should know that before you call me all the cruel bastards under the sun.

It's just that I'd felt I'd taken the show with the Sky Riders as far as it could probably go, and that maybe it was time to go solo.

I have to give Bob his dues though because, when I bumped into him some years later, he was proudly wearing his bright orange 'Sky Riders' jacket and he was still as friendly and as cheerful as he was when he was on tour with us.

He bore me no malice or ill-feeling whatsoever. To be honest with you, I don't think he knew what 'malice' or 'ill-feeling' were.

Changing the subject slightly, it must have been around that time that I was invited to do some shows in South Africa.

Younger readers, who might think that that represented a fantastic once-in-a-lifetime opportunity for me, might be surprised to learn that I declined. However, the more senior among you might recall that, until relatively recently, South Africa was in the vice-like grip of *apartheid*.

For those who are unsure of what that was, *apartheid* was a policy of racial segregation aggressively administered by the government in Pretoria.

Examples of that malignant dogma might include the institution of 'whites only' jobs, 'whites only' washrooms, or even 'whites only' park benches.

Mercifully, and thanks in no small part to the magnificent efforts of people like Nelson Mandela, a swathe of constitutional chemotherapy in the late 1980's and early 1990's wiped *apartheid* from the face of South Africa.

Now, you might be asking what all of this has to do with me. The answer to that simple; Donna, with her New Zealand origins, had coloured skin.

Okay, I'll admit that her complexion did increase in its pallor after she'd spent some time in the largely cold and typically sunless United Kingdom, but she was still dark enough to have made life unacceptably uncomfortable even before we'd left the airport in South Africa.

There was absolutely no way that I was going to subject her to such inhumane degradation so, despite Donna's protests that I should still consider travelling there alone for the benefit of my career, we stayed at home and I haven't regretted that decision to this day.

It's incredible to think that such a repugnant doctrine of social separation as *apartheid* could prosper in the late twentieth century, but prosper it did.

Lamentably, the outdated philosophies which fed it and gave it life are still with us today and I strongly suspect with profound sadness that they'll be around for many decades to come.

I speak with some authority here, because Donna and I experienced them up close and personal.

It all happened in August 1986 after another successful world record attempt, that time at the Royal Victoria Docks in London.

I cleared two hundred and forty one feet, an exploit which has since been surpassed, and as a result wrote myself into the Guinness Book of Records for the second time.

But I don't remember that weekend for that.

I also set another obstacle record by clearing twenty juggernauts but, again, that's not important.

I even came close to killing myself by walking backwards up my take-off ramp the day before the jump in order to protect it from any rain, and would have easily plunged the thirty feet onto the concrete below had I not had the presence of mind to look between my feet once I'd reached the top.

Even that, however, is extraneous.

All that stirs me from that flying stop-off in the capital was a visit to an unnameable small-fry music emporium located in a grubby alleyway in the west end.

Donna and I wanted to buy a souvenir to remember our time in London, a single or maybe even a CD album to make us smile every time we put it on.

So in we went.

We were both contentedly flicking our way through the racks when the rather rugged, unshaven and sweat-stained proprietor sidled up to me, and said:

"Is she with you?"

"I'm sorry?" I replied, genuinely confused by the man's sharpness and manner.

"Is she with you?" he repeated, pointing at Donna.

"Yes," I answered with mounting irritation. "*That* is my wife."

"Yeah? Well, I don't want *her* kind in here," he snarled. "Get her out!"

I'm proud to say that I don't often lose the plot, but I certainly mislaid it at that moment. I can't really recall the exact words that I screamed in his face, but I'm pretty sure that I quickly turned the air blue and then carried on until it assumed a shade of very deep cobalt. He backed away and raised his hands as though he was offering to repent or apologise, but what had been said had been said, and there was nothing that he could utter or do that could render it null and void.

Donna, as I've already recounted, had naturally dark skin.

To me and the vast majority of reasonably-intelligent people like me, harbouring prejudice on the basis of someone's skin tone is abhorrent. To that bloke, though, making such repulsive judgements was clearly a central ethos of his life.

I would like to think that, after my tirade, he would have thought more carefully about his interjections the next time that a person of colour dared to venture onto his premises.

Sadly though, I very much doubt it.

Maybe he's reading this right now. Maybe there are some blurry recollections of our visit to his shop wafting through his bigoted and otherwise-vacant mind.

If so, then I'm afraid I have to ask: do you remember me, my friend?

No?

Well, maybe this will jog your memory: I'm the one that spat on your counter before I pulled my precious wife from your disgusting shop.

I've a strong belief that that unsavoury incident completely cemented Donna's growing feeling of homesickness which, if I'm truthful with myself here, had never lessened since her arrival at Heathrow in 1982.

So, fearing for the very future of our relationship I decided that we should sell up and, with the nine-year-old Shane accompanying us also, emigrate to New Zealand where we'd look to rebuild everything almost from scratch.

Of course, that process would also have to include the re-launching of my career but, as work from the various UK agencies had become worryingly patchy, I didn't consider that to be such a bad thing.

On the night before we flew out I offered my father a lift to his church (he'd quite actively developed his religious side in his later years). When I parked up there I realised that *that* would probably be the last time that I'd ever see him as, at the time, I had absolutely no intention of returning to South Wales.

"I love you, Dad," I called through the wound-down car window as he opened the church's imposing wood-panelled door.

He paused before turning to face me.

"I love you too, boy," he replied before stepping inside and shutting the door.

To be perfectly honest with you I didn't expect *any* kind of response from him.

After all, the last occasion he'd shown that level of affection was, as you'll recall from an earlier chapter, eighteen years previously during our one-off trip to Neath's old fleapit cinema to see *One Million Years BC*.

Still, those five unexpected words remained with me during the drive home, and also through the waking hours of our flight to Auckland the following morning.

With our hurried preparations we'd left ourselves with no time to purchase a property out there or even rent one so, at the outset, we relied on the charity of Donna's mother to put a roof over our heads.

We were hugely appreciative of that gesture in the early days, but I knew that it couldn't be a permanent arrangement.

I had to find work.

I had to start earning money again.

Not being one for doing things by halves Donna and I threw ourselves in at the deep end and organised a three-show, north-to-south tour of the country.

My plan at each of those shows was to try and break a world record.

The first gig was scheduled for Avondale Racecourse in Auckland (do you remember it?) for January 1987, and that would be followed by performances in Wellington and, finally, Christchurch.

We managed to secure a loan of six thousand dollars from a local businesswoman for the Auckland show and I knew that, with a well-attended performance in glorious weather, we'd be able to pay that back comfortably *and* have more than enough to take into the Wellington performance.

Now, what's that old saying which tells you what to do if you want it to rain?

Organise a barbeque, or a golf tournament, or a cricket match?

Perhaps even a stunt show in Auckland?

In New Zealand, January is meant to be the sunniest and hottest month of the year. The trouble is, with the north of the country (and therefore Auckland) situated at a subtropical latitude, the threat of rain always lurks.

And this isn't like the joking rain we experience in the UK, where we brush ourselves down and moan after being out in it and the dog shakes himself off over your furniture. No, this is *proper* rain, where umbrellas are totally superfluous and the typhoon-strength winds will blow you all over the place if you're stupid enough to venture out in it.

Yes, I can tell that you've guessed what's coming next.

My show, because of that wind and rain which was totally unanticipated at the time, turned out to be a complete and total washout.

I was left with an absolute disaster on my hands, and how we succeeded in reimbursing that businesswoman her six thousand dollars I'll never rightfully know for sure, but we did.

Sadly, we were left with nothing to set up the show in Wellington, so that was the end of that.

Left with no other option, we cancelled the entire tour.

The embarrassment, though, didn't end there.

My face was subsequently splashed all over one of New Zealand's Sunday newspapers, so the entire country knew how much money I'd lost and how broke I'd become.
Donna wasn't spared either as she was forced to work in one of Auckland's larger department stores, which was most certainly not how she'd imagined her dream return to New Zealand to shape up.

Nevertheless, even negative exposure can have some positive outcomes.

She secured for herself a television commercial for Wattie's foods and in which she appeared alongside Shane (I've tried for many years to get a copy of that so I'd be keen to hear from anyone who might be able to help).

I also did a commercial for Bernard Matthews beef, as well as a couple of slots on radio.

But it wasn't enough. Nowhere near, in fact.

The money and the bookings were drying up and, with our adventure destroyed in the most agonising of ways, it was time to return to South Wales.

So, in the autumn of 1987, the three of us disconsolately made our way back to Heathrow, but now comes the silver lining.

Between 1982 and 1988 Donna had suffered no fewer than eight miscarriages, with each one leaving a deeper emotional scar than the last.

While in New Zealand we visited some medical specialists and were advised by a number of them to consult Dr Peter Bowen-Simkins, the world-renowned Swansea-based gynaecologist who was an expert in fertility treatments.

We met with him at his practice which was based in Singleton Hospital, and Donna began her treatment with him almost immediately.
In February 1988 she learned that she had fallen pregnant with her (and our) first child and, in the November of that year, Natalie was born.

Two-and-a-half years later in the July of 1991, and without the need of any additional treatment, she presented me with our second daughter, Natasha.
We had become a wonderful family of five, but the happiness that brought was to be cruelly short-lived.

CHAPTER 19: TWELVE WORDS

Our lives, so we are persistently reminded by those tabloid-tethered philosophers who evidently have far too much spare time in their own, are precious and every moment should be savoured as though it is our last.

Yeah, right!

I hope you'll overlook my cynicism, but I suspect that anyone who has been forced to watch feebly as one of those so-called 'priceless moments' slips away forever will tell you that *that* is much easier romanticised about than achieved.

Of course, those rare and transitory periods where one can contentedly bask in the glow of good fortune should be milked for all they're worth, but one must always be prepared for the advent of those mahogany-brown and shit-scented clouds that seem to gather all too quickly, ready to dump their sizeable load on one's happy parade.

Please don't get me wrong here, since my glass is always half full even when it's been bled all but dry, but dreams and reality are two astonishingly different things and, as our years spent in this increasingly-unsympathetic and punishing world trundle by, so the mesh of barbed wire between them seems to grow just that little bit thicker.

For each one of us who is able to enjoy some respite skipping through that imaginary meadow which is packed up to the hilt with fluffy rabbits, rainbows and castles in the air, there is always some hapless bugger for whom the luxury to so fantasise might as well be a million miles away or more.

And no matter who we are, or who we pretend to be, we can reliably bet our last quid against very short odds that those unbearable and tortuous times will hunt us down in the end.

My own personal confrontation with Fate's turf accountant began in the summer of 1992 and, before you read on, you should know that this remains by some considerable margin the darkest and most harrowing phase of my life.

It all began with the organising of my first sustained tour of Scotland which, in between the inevitable late-night feeds and nappy changes, Donna and I had tried to meticulously plan out for the July of that year.

Donna, though, had decided that she wouldn't be coming, citing concerns over such a long journey there (and back, let's not forget) for Natalie and Natasha, plus her reservations over how their presence might distract me from what I was actually going there to do.

I tried to persuade her that, in fact, the opposite was true (which it was), but she wasn't having any of it.
I wondered at first whether her obstinacy might have something to do with her father.

He died when she was very young so she never truly knew him and only rarely spoke of him, but she had mentioned some years previously that he'd hailed originally from Scotland.

It was only a theory, and one which I was reluctant to share with her for reasons of sensitivity. In the meantime, however, she was sticking to her guns: she wasn't coming with me, and that was that.

Then, maybe a week or so before my departure, she abruptly changed her mind and demanded, quite forcibly I should add, that she wanted the girls to be there as well.

That totally disoriented me because, for Donna, such a full-scale shift was almost impossibly rare; once she'd made up her mind on something there was generally no shifting it, and woe betide anyone who dared to try.

But, shift it did.

I was thrilled of course, ecstatic even, but still rather perplexed. Notwithstanding, one should never look a gift horse in the mouth so I played ball, but with full expectation of her having yet another change of mind (which, incidentally, never happened).

So, with that now fully explicated, let's get back to the tour itself.

We'd previously arranged with the various authorities and councils in Scotland that our first port of call would be New Deer, a remote but delightfully traditional Highland village situated in what is now Aberdeenshire and with a population of no more than six hundred. The place is also located close to the North Sea coast, a factor one is immediately reminded of whenever one is foolish enough to wander around into the open air clad in fewer than four layers of clothing.
Myself, Donna and our two daughters travelled up there in our faithful but pitifully-underpowered Austin Princess (which, for those younger readers who may be wondering, is a car) while the remainder of my supporting entourage trailed behind in a large Mercedes van which we'd hired solely for the tour.

Our good friend Brian was in there along with his partner Hayley and *their* two young children, as was Chris Barry, my new roadie, and *his* partner Camilla.

Oh yes, my two bikes and the accompanying 'Adam Dare' costume (the latest in a line of creations designed to keep my act suitably fresh) plus all the stunt gear had been shoehorned in there as well.

Brian's father had kindly loaned me his caravan, which the Princess towed valiantly but not without a few grumbles up the M6 and which would be our sleeping-quarters-cum-baby-changing space during the fortnight ahead. Shane, in case you were conjecturing, was in his fourth year of secondary school at the time and remained behind with his mother to complete his end-of-year exams.

We'd been informed before we departed that a fallow field just outside New Deer had been set aside for our temporary accommodation and so, nearly six hundred road miles and heaven only knows how many hours and service stops later, there we all sat in the weary throes of a well-deserved rest, playing cards and telling jokes with only cud-chewing cows and a howling gale for company.

As far as my show the following day was concerned, everything passed off absolutely according to the script: sunshine, vroom-vroom, jump, cheers, vroom-vroom again, jump again, louder cheers, paid, pack up, gone.

Further apologies now must go to you, dear reader, and to the good people of New Deer for the brevity of that previous account, but we were all still fatigued after our long drive there and I just wanted to get the job done. It is, nevertheless, a part of the country that is blessed with the most spectacular scenery and I would readily recommend a visit there to anyone.

Next on our itinerary was Nairn, which is about fifteen miles north-east of, and along the coast from, Inverness.

Having left New Deer at one in the morning we arrived about an hour later at Nairn's trailer park, an at-one-with-nature facility established for the innumerable visiting ramblers, groups of weekend golfers, a handful of birdwatchers and one motorcycle stuntman.

That, though, was where the good humour ended because, while there, my life would be changed and almost ruined forever, and as such nothing would ever be the same again.

We reached Nairn on 19th July, 1992.

The first portentous suggestions that something wasn't quite right surfaced soon after we'd pitched up, and mere hours before my performance.

At about three o'clock in the morning I decided to head over to the trailer park's shower block, just to spruce myself up a little with a good scrub as I knew the following morning would be extremely busy for me and I probably wouldn't have the time to wash properly then.

After I was all done I dried myself off and re-dressed before making my way back.

I couldn't have been more than a dozen paces from the door to the caravan when, terrified, I stopped in my tracks, rigid.

A cold, numbing shudder tore through my spine. My heart skipped a beat or ten, and I began to breathe heavily with mounting apprehension.

Though the night was moonless and thus virtually pitch-black, I was still able to make out a silhouetted figure sitting in the front passenger seat of the Princess.

Nervously I began tip-toeing over to the car; whoever was in there must surely have seen me I guessed, but there was no obvious reaction as I approached.

With my right hand trembling almost uncontrollably I reached for the passenger door's handle; as before, there was little suggestion of movement from within.

I yanked the handle and swung the door open with all of the might that my rapidly-waning courage could muster and with every expectation of then being lunged upon by whoever was trying to steal the car, but the 'intruder', who I recognised instantly, continued staring through the front windscreen with teardrops trickling down her cheeks.

"What the *hell* are you doing out here?" I yelled with both relief and anger (but mostly relief) at the visibly-startled Donna. "Don't you know what time it is? Or have I done something wrong?"

"Just leave me alone," she whispered. "Something terrible is going to happen tomorrow."

"What? Oh, don't be ridiculous Donna! *Nothing* is going to happen! I've been doing this for years now, you know that! It's not as though I'm even going for a record here! It's just me, the bike, and half-a-dozen cars! *You* could probably do it, seeing as you've watched me so many times!"

"No, I mean to *me*. Something bad is going to happen to *me*."

At the time I really couldn't fathom where *that* had come from. Was it simply tiredness from the journey up, followed by a post-midnight jaunt over to Nairn? Either way, whenever I've had cause to be annoyed I've always tried my level best not to let it show, but I *was* annoyed that night and, regrettably, it *did* show.
Donna, though, was utterly unmoved.

She remained sat as a passenger, shaking her head mournfully and gawping at something in the distance that wasn't there and never would be.

"So, are you coming in now?" I asked her with admirably-restrained impatience. "It's getting cold out here!"

She *did* come in and she *did* eventually sleep, but only after she'd spent a further half-an-hour alone in the car and gazing out over the bleak and shimmering expanse of the Moray Firth. Her mood, perhaps unsurprisingly, hadn't improved greatly, if at all, by the morning. In fact, if anything it had turned even more sombre.

Then, the realisation hit me.

Of course! It was all to do with her Scottish-born father, who had passed away when she was an infant!

Why didn't I think of that before? Was she sensing his spirit, calling to her from somewhere out there? Was she being slowly overwhelmed by her first visit to his homeland?

Prudently I thought much the better of questioning her outright, so I kept my hypothesis very much to myself.

Nonetheless, in my own mind the connection had been made, my conscience was clear, and I could return to my preparations for the day ahead.

I met the show's organiser and introduced him to Donna but she seemed less than enamoured by him, almost to the point of being wary and distrustful, but at the time I thought little of it.

While Chris and Brian helped me to get everything ready later that morning they badgered me almost constantly about the change that had come over Donna since our arrival in Nairn.

I can't remember exactly how I fobbed them off, but I know for sure that I wouldn't have complicated the issue by revealing that particular aspect of her paternal family history. Instead, and being as I am a stereotypical man, I'm certain I would have plumped for the usual things: tired because the two girls were keeping her up all night, headaches, time of the month, the standard stuff that can be found in the blinkered male's cerebral hideaway.

Yet, I do recall that, while the three of us were setting up the ramps, Donna was seemingly enjoying a relaxing meander around the show's stalls with Hayley, Camilla and all the children so at least she was making an effort to get herself back onside.

In spite of my clumsy deduction though, that single show of unity was by itself not enough to dispel my own nagging doubts regarding her belief in what I'd driven us all the way up there to do and, for the first time, I found myself musing over whether indeed it would have been better had she remained in Skewen.

I simply had to speak my mind because the whole thing was starting to drive me crazy, and I had my chance to do so once she'd returned from her open-air window shopping.

"So, come on," I gnawed at her but only when we were well distanced from prying ears.

"What's up?"
"I don't know," she shrugged. "I really don't like this place though. And I don't like that organiser either."

"I know but, look! All I have to do here is a few jumps and then that's it; job done! We've got some free days before we have to head up to John O'Groats so we can relax a bit and spend some more time together. I know there's not much here for you and the girls to do but just hang in there, okay? For my sake, that's all I'm asking for."

"Alright," she sighed. "If it'll help to keep the peace, I'll lighten up."

I smiled and so did Donna but, while my smile was genuine, hers most definitely wasn't. Something had bitten her deeply but I had no time to dwell further on whatever that might be because Chris was about to lengthen my glitch list substantially with these heart-stopping words: "We've got some problems with the jump bike."

What?! How could that happen? I quailed. After all, when the bike was packed away after I'd done the New Deer gig it was most definitely in tip-top working order.
"There's about a dozen nuts loose on it," Chris explained gloomily as I followed him behind the Mercedes van and to where my bike was resting on its stand. "It's not firing properly either, and the handlebars are all out of alignment as well."

He moodily continued to highlight the many issues, but I'd long since stopped listening. I hadn't made any subconscious link between Chris's trials and tribulations and Donna's continuing desire to just get the hell out of there, and I had no interest in doing so either because my curtain call was less than five hours away and I harboured little desire to embroil myself in any preternatural nonsense.

"Just get it fixed," I snapped at Chris, rudely cutting him short while he was still in mid-flow. "I'm not bothered how you do it, just get it bloody sorted! That's what you're here for!"

I'd never barked like that at him in all the years I'd known him but, by that point, I was so tense, defocused and irritable that, and I say this with all due respect to that town and its wonderful inhabitants, my head was well and truly in the shed and all I wanted was to exit Nairn post-haste.

The minutes dragged both before and after the gates to the show opened at midday. I'd wasted the early part of the afternoon pacing back and forth between Donna with her growing need for reassurance, and Chris with his.

Everything was getting too much for me, and I could feel the pressure building.

To be fair to him, though, Chris certainly did his bit.

By the time I'd changed into my 'Adam Dare' get-up he'd somehow brought the bike back to proper working order.

You're the main man, I thought, and I told him so.

He seemed mildly appreciative but I think he was still miffed with the manner in which I'd lost my cool with him earlier in the day, and rightfully so I suppose, but the rebuilding of those bridges was something that would have to wait until Nairn was firmly at our backs.

I had work to do, after all.

After I'd mingled with all those that had come to watch, and gleefully signed an autograph or two as well, I was ready for the off.

So, Take One: Chris Bromham, as his alter-ego 'Adam Dare', jumping over six (I think) vintage cars in Nairn, northern Scotland.

One issue that even the hardiest of souls will have with northern Scotland is that it can be a trifle breezy, and one of those all-too-frequent and icy blasts from the sea caught me in mid-flight and caused the bike to drift off course. Thankfully though I grounded it without too much difficulty, and Chris was soon on hand with his box of magic tools to effect the running repairs.

He was at least more responsive and amenable than previously which is more than could have been said for Donna who, while applauding more-or-less mechanically and carrying barely a trace of emotion on her face, endured like a statue beside my landing area with our girls.

All of the other spectators were much more passionate, with a multitude of 'oohs' and 'aahs' and other animal-like noises emanating from the hundreds that had assembled there.

In spite of that, I only had eyes for Donna. I looked at her for a moment or two, but she was staring clean through me and at something that didn't exist one hundred yards away and behind my head.

On to Take Two: as per Take One, but with eight cars rather than six.

There was another gust and, yes, again the wind took me adrift.

Still, I again managed to land properly which brought an even more enthusiastic reaction from the admiring crowd.

Enter Mr Barry with his Super Spanners; twist, tweak, tighten, top-notch again.

In the meantime Brian had scurried onto my take-off ramp to reposition a couple of the then-loosened boards.

Take Three: Ten cars, but the conditions were making it feel like twelve or more.
I'd grown increasingly restless by that juncture because I was already touching down an uncomfortable way up my landing ramp and I knew damn well that those vintage cars I was trying so hard to fly over weren't cheap but, fortunately, I finally had some brief but welcome respite from those troublesome sea squalls for that third and final attempt.

I sailed without a hitch from take-off ramp to landing ramp, and was saluted with approving roars from those watching on.

The loudest roar, though, was inside my own head.

I'd done it!

Despite the very best intentions of the invisible powers-that-be that revel in repeatedly wreaking untold havoc in our hearts, our minds and our world, I'd done it!

Fate's bookie, I resolved and with considerable satisfaction, would have to wait a little bit longer before he could take that quid off me.

I'd more-or-less successfully negotiated each of the three jumps, which meant that Donna's forecasts of doom could be forgotten once and for all and I could offer my sincere apologies to Chris within an air of cordial celebration.

Tragically, and still incredibly to me now even after twenty-two years have passed, neither of those things would ever happen.
Once the organiser had crossed my palms with the amount of silver stated in the contract, Donna put her arms around me, kissed me, said 'Chris, I love you, and don't you ever forget it or me'.

She then strolled off forlornly toward the stalls with Natasha in her pram and Natalie shuffling along just in front of her.

She didn't say 'Great show!' or 'Well done!' or 'My hero!' or anything like that.

All she said was 'Chris, I love you, and don't you ever forget it or me'.

I don't believe I considered those twelve words to be overly significant at the time but, Jesus! I've thought of them every day since.

Soon afterwards, and with a swelling sense of unease, Brian and I deconstructed the ramps and began packing them away.

Many minutes then passed.

Donna hadn't returned, and there was no sign of her anywhere.
My anxiety was tightening its grip.

I hurried over to Chris who was cleaning down my bike and giving it a good once-over, and asked him if he knew where Donna had gone.
He replied that she and Camilla had taken the girls to the local newsagent's on the main road, to buy me a card for my birthday the following day.

With all that had been going on inside my head I'd completely forgotten about that.

Sadly, and despite all that had been going on inside *her* head, Donna had still remembered.
I then heard my name being shouted.

'Chris!' Brian shouted as he ran towards us as fast as he could. 'You'll have to come quickly! Donna's had an accident! She's been knocked down!'

The residues of those feelings that pushed everything else into a hazy nothingness when I heard those last two sentences have never really gone away.

It wasn't the words 'knocked down' or 'accident' that produced them on that day. It was Brian's use of past tense, and the inevitable sense of helplessness so produced, that did it.

I was an emotional wreck even before he'd had ushered me into the Mercedes van and driven me to the scene as swiftly as he could.

Even with his sterling efforts we could only get to within three hundred yards of where a small horde of extremely concerned faces had congregated because the traffic on the main road had completely ground to a halt. So, I sprinted the remaining distance and past a large exhibition trailer, which for some strange reason had its aluminium side canopy only half-opened, and with the already-exhausted Brian lagging wearily behind me.
While I ran I kept thinking: *Oh God, please don't take her away from me! Please don't let this be happening!*

An ambulance and a couple of police officers were already there by the time I reached her.

And there was Donna, laying on her side on the pavement in a crumpled heap and surrounded by hungrily-intrusive onlookers as the small squad of visibly-shaken paramedics were attending to her as best they could.
Natalie was leaning over her, crying.

As I could see no blood I simply couldn't work out what had happened but, thankfully, she was still conscious.

She somehow realised I'd knelt down beside her, and she groaned: "Are the girls okay, Chris?'
"Yes, darling!" I responded almost hysterically. "Yes! They're fine!"

"That's good," she whimpered. "I want to go to sleep now."

She started drifting in and out on consciousness and muttering 'Chris, the pain in my legs' during those ever-shortening periods when she was sufficiently cognisant to so do.

The paramedics, perhaps realising that time was working against them, gently lifted her onto a stretcher and then straight into the back of the ambulance. I clambered in with her and, after Camilla shouted to me that she would look after the girls, an extremely worried-looking bloke dressed in a road safety uniform pushed his way to front of the crowd and started staring at both me and my beloved. It appeared as though he was about to say something but, before he could, the ambulance's doors were slammed shut and, almost immediately, we sped off to the hospital.

The paramedics had already secured an oxygen mask to Donna's face but, even though she was unconscious, her breathing was disturbingly laboured and intermittent.
I gently lifted her arm, from which the skin had been torn cleanly from her elbow, and discovered a hole in her side which was comfortably the size of my fist.

I glanced at the female paramedic, and she glanced back at me.

She said nothing, but sometimes a silence and a breaking of eye contact can tell you everything that you need to know.

No blood was gushing from Donna's wound, indicating that her circulation was failing.
I understood what I was looking at, and I think the paramedic realised that as well.

Even after twenty-two years this is extremely hard for me to get down on paper but I knew at the outset that this moment would have to come, and perhaps by relaying to you exactly what happened that day to my treasured wife and the mother of my daughters, it might help to bring some closure to the whole dreadful affair.

So, I'm going to try.

Do you remember that exhibition trailer I dashed past when trying to get to Donna? Do you also remember me telling you that its side canopy was half-open, perhaps to no more than forty-five degrees?

Well, that trailer had been parked at the show and had, once its business day had come to an end, been towed toward the main road in readiness for being driven away.

It seems that the imbecile who was doing the towing (I'll call him Peter for the sake of clarity, even though I *do* know his proper name) had closed the side of the trailer but couldn't get the bolt which secured the canopy firmly in place to fit.

Despite that, he still decided to jump into the cab and drive off.

As he reached the speed limit for that road the canopy flew open to the angle I've already detailed but, of course, Peter was completely oblivious to that minor circumstance.

And so, as he went merrily along the canopy took out one road sign, then a second.

Next it struck Donna mere seconds after she'd passed Natalie to Camilla, leaving the impact wound in her side that I described a few paragraphs ago.
He was finally being flagged down by a member of the public, but only after he'd travelled a further one hundred and fifty yards along the main road.

The guy was actually a uniformed road safety officer, if you can believe the irony of that, and it was only after he'd dealt with his precious canopy and finally fastened it that he ambled over to an ambulance which had mysteriously stopped one hundred and fifty yards behind him.

Perhaps as he pushed through the small but shocked crowd which was noiselessly watching a beautiful, dark-haired woman being stretchered into the back of the ambulance, he'd made the crucial association that he should never have had to make.

Perhaps there was something he then wanted to say to the woman's husband, who was sitting next to her powerless and with tears streaming down his cheeks.

If there was, then Peter's moment was to pass forever with the slamming of the ambulance's rear doors and the wail of a siren as the innocent victim of his negligence and stupidity was quickly driven away.

CHAPTER 20: A LOST LIGHT

As soon as we'd screeched onto the grounds of Raigmore Hospital in Inverness and reversed in front of the entrance to A & E (Accident and Emergency) a fully-briefed medical team rushed from the building, flung open the ambulance's doors and wasted no time in rolling Donna's stretcher inside.

"Don't worry," our driver mouthed as he parked up. "I've seen people with worse than that."

Oh, really?

I wonder if he would have chipped in with such an offensive comment had it been *his* wife laying there rather than mine.

I suspect not but, regrettably, such is the offhand world we live in.

The medics wheeled Donna through a pair of double swing doors and down a short corridor before vigilantly manoeuvring her into one of the side rooms within the casualty unit. I followed a couple of strides behind but I was frightened and confused and, in all honesty, I would have screamed aloud with the trauma and distress with all that was happening were it not for believing I hadn't a breath left in my body.

The room was small, windowless and illuminated by garishly fluorescent strip lights, and was much like the one in Tonna hospital where I had my tonsillectomy all those years before, but it also had a bed upon which the team had already rested Donna by the time I'd faltered in there.

It was also thoroughly equipped with, as was my hope at least, everything they would need to save her life.

They wasted no time at all in stripping her down to her underwear.

"Do you mind if we remove her bra?" I was asked by one of the more junior doctors.

I've been asked some pretty brainless questions in my time but that one took the biscuit!

"Y*es*!" I yelled back as a less-than-gentle reminder that Donna was ebbing away. "Just cut it off!"

In the meantime their efforts to save her had become perceptibly more frantic.

"Tell them about my legs, Chris," she kept murmuring, her voice weakening further with every word. "Tell them about the pain in my legs."
My own voice was faring no better. "I will. They're doing everything they can, sweetheart. Everything they can."

All *I* could do was watch their increasingly desperate work, and when *that* became too much to bear I closed my eyes. I quickly opened them again because the team's already-heightened level activity was intensified anew: Donna had begun to convulse. Clearly this was a development they hadn't anticipated and, for the first time, I sensed that they were panicking and perhaps losing some control of the situation.

Abruptly, Donna then tried to sit up in bed.

She noticed me through bloodshot eyes and extended her arms as though beckoning me to her, but then she collapsed back down onto the mattress, seemingly lifeless.

One of the nurses quickly prepared a large syringe and plunged its long, thick needle into the right side of Donna's chest.

Her body shook and juddered for the briefest of moments.

I afforded myself the luxury of some optimism but then, as she again fell completely still, my hopes faded away once more.

Never have I felt so totally useless. I desperately wanted to help of course but, even in my wholly bewildered state, I understood that there was nothing I could attempt that wasn't already being tried.
I was then told to leave the room immediately.

Difficult though it was I wanted to stay but, blearily appreciating their need to be left alone to do whatever it was they had to do, I tottered into the corridor and slumped onto the nearest bench.

Some more of the hospital's staff hurried in to the room, while others scampered away before returning with whatever apparatus or equipment they needed.

Moments later the bra-removing doctor came rushing out, and I grabbed him by the arm before he could disappear into the depths of the hospital.

"Is she going to be okay?" I muttered almost inaudibly and fearful of his reply but, instead of giving me the straight answer I still yearned for, he looked at me fleetingly before dropping his gaze to the corridor's floor.

Only then did the realisation of what was happening, and what was very likely going to happen, begin to set in.

I released him, and off he dashed.

Please forgive my use of a well-trodden cliché, but every minute that then crawled by seemed like an hour, until…

"Chris?" came a familiar voice from near the entrance to A & E.
At that moment I didn't really want to be speaking to anyone but Chris Barry was a true friend and not one to be offended for long by one of my pathetic outbursts over something as insignificant as a faulty motorbike.

Camilla stood silently beside him, palpably distraught.

"Where is she?" he whispered as he placed his hand on my shoulder.

I nodded in the direction of Donna's room where the doctors and nurses were still scurrying to and from. I fully understood that both he and Camilla wanted to find out how Donna was and what her chances were, but I'd been in a similar position to the awful one that they now found themselves in and I knew all too well that some questions are best left unasked.

"Where are the girls?" I mumbled.

"They're with Brian and Hayley. They're safe and fine, Chris. Don't worry about them."

And so the three of us sat on the bench, and each reluctantly forced to accept that all we could do was wait.

Soon afterwards a small crash team appeared. They were pushing a trolley with some urgency toward, and then into, Donna's room.

My heart sank.

That's it then, I conceded to myself. *She's gone.*

I stood up and started pacing up and down the corridor, in the numbing anticipating that the next message to come from the room would be the last.

The crash team's agitated senior doctor then emerged from the room and, clearly realising who I was, approached me.

"Mr Bromham?" he enquired. He also introduced himself of course but I was far too concerned about Donna to be paying attention to such a minor detail and I'm ashamed to say that, to this day, I cannot recall his name. "I must tell you that your wife is in a critical condition and requires emergency surgery. She's being prepared for theatre now."

As if on cue Donna was veered out of the room by her attendant doctors and nurses, and the doctor that had spoken to me joined them straight away.

Within seconds she'd been wheeled around a corner, and that was that.

Chris glanced at Camilla, and then both regarded me. Each of our expressions carried the same cautiously guarded but thoroughly pained sentiment: *at least she was alive*.

By that time I'd been at the hospital for some three hours and I remained there, praying for a miracle with each minute that inched by, for the next thirty.

The compassionate administrative staff had allocated me a small but bleak family room to stay in, just a little way down the corridor from Donna's operating theatre. It had a bed, where I spent half of my time laying, and a sofa, where I spent the other half. There was also a window so I could stare blankly at the outside world for hours on end if I so desired, provided I didn't mind the wind which howled through the holes in the rotting frame, and finally a table which held a wooden bowl half-filled with fruit and the most recent and totally disregarded hospital menu.

I had no appetite obviously and couldn't face hospital food in any case, so I didn't have any kind of meal while I was there. All I had was one cup of tea and, to be brutally frank, I didn't really want *that*.

The only thing I craved was some news about…

"Mr Bromham?"

Through not eating or drinking properly I'd grown exhausted and words, even when they were spoken next to my ear as *those* were, seemed disconnected and meant for somebody else standing far away. However, I managed to make out the blurred outline of one of another of the hospital's doctors standing over me, and sensed that my shoulder was being gently rocked back and forth.

"Mr Bromham?" the detached voice parroted. 'I've just come from theatre. Your wife has now been transferred to intensive care. Would you like to come and see her?'
His question had much the same effect as taking a deep waft from some smelling salts. I'd been hauled from my stupor and, while my legs were weak and my mind still scrambled, I eagerly trailed the doctor along the corridor.

As we walked he said something about Donna needing three operations, and that her spleen had been removed along with the lower half of her left lung, and that there was significant

damage to the pancreas and kidney, and something else about eighty pints of blood and uncontainable haemorrhaging, but in my eagerness to get to intensive care I stupidly allowed all of that to wash over me.
That doctor had asked me if I wanted to *see* Donna.

Foolishly I'd misinterpreted that as an indication that I could actually *speak* to her.

I was apprehensive of course about how Donna would look but the prospect of talking to her, a thought which you'll remember I myself had planted in my own head, overrode everything.

"Which one is she?" I asked the doctor as I stood behind the window to the intensive care unit, glancing in turn at each of three people lying in their beds.

"She's there, Mr. Bromham," he replied, "over by the window. However, I have to inform you that she is currently on life support, and will remain so until...."

"Until?"

The doctor answered as openly, as sensitively and as diplomatically as he could.

"Until that life support is no longer required."

I looked again but, as I followed the doctor into intensive care, I simply couldn't allow myself to believe what I was seeing.
I shuffled over to Donna's bed where a pungent stench of blood, other bodily fluids, antiseptic and a multitude of chemical solutions hung heavily.

This can't be her, I remember thinking to myself. *It simply can't be*.

Her entire body was swollen out of all proportion, and almost out of all recognition. She was also laying on her back, and in the crucifix position. Her torso, abdomen and thighs had been wrapped in some form of aluminium foil. She'd been attached to at least six intravenous drips and she had innumerable needles and tubes piercing the skin on both of her forearms. A ventilator was helping her to breathe, while a heart monitor in the corner beeped just once for every two beats of my own. Those parts of her skin which *were* free from the foil contrasted sharply in colour from black and the most gut-wrenching shades of red and blue, and through to sickly yellows and the palest of white.

Her puffed-up hand, which I gently but hesitantly held in my own, felt like marble.

Deeming her to be entirely unaware of my presence I leant over and whispered 'I love you' in her ear but, as I did so, her body flinched and her eyes flickered open.
That startled me; looking at her I found it almost impossible to accept that she was capable of consciousness.

I would have given anything to be laying in that bed instead of her.

I asked her if she wanted me to call her family in New Zealand.

She nodded, but wearily.

"Do you think you can make it?" I asked her tenderly.

Very slowly, she shook her head.

I begged her to hang in there, and to fight to stay alive. I pleaded with her to think of the girls, and to hold pictures of them in her mind so that, from them, she might garner sufficient fortitude to pull through.

Whether she did, or indeed whether she was able to, I couldn't tell.

What I *do* know for certain is that she nudged me three times with her arm, which was her secret signal for 'I love you', and then she closed her eyes.

I remained with her for a few minutes before being escorted back to the family room by a kind-hearted staff nurse. There, I gathered some money from my bedside table and blearily headed to the payphones in the reception area.
Donna had rung New Zealand many times of course, and over the years I'd learned her family's telephone number off by heart. So, once I'd rehearsed in my mind what I was going to say and how I was going to say it, I called them.

The link was certainly not the clearest and I ran out of change rapidly, but I stayed on the line for long enough to give them a disconsolate account of what had happened and how Donna was, and the number of the hospital's intensive care unit.
Their shock and distress with what I had to tell them wounds me as much now as it did then.

Never have I had to make a more emotionally difficult phone call and, once it ended moments later through either a steadily-deteriorating connection or the exhausting of my money (I cannot remember which), I ruefully placed the handset back onto the receiver and lumbered firstly back to intensive care, where I was informed that Donna's condition had not changed, and then back to my room.

I tried to sleep, but couldn't.

Those hauntingly recent memories of Donna sitting in the Princess at three in the morning, her sorrowful predictions, the tragic accident, her words as she lay on the pavement and the desperate sight of Natalie crying at her side, simply wouldn't go away.

My conscience was playing the blame game with me, and I was losing badly.

It was *my* fault that she'd travelled to Scotland with me and not stayed at home as she first wanted.

It was *my* fault that I hadn't listened when clearly she was trying to tell me something of importance, no matter how unearthly I might have considered the source of that 'something' to be.

It was *my* fault that I hadn't gone with her and the girls when she took that fateful walk to the newsagent's.
Everything, I convinced myself, was *my* fault.

In the very early hours of the following morning a nurse rushed anxiously to my room and told me to come quickly as they feared that Donna was slipping away.

As more time passed without a notable improvement in Donna's condition I realised that I had to prepare myself to hear those dreadful words, but they still floored me when they eventually came.

Shortly after I'd raced to her bedside the unit's telephone rang. It was Donna's cherished brother, Gene, calling from New Zealand.

What was I going to say to him? What the hell *could* I say?

When I called them just minutes previously all I told them that was Donna had had an accident and was intensive care after emergency surgery.

Now I had to tell her brother that she was close to death.

I managed it somehow though, along with some information that my broken mind could recall concerning the horrendous injuries which would surely claim her life.

Another nurse then came up to me while I was still speaking to Gene.

"I'm very sorry, Mr Bromham," she said quietly. "Your wife has just passed away."
I cried when I heard those words, and Gene heard them also I think.

I ended the call soon afterwards but with the promise to call back of course, and I spent heaven knows how many minutes staring at Donna as she lay motionless in her bed.

Everything was quiet, and serene, and tranquil.

The hustle and bustle of those wonderful doctors and nurses, who held back the inevitable with all of the knowledge and skill they possessed, had ceased.

The bleeps from Donna's heart monitor, though always disconcerting but somehow a source of reassurance during the darkest hours, had stopped.

She was at peace. Her pain was no more.

I held her hand. There was no pulse, and no twitching in her eyelids.

Nor were there the three little nudges from her forearm that I would have gladly sacrificed anything and everything to feel once again.

Staring onto her still beautiful features I remembered the many times we shared; my first sight of her on that trampoline in Auckland, her pushing me into the swimming pool there, getting married in our jeans and T-shirts, honeymooning in Bromley, a thousand more shows and so a thousand more of her beguiling hugs and smiles.

Everything had come flooding back.

I still had the memories of course, but there could never be any more.

Donna died at around five o'clock on the morning of July 21st, 1992. She was just thirty-one years of age.

I spent the next hours back in the family room desperately trying to come to terms with what had happened, and what I had lost.

It did truly feel as though my life had ended along with hers.
To their credit various members of the hospital's magnificent staff came and offered some words of sincere consolation and genuine support but, at the time, all of that seemed hollow and irrelevant.

I reluctantly listened to what they were saying to me but, the more I did so, the more I had to get out of there.

I simply couldn't stay in that hospital any longer.

I dressed myself of a fashion, took possession of Donna's handbag and some other personal effects that had been recovered from the scene of her accident, waited until nine o'clock or thereabouts and, while I headed back to Nairn carrying the small bag which held Donna's things, I wondered about what on earth I was going to say to Natalie and, ultimately, Natasha.

Chris and Camilla had visited the hospital since Donna's death but, through their desire to give me some space to grieve and reflect, they had since returned to the trailer park. That meant that Brian and Hayley, who had taken care of our daughters over the past few days while I was forced to watch helplessly as their doting mother passed away, were also aware of what had happened.

Natasha, being just one year of age, was obviously too young to properly understand; the four-year-old Natalie, to my knowledge, had been told nothing beyond what she'd already witnessed.

Walking toward the caravan I could hear Natalie's voice as she played nearby with Brian and Hayley's children.

Brian himself was pottering around with the gas bottles outside the caravan and, on seeing me meandering along the park's narrow gravel road, met me halfway and offered a supportive embrace.

Hayley, carrying Natasha in her arms, joined him moments later.

Words, being as they were wholly inadequate, were not spoken.

Natalie then noticed me and came dashing over to hug my leg.

At that point I almost completely broke down, but I just about held it together for long enough to pick her up so that her gloriously pure expression of innocence could look upon my thoroughly anguished one.

"What's wrong, Daddy?" she said to me, with the uniquely ingenuous puzzlement that children lose all too quickly as they pass through this awful world. "Why are you crying?"

There can be few questions where answering with the truth can be as hurtful and as damaging as doing so with a lie.

That, however, was one of them.
But, being as I had insufficient mental cohesion to respond either way, I simply carried her quietly to the open door of Brian and Hayley's caravan and put her down so she could run off and carry on playing.

I couldn't watch her though, nor could I listen to the unwitting joy of a child whose devoted mother had just been snatched away from her forever.

So, I crumpled down onto the little plastic doorstep and, with everyone keeping a discreet distance, I opened the bag that I'd carried from the hospital.

I naturally recognised everything in there and, being only human after all, I thought back mournfully to those times when she had bought herself *this*, or I had bought her *that*.

There was only one item in there that I'd never seen before.
Within a small, white wafer-thin bag there was a birthday card, and I realised immediately that *that* was the card that Donna had gone to the newsagent's to buy for me (my birthday, immaterial though it then was, had fallen on the previous day).

The verse on the card, which I kept in its original cellophane wrapping and still have to this day, reads: *Always as close as the love in my heart.*

Once the significance of that simple sentence had taken hold I bawled out loud until my eyes were all but dry.

CHAPTER 21: THE AFTERMATH

Maybe those Fleet Street philosophers have been right all along.

Maybe life *is* priceless, and that every precious moment contained therein *should* be savoured and exploited to the max.

The problem with that notion as *I* see it, writing it as I am nearly twenty-two years after those terrible events in Nairn, is that we humans are highly emotional creatures and are, as such, all too often incapable of stepping back from a situation so that a bigger and more objective picture can be spread out before us.

Historically our penchant has been to adopt one single overwhelming sentiment which is inherent in *one* particularly intense situation, and then carry that forward to the *next* situation, and the next, and the next.

In other words we shut ourselves off, say 'screw everyone else' and watch life pass us by.

Perhaps the most remarkable aspect of these sentiments is that, when we grant them free rein to consume us completely, they tend to become exclusive to *us* and, as such, we do not allow them to be harboured by anyone else.

For example, when we are angry then no other person, or so we perceive, can be angry except ourselves. When we're blissfully happy and skipping through the long grass believing that the world can treat us no better, then we grow selfish and demand that no-one else is given leave to share in our bliss.

These emotions then stay with us. Temporarily perhaps, depending on our resolve and strength of character, but they stay.

They linger.

They can cloud our judgement and challenge our sense of perspective, until such time as another event endows us with an entirely new set of perceptions with which to effectively dismiss everything that lies one inch beyond our noses.

And if there exists one single emotion that the human mind can employ if it desires to blank out the universe around us then, surely, that emotion has to be grief.

Grief has the power to partition our lives into the dark and the light, just as certainly as the sun segregates our mortal domain into night and day.

Grief can make you see everything differently, quite possibly to the point where you actually see nothing at all.

Grief, we can be safely assured, will come to us all; it doesn't discriminate between saints and sinners, nor does it generally forewarn us of its arrival.

In my *own* case, grief totally incapacitated me at Nairn and, despite the many positive developments and events which have delineated my life during the two-and-a-bit decades since (the most important ones of which I shall relate in due course), it hasn't really gone away.

Perhaps it never will.

That may be something of a blessing because, for all of those yawning scars that grief can leave in its destructive wake, it can also leave you that much more grateful for those many modest things that enrich our lives, and which we otherwise and so frequently take for granted.

And, although I maybe couldn't appreciate it at the time, I had (and have) much to be grateful for.

For instance, I had (and have) a son and two beautiful young daughters.

While I sat clutching my birthday card on the doorstep of Brian and Hayley's caravan, watching Natalie playing hide-and-seek and Natasha sitting on her blanket and throwing the pieces of her plastic tea service around in the soothing glow of the mid-morning sun, I understood that, for *their* sakes, I needed to pull myself together.

After all they had, in the space of just two days, become entirely dependent upon me and me alone.

I needed a focus. I needed something with objectives, something with a purpose and a definite goal.

So, I decided to head back into Nairn to find out exactly what happened to Donna because, even though I've documented some brief details for you, on the morning of her death I still didn't know the truth.

Now, I knew that the exhibition trailer that had hit Donna had been impounded at the town's police station and so, with Chris Barry as my driver-cum-photographer, we went over there.

On our arrival we were greeted (if that's the right word) by a Sergeant Macready.

I introduced myself, but his eyes narrowed. He'd recognised my surname because, naturally, that was Donna's surname also.

I asked to see the vehicle that had struck her.
"I'd rather you didn't, Sir," he replied curtly and with a thinly-masked mulishness when he noticed the camera that Chris was holding in his hand.
Excuse me? What was that again? *I'd rather you didn't, Sir?*

We were there, I reminded him rather more vehemently than I ordinarily would have done with an officer of the law, to find out what happened to my wife and, as such, I needed to inspect that vehicle. I *demanded* to do so in fact and, quite honestly, I didn't give a flying toss about what Sergeant Macready rathered we did or didn't do.
"I insist on seeing it," I pressed.

"No, Sir," was the insipid response. "I'm afraid I can't permit that."

So, copper or no copper, I barged past him and strode resolutely toward the station's yard.

And there it was: the trailer that had killed Donna.

Chris immediately set about his work, photographing its exterior from every attainable angle, while the flummoxed Sergeant Macready stared at us from the entrance to the pound.

He really wanted Chris to stop taking those photographs.

Then again, *I* really wanted Donna to still be alive but, sadly, we don't always get what we want.

To be fair to him though, he became slightly more conciliatory once we confirmed that we'd seen all that we wanted to see and to the point of providing us with considerably more information relating to the circumstances of Donna's accident, which we learned had been drawn from eye-witness statements.

What follows is the critical chain of events so gleaned, along with those additional facts which my later research has enabled me to weave in.

The trailer's driver, who I falsely named 'Peter' a couple of chapters ago so I'll stick with that here for continuity's sake, was actually a former policeman and, latterly, an officer with the Scottish Road Safety Campaign.

His trailer, for which he was solely responsible, housed a display which was duly paraded at the shown in Nairn.

Once Peter had finished his work for that day he packed all of his paraphernalia back into the trailer.

His final chore before pulling away from the showground *should* have been the securing of the eight-feet-square and two-inch-thick hydraulically-operated aluminium canopy, which was double-hinged near the roof of the vehicle. However, for reasons which have never really been completely clarified Peter was unable to secure the canopy correctly.

Catastrophically, that didn't dissuade him from jumping into his van and towing the trailer toward the main road.

On pulling away from the junction at the entrance to the showground the canopy flew upwards like a bird's wing, catching a 'Give Way' sign and tearing it from the ground.

Of course, because the trailer was wider than the van he was driving Peter couldn't see any of that in his side-view mirrors.

By that time Donna was making her way across the forecourt of the petrol-station-cum-supermarket where she'd bought my birthday card. She'd walked about twenty feet along the pavement when, thanks be to God, she passed the pushchair holding Natasha to Camilla, presumably so that she could 'be mother' for a while.

Natalie was there, as were Hayley's two children and also Brian, who'd hurried to join them all once he'd stored my ramps away.

Behind them, Peter was getting ever nearer.

The canopy of his trailer had opened to around forty-five degrees and all but covered the width of the pavement on which the group was walking.

Brian was the first to become aware of the imminent danger.

On seeing the canopy heading towards them he pulled Camilla from the pavement, an act which thankfully saw Natasha's pushchair roll onto the adjoining grass verge and out of harm's way.

Natalie also managed to get herself clear.

Donna, obviously sensing that something was wrong, was more concerned with what all of the children were doing and so, by the time that Peter was level with her, she'd given herself absolutely no time to escape.

The edge of the canopy caught Donna on her left side, between her ribs and her pelvic bone, leaving a horrific indentation which, as I've already mentioned, was about the size of a clenched fist.

She was lifted from the ground as he carried on driving forward, and was thrown like a rag doll onto the canopy's face before she tumbled heavily to the ground some yards from where the trailer had first struck her.
Even then Peter continued onward, utterly oblivious to what he'd done.

Motorists behind him and approaching him from the front flashed their lights furiously and sounded their horns in an attempt to flag him down.

Who *he* believed they were trying to stop is really anyone's guess.

Eventually though, he must have twigged; about two hundred yards beyond the petrol station he pulled into a bus stop.

The canopy, after hitting the 'Bus Stop' sign, was ripped away from one of its hinges.
Peter got out of his van to inspect the damage, presumably still unaware of his role in what had happened further down the main road.

As I reached where Donna lay I noticed him approaching the scene of the accident, but I paid him no more attention than that. I had no idea who he was or what he'd done and Brian, because he was shattered with all the running that *he'd* done since Donna was hit, was some paces behind me and so wasn't able to enlighten me further.

That, I have to say, is probably just as well because if I'd been aware of Peter's part in the chaos that we could see all around us as we sprinted on, I might just have taken a detour and laid the man out.

But then, 'an eye for an eye' cuts no ice in the courtrooms: *I* would have been the villain, and *he* the innocent victim.

Justice?

Please, I challenge you.

Show me where justice can be found. Let me see it with my own eyes and then maybe, just maybe, I'll have some faith in it.

I said as much to Sergeant Macready when I asked him where Peter was. He didn't answer me, which makes me wonder whether he'd been detained for questioning in that self-same police station, and was very possibly still in there.
With the benefit of hindsight though, it didn't really matter.

Donna was dead, and no amount of interrogation, recrimination or so-called 'justice' could ever change that.

Nevertheless, after our visit to the police station I felt slightly more invigorated.

Not much more you should understand, but just enough to get one or two of the tinier mental cogs turning again.

In fact, they didn't just turn. They clunked around all night long, which meant that I couldn't sleep.

Then again, I didn't try to.

There was a knock at my caravan's door late the next morning.

Trevor and Michael, my brothers as you'll no doubt recall, had driven up from Skewen through the night to be there, and they'd brought Shane with them.

It was wonderful to see my brothers of course, and I thanked them for travelling all that way, but I'm sure you can fully imagine and appreciate my reaction when I saw my son, so I'll say no more.
We cried and talked and cried all over again and Shane, who at fifteen years of age was certainly old enough and also heedful enough to comprehend the magnitude of what had taken place, became a strapping pillar of support throughout his stay.

Michael then suggested that they take Natalie and Natasha back to Skewen.

Being their father I was unsurprisingly reluctant and probably dismissive of his idea at first but, after listening to his lucid reasoning and then realising that there was simply too much to sort out in Scotland, plus the scope for administrative complications and emotional upheaval contained therein, I agreed.

Besides, Natalie was missing Donna and repeatedly asking me where she was.

I couldn't tell her the truth because heaven only knows what that would have done to her, but I feared that she would find out sooner rather than later while we remained there, and most likely from someone considerably less sensitive than myself.

So, once my brothers had spent the remainder of that morning and the bulk of the afternoon doing their level best to make me feel human again, they departed on the long journey back to South Wales with Natalie and Natasha staring at me with tender confusion through the rear window as Trevor pulled out of the trailer park.

Shane, however, decided he was staying with me which gave me a phenomenal and timely boost.

That only lasted until the following morning though.

"Mr Bromham?" asked the police officer who'd come to the trailer park around lunchtime on Thursday 23rd July. He also told me his name and rank, but my scrambled brain was in no fit state to retain such trifling information, so I'll refer to him here as 'Constable McKee'.

"Yes?" I cautiously replied, and at the same time trying to think of what I'd done wrong.

"I apologise for the intrusion at what must be a difficult time for you, Sir," Constable McKee droned, "but I'm afraid I must ask that you accompany me to the mortuary. It's for the purpose of formal identification of the deceased, and is a standard procedure that needs to be adhered to before the authorities can release the body. As I say, I am genuinely sorry."

Genuinely sorry, did he say?

Maybe it was just my inability to reason clearly which got the better of me at the time, but I just couldn't believe what I was hearing!

I spent nearly thirty-six hours at Nairn's hospital watching Donna's life fade away, and now they wanted me to go back there and say 'Yes, that's her'!

I've never been a strong advocate of 'shooting the messenger', especially when that messenger is making an emotional request which he or she hasn't directly sanctioned, but I *did* go so far as to tell Constable McKee that what I was being asked to do was ridiculous and, to me at least, unnecessary.
But he'd been trained well.

He didn't bite, or challenge my right to speak to him in that way, or mollify me to the point of belittlement. He was calm, composed and as empathetic as his uniform required him to be, and it has to be said that the pacifying influence such a professionally-adept approach frequently exerts upon anger is extraordinary.
"Alright," I said when it really wasn't, and he *knew* it wasn't, "I'll come now."

Chris and Brian travelled with us as I feared I would be requiring some special support to get myself through the ordeal and I'm glad that they did because, when we entered the mortuary and I saw a metal table upon which a body lay covered from head to toe in a clinically-white sheet, that was me finished.

I couldn't, and absolutely *wouldn't*, take another step. Instead, I collapsed into a nearby chair and dropped my head into my hands.

"It's okay," the female mortician whispered to Chris and Brian while Constable McKee, having removed his helmet, observed proceedings from a discreet distance. "Either of you can complete the identification. That would be perfectly satisfactory to us."

Once they'd both nodded their agreement, the mortician pulled back a corner of the sheet. I couldn't look but Brian did and mumbled: "Yes, that's Donna."

Chris also looked but, as far I can recall, added nothing to that confirmation.

Brian then signed a form which the mortician presented to him on a clipboard, and that was that.

The next task was to get Donna's body back to South Wales.

I rang each and every number within the 'Undertakers' section of Nairn's Yellow Pages, but not a single one of the firms I spoke to was prepared to drive her body home.

In the end, and as a last resort, I asked my family in Skewen to contact the various undertakers there in a desperate attempt to persuade one of them to drive up to Scotland and collect her.

Thankfully, two firms said that they were prepared to accept the job.

I chose a small Neath-based practice as they offered more in terms of shouldering the numerous responsibilities that, under 'normal' circumstances, would fall squarely upon me.

And so, comforted with the knowledge that Donna was going to be in very good hands, I called a meeting with Chris and Brian to decide on how best to proceed with the tour.

Chris was absolutely incredulous. "What the hell do you want to do that for?"
"Because I've never failed to do a show," I replied. "Besides, I can't face going home and sitting around sulking all day long. That'd just be too much. I'd go crazy within a week. At least up here I have a chance to clear my head a bit."

"Okay, I can accept that, but what about the funeral?" Brian (I think) asked.

I said that my family had offered to make the necessary arrangements, and that Donna's body would be held in Neath's Chapel of Rest until my return.

They spoke between themselves for a few moments before agreeing to help me continue with the tour, but even then I still believed they thought I was barking mad.

So, during the late afternoon of Friday 24th July we wheeled our cavalcade back on the road and, after following the A9 and crossing the Kessock Bridge at Inverness, headed northwards to John O'Groats.

They can provide an astonishingly palliative setting for the melancholy mind, the Scottish highlands.

There is an inimitable splendour to the openness of their wild and rugged terrain which offers the sorrowful eye a shrill but humbling sense of perspective. It can stimulate a strong feeling of remoteness, but rarely one of solitude; the sprawling landscape with its indistinct horizon reminds you that isolation and loneliness are in fact two quite different things.

One is also prompted to consider one's place in the world since, while we naturally exude an air of self-importance in the company the others, one brave glance through the dispassionate lens ground from those mountains and lochs will offer a fresh and sobering insight into the word 'insignificant'.

Yes, I certainly did a lot of soul-searching during that one-hundred-and-thirty-odd-mile run between Nairn and John O'Groats.

Donna was precious and irreplaceable, and nothing would ever change that.

But, because 'precious' and 'irreplaceable' are subjective sentiments, and especially so when one applies them to loved ones lost, they are powerful and formidable enough to cocoon us in a prison without bars.

And we call that prison 'grief'.

I, however, am no jailbird.

Obviously, Donna's death was an immense loss to me and it has remained so to this day. I mourned her deeply of course but, even so soon after her passing, I realised that *that* process would need to be just another component of my life rather than becoming the principal shaper of it.

I had responsibilities: my beloved daughters, Natalie and Natasha, had been left to grow up without a mother and so, in the space of a tragic week, I had become two parents rather than just one.

My son Shane, who sat beside me in the Austin Princess, was at the time of his life where he would be making important decisions and ploughing his own furrows.

He would need clear-headed guidance and support, but if I allowed myself to fall apart before his eyes then there was the risk he would turn his back on me and seek those things elsewhere.

No, I decided firmly as we finally caught sight of the octagonal crowns of the John O'Groats House.

Life, by some means, would simply have to go on.

We quickly found the spot we'd been allocated and parked up.

Everyone slept apart from myself so, come the following morning, I looked a bleary-eyed and unshaven mess.

The show wasn't too large but it still needed to be organised.

It's just a shame that that onus had to fall on possibly the coldest and most pitiless woman that it has ever been my displeasure to meet. I know her proper name but glorying at the sight of it in print is a privilege I'm not entirely convinced she deserves, so I'll just call her 'Sally'.

'Oh, hello', said Sally as she blustered up to me with her folders in one hand and a bottle of mineral water in the other. "You must be Chris. I'm sorry to hear about your wife. Very sad indeed. But, never mind. The show must go on so, chop chop! We're tight for time at the moment, and they're all waiting for you. I'll see you in a few moments. Oh, by the way, there are a lot of photographers here today and some of them have come from Glasgow so, if you could manage a quick one-two with your razor then that would be brilliant."

I was absolutely dumbfounded.

As I watched her head back towards the showground with that pretentious cross-legged gait that catwalk models use, I wondered whether I'd actually heard what I *thought* I'd heard.

I looked first at Chris, then at Hayley, then Brian, then Camilla and finally Shane.

Their flabbergasted expressions confirmed that, yes, I'd heard correctly.

"Right, that's it," I stated, but loudly enough so Sally would hear. "I haven't come all this way to be humiliated by some jumped-up, downmarket checkout girl like…like *that*. Come on, we're going home!"

Sally was gawping at me from about fifteen yards away.
"Got a problem?" I snarled.

She did indeed have a problem, and a colossal one what's more.

She had a showground packed with hundreds of people, who'd presumably travelled from all parts of the Highlands and possibly beyond, to watch me perform.

Ah yes, and let's not forget those photographers (some of whom had come from Glasgow, remember) whose promotional shoot for my aftershave would have to wait for another day.

Regrettably, and with thanks going entirely to that pompous gob-on-a-stick, they would all have to endure to a grovelling apology instead.
"But you won't be paid!" she squealed.

"And once I've gone without doing a single jump," I said blandly, "neither will you!"

Did I care about what I'd decided to do?

Well, in some ways I did, because that was the first time I had *ever* flatly refused to do a gig after turning up at a venue.

On the hand, her virulent words and complete lack of empathy filled me with disgust right the way down to the pit of my stomach.

I simply *couldn't* stay there. I *had* to leave.

So I did, and with no dissent whatsoever from my clearly-relieved entourage.

With my blessing and a handful of loose change Camilla found a telephone box and cancelled the remainder of the tour.

The lady who was organising what should have been our *next* show, instead of being irritated by the late cancellation, was compassionate to the last and understood completely having already read the reports of Donna's accident and passing in the Scottish newspapers.

Sally, on the other hand, could hardly have cared less about my personal circumstances so within half-an-hour, and entirely because of her atrocious attitude I should add, we were doing what the overwhelming majority of vehicles leaving John O'Groats must also do.

We were heading south.

CHAPTER 22: PICKING UP THE PIECES

So, where did all of that leave me?

Not in a good place sadly, and that's being tactful.

For example, from the time of my first setting foot in Raigmore Hospital to our arrival back in South Wales I really don't recall eating more than a couple of sandwiches and a small plateful of chocolate biscuits. Throughout that impossibly-horrendous week I think I might have showered just the once, shaved just the once and stopped crying just the once.

Perhaps, dear reader, in your own mind you're berating me and waving a stick because you've coped with the loss of a loved one far better than I've described here.

If indeed that's the case, then so be it.

I can't change who or what I am I'm afraid and, despite the sterling efforts of many who have entered my life as documented thus far, I stubbornly refuse to sell my soul in order to do so. As far as I am concerned Death always leaves a formidable but tormenting trace and, quite possibly, I'm that much more susceptible to its indistinct influence and its disorienting impact than others might be.

I'm not entirely convinced that I owe anyone an apology for that because, when all is said and done, we're all different.

Nevertheless, when I turned the key in the lock of the home Donna and I shared in Aberdulais and stepped inside, that trace I've mentioned existed all around me.

Everything was exactly as it had been when she was last there.

Her slippers were side-by-side in the hallway, and in the space normally reserved for the trainers she'd worn at Nairn.

Her rinsed-out coffee mug rested on the draining board and next to my own.

Some of her clothes were heaped in a pile by the side of our bed, just where she'd discarded them.

The smaller of her two make-up bags was open, precisely as she'd left it.

The novel she'd been reading, complete with its bookmark, sat gathering dust on the bedside table, never to be completed.

So the list would go on, if I'd the courage to let it.
Within each room, and with virtually every object or fitting contained in those rooms, Donna's uniquely-beautiful spirit endured.

And yet I couldn't stay there, either for that afternoon or any of the ten thousand afternoons to come.
I had to leave and never return.

Even though it meant I'd have nowhere to live, I absolutely had to get out of the place.

Once I'd explained the situation to my mother she offered me my old bedroom in Southall Avenue but, welcome though that offer was, I couldn't face being around people so soon after Donna's passing.

So, I donated that room to Natalie and Natasha while I lived on the driveway and in the caravan that Brian's father had loaned to us for the tour of Scotland (a loan which he'd graciously extended for another couple of months).

It was from there that I completed all of the arrangements for Donna's funeral.

I had no money at the time and harboured little hope of earning or borrowing any so she was buried, on July 29th 1992, with the help of social security benefits.
In the weeks which followed I tried to hold myself together as best I could, for the girls' sakes if for no-one else's.

I'd already thought long and hard about getting back on the bike and doing a show or two wherever I might land a booking but as the months dragged by, so the desire to prolong my calling began to fade.

Gradually, my life was drained of all passion for stunt riding. There was no adrenalin there, no kick, and no fervour for breaking records.
To compound that, many of my associates on the circuit were giving me the cold shoulder, not out of any malice or spite I suspect but more probably because they didn't know how to handle the situation I was in and none of them wanted to be the first to test the water.

Hence, and totally demoralising though it was to accept at the time, I deemed that my career was finished.

Sixteen long years had gone by since I took my enduro bike to that ammunition dump in Swansea and wondered whether maybe, just maybe, I could ride my way to fame and fortune.

Nearly half a lifetime later, I had my answer: I was back exactly where I started and with barely a penny to my name, and I feared that everything I *had* achieved in those sixteen years would be completely forgotten by everyone in less than twelve months.

I'd worked so, so hard to make sure that as many people as possible recognised the name 'Chris Bromham'. The last thing I wanted was to go back to being known as 'Chris who?'

More importantly, I needed to feed and clothe and care for Natalie and Natasha when I was barely in a fit state to do those things for myself.

As my own wellbeing suffered so did that of my parents: my mother had developed osteoporosis while my father's emphysema had grown progressively worse.

Then, to cap it all, Natasha was rushed into hospital with a massive asthma attack.

Her blood, so the doctors informed me, wasn't oxygenating and that her prospects for survival weren't good.

Hearing those words absolutely destroyed me.

Seeing her laying in that bed connected to countless tubes and drips, just a year after her poor mother had suffered similarly, pushed me to the edge.

Was I going to lose Natasha, who was only three years of age you'll remember, in the same dreadful way?

Everything was becoming too much for me to deal with, and the acute depression which had already set in was starting to grip harder than ever.
Natasha eventually spent four long days on a ventilator in intensive care, and then a further four on a general children's ward so that the doctors could monitor her reaction to their round-the-clock treatment.

Without their intervention she would certainly have died, and so I want to place on record my eternal gratitude for what those doctors did.

I was naturally elated that Natasha had survived that near fatal scare, but the effects of that trauma upon me, especially when considered alongside everything else, had taken their toll.

I wasn't myself.

Looking back, I'm not sure I knew *who* the hell I was.

Things got so bad that I'd often find myself ambling aimlessly around the streets of Neath and Swansea like some hapless vagrant, seeking to enlighten people about what I was going through when I didn't even have the slightest idea who I was talking to.

With hindsight, it was of no consequence to me that they were complete strangers; all I wanted them to do was lend me their ear. It didn't matter if they were men or women, young or old, or 'proper' tramps as opposed to the part-time one that I was attempting to be. They didn't have to console me or humour me as if I were a child. They didn't have to say 'what a shame', or 'oh dear, that's just awful' or 'it must be terrible for you'.

After all, no-one pesters a complete stranger in order to hear something that they already know.

All I wanted them to do was listen, and I wanted them to listen because I needed the liberating feeling that that can sometimes bring.

I didn't (and don't) do heavy drink or any substances of an illicit nature, but I desired something that would likewise unshackle my emotions and take some of the pain away, if only for a fleeting hour or two.

I found it good to speak openly and get things off my chest.

Some people would offer me their polite but short-lived attention, while others were so oblivious that I may as well have been jabbering away at a brick wall.

Which, incidentally, I once did.

Perhaps not surprisingly it wasn't long before those one-way conversations became increasingly tedious and lost their earlier appeal and so, instead, I sought comfort and solace in the female form.

Maybe I was subconsciously seeking a fresh love, and a new soul mate. Had the women with whom I 'socialised' wanted the same thing, then possibly my rather questionable plan might have met with greater success.
As it was, the ones I seemed to prefer chasing around were into everything except commitment and offered me no solace in my grief,

But women have always been a weakness for me and, if you think back to the earlier chapters and to some of my exploits in more carefree times, you'll maybe come to appreciate the motives behind what I was doing.

Where some people yearn for alcohol to get them through life while others might hanker for *Coronation Street* or *The Jeremy Kyle Show*, I longed for women.

Different people deal with things in different ways and, like all addicts, I was craving a 'quick fix' day after day after day.

The trouble was, like any recreational drug you'd care to mention, it didn't work.

Then, one evening, while I was at home having some nervous breakdown or other my father said something which has rankled with me ever since.

He said, and please excuse me here because the wording is not completely accurate: 'You must be very evil! This only happens to evil people!'

Gee, thanks Dad! I really needed *that*, didn't I?

What he said affected me so much that, one night not long afterwards when I was heading home through Swansea, I decided to drive my car straight into a lamp-post with my foot pressed hard to the floor.

And why did I want to do that?

Because I'd reached that point where I'd had enough of everything, that's why.

It was almost like old times: just me, my machine and something I had to do, but that time there were no cheering crowds, no promoter wishing me well and no safety ramp if I cocked it up.

The human mind, though, has a remarkable aptitude for self-preservation.

I knew where my hands needed to be on the steering wheel to ensure I slammed into that lamp-post and killed myself outright, and *it* knew where my hands needed to be to avoid it. Sure enough, *it* made sure my hands were in the right place and, instead of forfeiting my life, all I lost was a headlight, a wing mirror and a few quid paying for minor dents and paint-scrapes.

So, was my botched attempt at suicide a selfish act?

Yes, of course it was, and I still view it as such to this day.

But then I discovered the impetus to carry on living that I so desperately desired and it came, as it can so often do, completely out of nowhere.

Those well versed with the Swansea of the early 1990's might remember a nightclub called *Martha's Vineyard* (or just '*Martha's*') which stood at the junction between the Kingsway and Christina Street.

The site is now occupied by a pay-and-display car park, which some might regard as a significant improvement.

Anyway, while Martha's may not have been the most convivial of places, it *was* where I managed to pick up many of the women of which I've already spoken.
However, on the night on Thursday December 1st 1994, there was *one* woman in there who exuded considerably more class than any of the others present, and that *certainly* included the minger (pronounced 'ming-a', that's a Welsh synonym for 'ugly bimbo', as are 'boiler' and 'monster') who was clinging onto my arm like some four-parts-pissed koala bear.

Once *she'd* decided to clear off ('D'ya fancy a kebab, luv? No? Okay, well, me an' the girls are goin' for a kebab, so I'll see ya later, yeah! Come on then, y'floozies! Less go! Oh no, hang on a bit! My tights are coming down again!', etc.) I could finally make my move.

I introduced myself and so did she, as 'Anna-Marie'.
Quite naturally I bought her a drink and we chatted away for a bit, but the place was simply too loud and the dense cloud of cigarette smoke was almost choking so, after we'd exchanged phone numbers, I left.

I felt good about myself when I departed Martha's, much better than I had for many months I believe it's fair to say, and so I resolved that I should celebrate by having a peaceful drink in the nearby *Liberty's* bar.

Probably because it was smaller, quieter, far less crowded and usually more problematic to smuggle in and consume some of the world's more exotic tobaccos, *Liberty's* tended not to be quite as popular as *Martha's Vineyard*. That meant that its patrons could think, reflect and, on rare occasions, be very unpleasantly disturbed.

"Ooh, hiya luv!" the koala bear shouted from Liberty's doorway. "Now there's a nice surprise innit, seein' you in 'ere like!"

I resignedly peered over to where she was standing, but it wasn't an attractive sight.
She had a long smear of coleslaw down her front which presumably had been jettisoned from deep within her king-size doner, and she'd yanked up her tights so vigorously that she'd actually ended up laddering them around her knees.

Wholly undaunted by my valiant show of indifference within seconds she'd clutched my arm and was pestering me to get her a drink with breath that reeked of onion and halal meat. Then she belched, and from which I concluded that she must have drowned her kebab in barbecue sauce as well.

I was so pleased that Anna-Marie wasn't there as well because, if she had been, there's no doubt that my telephone number would have been despatched to the deepest recesses of one of the Kingsway's innumerable wheelie bins.

Women are often remarkable, though, for invariably tending to do the last thing that you expect them to do.

"Oh! Erm…hello again," said Anna-Marie from over my shoulder and, having eyeballed the questionable company I was keeping, with markedly less enthusiasm than she had done in *Martha's*.

My God! What was *she* doing there?

I had to think quickly.

I wanted Anna-Marie to stay, but the monster simply had to go.
How could I do it?

Deftly, I slipped my hand into my trousers and, after something of a struggle, I whipped out the one thing that I hoped would provide the solution.

"Is *this* enough for you and your friends to have a bit of fun with?" I asked the boiler.
I think she heard my question but it was hard to tell. She just stood there for a moment or two, seemingly hypnotised by the five-inch-long treasure that I was teasing between my fingers.

"Bloody right it is!' she squealed with her eyes fairly popping out of her head.

No more than a fraction of a second later she'd snatched the ten pound note from my hand and was gone.

I never saw her again and so, therefore, I'd probably have to consider that the best tenner I'd ever blown and even more so because, to my amazement, Anna-Marie stuck around through it all.

Having been left in Liberty's in almost idyllic peace we talked over another drink, then we talked some more in my car while I drove her home, and finally we chatted the next day on the phone when she called me.

As our friendship grew (I call it a friendship but we could both see where it was heading and I imagine so can you by now), so did my confidence and self-esteem.
My belief in myself had started to return.

Very gradually, I began pulling myself up from the depths where I'd spent the previous two-and-a-half years.

With each day that went by I could once again see that there was beauty in the world, and happiness, and a multitude of reasons to get myself out of bed before one o'clock in the afternoon.

I was, at long last, being the two parents that both my son and daughters needed me to be.

Yes, I was still flat on my arse financially and still missing Donna, but should that stop someone from being a true and loving father?

No, of course it shouldn't.

Hauling myself back onto my proverbial feet was a slow and arduous process, but I could somehow sense that I was definitely taking more forward steps than regressive ones.

I was back, and so was my appetite for stunt-riding; for the first time in nearly three years, I felt ready and willing to get back on a bike!

And so much of that was down to Anna-Marie, through the support she'd given me, the seemingly-unlimited understanding she exhibited and the loyalty she never failed to show.

Then, just as all seemed to be going so well, the next hammer blow: during the early summer of 1995, my father finally yielded to the emphysema which had blighted his health for so long.

Bless his heart.
I doubt it could be said that we had a typical father-son relationship but he was still my Dad and he was still a good man, although perhaps he found the revealing of that side of his character more challenging that it should have been.

I was never entirely sure what *he* really thought of *me*, but *I* loved him much as I love my own children.

Backtracking slightly, earlier in that year I did an interview for a women's magazine (I can't remember which one) in which I talked about my life since Donna's death, Shane, the girls and my desire to re-join the stunt-riding circuit.

Following its publication the magazine's editor contacted me and said that some bloke called Mike Fisher wanted to manage me, and as such had requested my contact details.

I said, fine, feel free to pass them on and, within hours, Mike was on the phone.

I warmed to him and his friendly Cockney tones almost immediately.

Even after only a couple of minutes of conversation it was clear that Mike, having read my piece in that magazine, had complete confidence in me and in my ability and motivation to get myself back on the road and working once again.

Perhaps more crucially for me at that time, he'd had twenty years of experience in the management game; if you considered yourself to be any sort of celebrity in the 1970's and 1980's but Mike didn't know you, then the chances are you weren't worth knowing. I'm sorry to put it like that because I know it'll probably come over as conceited, but it's a fact; the man had more connections than a railway timetable.

That, though, was exactly what I needed to get my career started anew.

You see, I'd been out of the loop for too long, and things had changed. Some of the agencies I'd previously dealt with had long since closed, while others were in the hands of people who were completely unknown to me.

I was serious about getting back onto the saddle but I knew that I'd need a tremendous amount of help to make that happen: Mike was the man who'd offered to provide it.

So, between us, we set about scheming my comeback, but things didn't come easy.

Firstly, having not owned a bike for a good while, I had to reclaim an old faithful (the one I'd used to clear two hundred and forty one feet at Victoria Dock in 1986) from a motoring museum.

After signing an agreement that obliged me to return the bike to the museum after I'd used it, the next task was to try and muscle in on a suitable show somewhere.

That wasn't straightforward because I'd been off the radar for a while and, with all that had happened in my life in the previous three years, finding a promoter willing to take a punt on me wasn't the given that it once was.
Nevertheless, and with my endless thanks going to one of my benefactors at the time (a great guy and devotee called Ken Church), the maiden appearance of my return to action was to be at one of my old stamping grounds – Norman Park in Bromley.

As with my honeymoon gig there all those years before Bromley council were utterly brilliant and thoroughly supportive in every meaningful respect: only the burden of riding of the bike had been left on my shoulders.

Everything in Bromley was set for a weekend during the scorching August of 1995.

Even the Princess of Wales had expressed an interest in bringing her sons William and Harry to Bromley to watch me (and for which the council had offered to spray the sun-bleached grass a luscious shade of green!) but, unfortunately, her arrangements had apparently been shuffled around a little at the last minute and so she didn't make it down.

Despite that disappointment the show still went on, but with a bike that was a long way past its prime.

Putting it bluntly, it was well and truly buggered.
It had, after all, sat idly on a stand in that museum for the thick end of a decade. Yes, it had been cleaned and polished, but its mechanics hadn't been maintained to the level where it could have been safely ridden out of there.

Even so, I still succeeded in rattling off three jumps in Bromley, the third of which ended up with me being kicked over the handlebars because the rear shock absorber had abruptly disintegrated, thereby leaving the back tyre to lock against the mudguard and act as a brake (and that was the one and only occasion where I winded myself on take-off rather than on landing).

So, I'd gotten away with one there, but at least I felt like a performer again!

I'd already conceded that a more significant event (i.e. one in which I went for a record) was still some way off so, instead, I acquired for myself a properly-reconditioned bike and filled in at a number of smaller events around the country, simply to get back into the swing of things.

Television work was starting to trickle in as well, all thanks to Mike of course and his seemingly inexhaustible list of contacts.

Do you remember the game show *You Bet!*, which ran for about ten years on ITV?

I appeared on that programme when Darren Day hosted an episode which was filmed at the Imperial War Museum at Duxford Airfield.

There, I was presented with the challenge of jumping ten cars over and over again, back and forth, in an attempt to break some obscure time record the precise details of which escape me for the moment.
Anyway, whatever my *own* final time turned out to be I missed out on that record by a mere two seconds. I was gutted as you'd expect, but it was great to feel the glow of that competitive fire burning within me once again.

The emotional wounds from losing Donna were still there of course and, if the truth be known, they've *never* left me, but at least I finally had a motive to get my arse out of bed every morning!

In the meantime, Mike was setting about excelling himself for the umpteenth time.

He'd opened negotiations with an American pay-per-view channel which, after buying in to some of his persuasive allure, was starting to show a real interest in broadcasting a fresh world record attempt.

To be fair to the facts here I freely admit that the two of us had spoken for some time about my breaking that twenty-lorry obstacle record that I'd bagged at Victoria dock in 1986, but Mike thought it would be much more fun (and potentially lucrative) if the rest of the world was watching as well.

I also realised that, in all likelihood, *that* was going to be my last significant jump and, predictably enough I suppose, I wanted to go out on a high and with an achievement I could cherish for all time.
So, through the unstinting efforts and generosity of my sponsors I took possession of a Honda CR-500, a machine which was fully capable of clearing twenty lorries plus one, given the usual caveat of favourable weather conditions.

Maybe then, with that last consideration in mind, Wales might not have been everyone's first choice of venue, but bringing down the curtain on home soil was important to me.

Consequently, Mike got down to some serious wand-waving and secured for me the showground in the scenic setting of Usk, located around ten miles north-east of Newport.

Pretty much as soon as that was finalised I drove up there and pegged out where I wanted my take-off ramp to start, for the benefit of the necessary army of scaffolders. Annoyingly though, they'd taken to position of those pegs to be the point where I wanted the ramp to *end* rather than begin, and so I instantly lost about three hundred feet of my run up.

It was my fault of course as I should have travelled to Usk when I knew they were getting everything set up but, for whatever reason, I didn't.

Come the day of the jump the pay-per-view channel had set up a sizeable mobile studio (one of those with a Jodrell-Bank-sized satellite dish stuck on top) at the showground.

I knew that my work was being beamed all across the United States, Australia and a number of other countries which had chucked some pennies in the pot for a slice of the pie. Frustratingly, after only my first practice jump I realised that the whole thing was a no-go. My run-up to the take-off ramp was too short and I just didn't have the power to get over the twenty-one juggernauts that had been parked in my way.

Still, I resolved to screw that CR-500 for all it had on the 'live' attempt.

I opened up the bike as much as I dared on the level ground, mounted the first ramp as cleanly as I could, powered along an horizontal track (an elevated runway, if you like) for a further one hundred yards or so, slammed onto the take-off ramp, got myself airborne, and…failed.

I'd cleared the first twenty lorries but not the twenty-first, which meant I'd only equalled my own record and not beaten it.

Shortly afterwards I was interviewed by local news reporters and asked whether I was disappointed not to have done what I went there to do.

I said 'no', and that I was pleased and proud to have equalled my record.

That, as you've doubtless already guessed, was bullshit.

I actually meant 'yes', and that I was absolutely bloody furious that, after months of painstaking and fastidious planning, I'd been let down by something as ridiculous as the scaffolding and take-off ramp being three hundred feet away from where they should have been.
But there we go. It wasn't meant to be, and I've learned to live with it.

Mike and I went our separate ways shortly afterwards which was a setback at the time because he and I had become good friends as well as being colleagues in business. He went on to manage Eddie Kidd and we didn't speak for some years afterwards but, despite that debacle in Usk, I consider that my life was getting well and truly back on track by that point, even if the time to hang up my leathers had finally arrived.

After all I had Anna-Marie, who was then my partner and adopted nanny and mother to my two priceless daughters.

I had Shane, who had completed his studies in college and, even though he'd left home by that point and still had one year to go in university, was still making me ever-more proud with each passing day.

I also had Natalie and, by some miracle, Natasha.

Finally, I had a future that was mine alone to shape.

I wasn't entirely certain as to what I was going to do with that future but, to me, the main thing was that I could look forward more often than I might dare to peer back.

Donna, though, has never been forgotten.

Around the time of that final jump in Usk I penned a poem in dedication of her life and love I held (and still hold) for her.

Other poems would follow but I think that that initial attempt at prose remains the most poignant, possibly for that very reason, and so I've included it here as a fitting epilogue to the most devastating time of my life. I wouldn't expect all who read it to enjoy it, but I trust you'll appreciate its importance to me.

Hell has no mercy
Hell has no smile
Hell has only darkness
Mile after mile
So be warned my friend
Be good in life to your fellow man
For the warmth you give to others
Will pass hand to hand
So when the light comes to seek you out
For all the good you've done
One day it will come back to greet you
In that heavenly wonderland

Me and Eddie Kidd taking a break on the film Riding High. I doubled for two of the characters Judas S Chariot and The Halifax Hellcat.

The late, great Dave Taylor. Britain's wheelie king. Performing together in 1978

Stealing a cheeky kiss from the wonderful late actress Diana Dors. This was my first personal appearance and I was so lucky to have met her. What a beautiful warm lady she was.

Singer Kim Wilde at the Larry Parnes party in London

Donna, myself and Tom O'Connor when I appeared on his TV show I've Got A Secret

With actor Tom Wopat from The Dukes of Hazzard

ME WITH
THE STREET HAWK BIKE

CHAPTER 23: THE FAN CLUB, THE DOGS, MY DAUGHTER AND HER SON

Although it splintered my heart at the time, selling the house in Aberdulais that Donna and I shared enabled me, in the June of 1998 or thereabouts, to put down a chunky deposit on mine and Anna-Marie's first home together.

Located in Birchgrove, which lies within Swansea's leafy north-eastern outskirts and on the western shallows of Drummau Mountain, it was perfect for us at the time.

Natalie (who was then ten years of age) and Natasha (seven) were growing up frighteningly quickly, just as all children tend to do these days, and so we really did need the additional space that our new abode provided.

From a purely selfish point of view it also had a large garage so I could safely store my remaining bikes and other artefacts and keepsakes from my career.

We had (and indeed have, because we still live there at the time of writing) fantastic views over the lower Swansea valley, and we're just a two-minute drive from the M4.

I think I should nudge this along now though because it's beginning to sound like an instalment of *Escape to the Country*.

What I'll state in closing though is, now that the girls have grown up, both Anna-Marie and myself are finding the place too big for our needs and that maybe the time is now right for us to move on.
Nevertheless, we've enjoyed sixteen wonderful years in Birchgrove and I think we'll both miss it immensely when we eventually sell up and go.

Mind you, we've had some tricky moments there as well but anyone that's ever been in a long-term relationship will know all about those, so I shan't elaborate on them further.

I first suggested to Anna-Marie that we should get engaged after we'd managed to patch things up after one such 'difference of opinion' in 1999.

Her reply went something along the lines of 'No, let's just go straight to the wedding'.

That's the way I've always liked my women: strong, single-minded and ready to spend all of my money at a moment's notice!

But, hey! Hang on a minute! Without her would I have even been alive to ask the question?

Possibly not and, with her answer, she was flourishing exactly the same commitment and devotion toward me as she did when I was wallowing at rock bottom.
So, I said to her, wedding bells it shall be!
We wed on August 7th 1999, although you may recall that Donna and I tied the knot on August 8th 1983. There was no intent from either of us to schedule things like that; it's just the way it so happened.

Our marriage took place at Neath registry office, as did mine and Donna's and in exactly the same room in fact.

That was also a coincidence, albeit a deeply thought-provoking one at the time.

The reception was a token affair with perhaps thirty or so guests.

We had a finger buffet in lieu of a cake and our honeymoon comprised a weekend in London with my girls. That may not sound like much, especially when these days we're used to hearing about celebrities being so offhand about spend millions on their big day, but while *their* shows of materialism have all the frills and pretence while perhaps lacking in true meaning, *ours* was the complete opposite.

Anna-Marie was happy, and so was I.

There were long periods during the early 1990's where I believed that my life could hardly be less bearable and yet there I was, a mere handful of years later, contented and bathing in the love of my new wife and two daughters, and wondering what the future had in store for me. That last line isn't quite the throwaway one that you might think it is because, remember, I'd retired and therefore wasn't earning the sort of money required to keep us all ticking over sweetly.

I'd managed to be sensible and build up some savings over the years but I didn't want to be reckless in chipping away at those, at least not just yet.

So, I had a brainwave, and one which had its roots way, way back in 1971.

From that year (I was fourteen at the time) I'd always been a massive fan of the late Marc Bolan and his extraordinary music. With T-Rex, his legendary band, he had two enormous worldwide hits in '71 with *Get it On* and *Hot Love*.

Older readers might be finding that a little nostalgia is creeping up on them now whereas the younger generation are probably wondering who the hell I'm talking about.

So, to those kids, here's some sound advice for you: turn off your rap and your hip-hop and your grunge and all the other tuneless shit that you listen to, go onto *YouTube* and check the guy out.

I can promise you here and now that you won't regret it.

Anyway, some years later and out of respect for what I personally thought of Marc and his work, I purchased his famous and instantly-recognisable 'Flying-V' guitar from the official Bolan Fan Club.
And how much did I pay for it?

Well, after a certain amount of haggling I succeeded in securing it for ten thousand pounds which to me, while certainly a lot of money in anyone's book, was an absolute bargain considering what that guitar stood for.

My family, naturally enough I suppose, thought that I was completely out of my tree paying that much for something I could easily pick up for a few hundred quid from any decent music shop, but *they* didn't understand and *I* didn't care.

I had the man's guitar.

It was *mine*. It belonged to *me*, and to no-one else.

Okay, so now that I've set the scene for you, let's fast forward to the year 2000, and to my subsequent decision to buy the Marc Bolan Fan Club outright.

"You must be completely out of your tree!" Anna-Marie said on hearing of my plan.

She did have a point I suppose, because the Fan Club would cost a damn sight more than the ten grand I'd splurged on that 'Flying-V'.

They did, after all, own the largest collection of Bolan ephemerae in existence.

Club officials would turn up at auctions where Marc's stuff was being sold off and, largely without exception, they'd walk away with whatever was up for grabs. They wouldn't bid as such, at least not in the accepted sense of the word, because money was no object to them. They'd just keep their hands in the air while the auctioneer was brandishing his gavel, and they'd keep them there until all of the other bidders had gracefully surrendered and put their own hands back into their pockets.

As the new owner of the Fan Club those spoils then passed to me: dozens of Marc's original master tapes, the outfits he wore on *Top of the Pops*, his writings and poems (some of which became lyrics, as you might expect) and boxes stuffed to overflowing with photographs.

Had the Fan Club come with the rights to his music as well then I probably would have made some serious money but, as it stood, all I was empowered to do was sell some merchandise, put out a fanzine twice yearly and offer memberships.

Not exactly profitable you might say, and you'd be right on so many levels, but at the time I believed it would be.
Sadly, and like many schemes of its type, it was doomed to failure from the start.

To begin with, Anna-Marie loathed (past tense employed, but present tense would also suffice) the music of Marc Bolan and T-Rex.

She's really more of a Duran-Duran-type I guess so, even though she put in so much effort to help me make the Fan Club work, it wasn't exactly a labour of love for her.
With hindsight, it was probably more like slow torture.

Given a choice between her listening to 'Planet Queen' or 'Planet Earth' the latter would win hands down each time, but she stuck with it (bless her) for my sake.

The next drawback of owning a Fan Club, and this one did catch us quite unprepared, is the amount of travelling around that's involved. From full-sized conventions to small-scale tribute gigs in the back rooms of squalid, smoky pubs, the Fan Club was 'obliged' to have a presence there and we met that obligation whenever we could, usually at our own expense.

Many of the actual fans were good natured and reasonably even-tempered when we weren't able to do right by them, but others were so difficult and so gallingly bloody-minded that the job was a whole lot more thankless than it should have been.

Some of them were also quite weird and insular, as obsessives can commonly tend to be.

By way of an example, I can remember arriving with Anna-Marie at some-hotel-or-other in readiness for some-convention-or-other and, after we'd toiled up the stairs with our luggage, we were met by a Bolan fan (how could we tell? Bolan make-up, Bolan hair-do, etc.) who did nothing but stare at us as we struggled to our room.

He didn't speak, or smile, or help, or give us a thumbs-up or anything even remotely sociable like that. All he did was stand there and gawp at us, and he found the creepiest possible way to it do as well.
We made it into our room and with some relief because we truly thought that would be the last we'd see of him but, no!

Just as I was about to close the door he barged in, grabbed hold of the 'Flying-V' which I'd brought with me, sat on the bed with it, strummed a few passable riffs, handed the guitar back, and then left!

Is that just utterly bizarre or what?

We didn't always have to go to the trouble of traipsing around the country to meet these characters. Sometimes they would come to us and, by 'come to us', I mean turn up without warning at our house in Birchgrove.

One such guy, who I'll call Tony to spare him any embarrassment, became something of a regular. The first time we saw him was after we'd arrived home one day after doing the weekly shop – we found him sitting in our kitchen! He hadn't broken in or anything so criminal. He'd actually been *invited* in by Shane who, because he'd been away from home for a while and had maybe lost track of our acquaintances, thought that Tony was a friend of the family.

One look at the total bemusement on our faces, however, would have confirmed otherwise.

To give Tony due credit, there was no harm in him whatsoever. All he wanted was to gaze at the 'Flying-V' and also some of Marc's stage clothes, and he'd driven all the way down from the north of England for the privilege.
He became a frequent visitor as the months passed but, even though Anna-Marie and I really got to like him in a strange sort of way, we just wish he could have called us before taking it upon himself to come down, as opposed to simply turning up unannounced on our doorstep.

And that, for us at any rate, was the way the Fan Club worked.

It wasn't particularly glamorous, and it wasn't cheap either: I estimate that I must have spent somewhere in the region of twenty grand on it without ever seeing any meaningful return on that investment.
So, it shouldn't come as any surprise that, in 2003, we sold the Fan Club on and I only hope that the next custodians were able to make more of a financial success of it than we did.

But I had two other reasons for wanting to draw a line under it.

Firstly, my dear mother died in 2001 and that really did knock me backwards and took away a good deal of the enthusiasm that I'd held for the Fan Club.

After spending three weeks in hospital with pulmonary fibrosis she was released on Christmas Eve to spend her final days with us in Birchgrove and, while she slept during the early hours of Boxing Day, she passed peacefully away, with my sister Gwen, at her side.

Secondly, and mere months after my mother's death, Anna-Marie started training as a canine beautician (that's a dog groomer to you and me) at a specialist academy in London.
Now, our Birchgrove home had one feature which was a godsend for any aspiring canine beautician wishing to start their own practice, namely a modern and spacious outbuilding which could be readily adapted into a well-proportioned salon.

Therefore, once she'd graduated from the academy and we'd bought the equipment that was needed to get things off the ground, she was able to dive straight in and open *First Prize Pooches* for business in March 2003.

Her plan was to be the best goddamn dog groomer in Swansea!
My plan was to steer as clear of it as I possibly could because everything I knew about what she did could be written twice and in large letters on the back of a postage stamp.

Still, thinking back, I guessed it was inevitable that I'd be pulled in there one day when she required a hand with some particularly difficult mutt.

Would it be a Staffordshire bull terrier that I'd be saving her from, I wondered? Or a German Shepherd? Or maybe even a Rottweiler?

No, it had to be a couple of bloody poodles, didn't it!

Don't laugh, it's not funny!

Apparently, a lady had brought them in for their monthly manicure and spoiling, and had asked Anna-Marie what time she should return to collect them. Anna-Marie, who'd obviously been distracted by something else or was perhaps a tad overeager to please a newish client, said an hour and a half.

I'm far from an expert in the field but even *I* know, from what I'd heard her say many times prior to that, that a single poodle would normally take two hours.

Naturally, everything in that particular situation had to be scaled up by a factor of two.

It's doable, providing the numbers of pairs of hands at your disposal also increases by a factor of two.
And so, she yanked me in.

She didn't have me doing any of the cutting of the fur or clipping of the nails or anything like that because each of the dogs would have looked as though they'd gone ten rounds with an English Mastiff if she had.

Instead, she stuck me on washing and drying duties which was fine by me because I certainly didn't have the confidence to handle anything more involved than that.

It seems, though, that I must have done a decent job that day because she's had me working in the salon pretty much every day since.

That's the best part of ten years, scrubbing dogs and towelling them down.

Let's wander over to the ball-park here and assume that we talking about three dogs per day for five days a week, and forty-five weeks a year for those ten years.

Based on those figures, I conservatively estimate that I've shampooed something like seven thousand dogs since Anna-Marie's timings went all pear-shaped with those damn poodles.

She did promote me to some minimal but light scissor work to break the monotony a touch but, even so, if you're asking yourself whether that's what I really wanted to be doing then I strongly recommend that you go back to Chapter One and start reading all over again.

No, of course it wasn't what I wanted to be doing, but you'll recall that I'd retired and so the only income we had was from *First Prize Pooches* and the prodigious effort that Anna-Marie was putting in to keep that business going.

I simply helped out as far as my limited abilities would allow and, at the time of writing, I still do.

Just prior to Anna-Marie telling me to throw on my gloves and overalls for the very first time, I'd actually started a little construction project of my own.

You might remember me talking and with some considerable warmth about the 1958 film *The Vikings* which starred Kirk Douglas, one of the heroes of my youth.

Well, that wasn't the only movie from that era to have had a powerful impact upon me. *The Time Machine*, which was released in 1960 and featured Rod Taylor in the lead role, left me awestruck when I first saw it and has stirred something within me on each and every occasion when I've watched it since.

The special effects are understandably crude by today's standards but let's understand that we're talking about a production which is now over half a century old.

In those halcyon days of cinema there were no computers to do everything for you.

As a film-maker you had no alternative but to rely on your craft, your skill and your ingenuity, rather than putting your faith in a ginormous hard drive, seemingly unlimited RAM and state-of-the-art graphics drivers.

The science-fiction films from the fifties and early sixties really did appear as though they'd been forged by extraordinarily talented people who'd stretched their resources and proficiencies to the limit.

Nowadays, and with some of the productions on offer (but *not* all), it almost appears as though they've not been touched by a human conscience at all.

To me they are cold, sterile and repetitive, and are only brought into being to satisfy our increasingly insatiable appetite for explosions, bloodshed, pain and death. That, of course, means they make lots of money, which enables the film company to buy an even bigger hard drive, more RAM and faster graphics drivers.

And so it goes on, sadly without end.
Right, that's quite enough of that. It's time to get off my soap box and get with the program again.

Now, the time machine itself (which was created by Bill Ferrari, MGM's Art Director at the time) was, to my longing eye at least, an object of true beauty with its gorgeously authentic Victorian design, its stunningly simplistic control panel and its big spinning wheel at the back.
I wanted to own *that* very machine, being as it was a genuine prop from a seminal movie, but later in life I learned that it had been sold off to an American actor and zealous collector of such memorabilia.

So, not to be defeated, I set about creating my own life-sized replica.

It was a challenging undertaking in its own right but I had other, less obvious motives for wanting to see that task through to its conclusion.

To begin with, I feel that the building of the machine was an essential part of the grieving process for Donna, being as it was something which could put anyone with a sufficiently pliable imagination in touch with times gone by.

Yes, I realise that the interval between Donna's passing and me starting work on the replica was over ten years but, as I've said before, we're all different and we all cope with personal loss in different ways.

If others are able to handle it better than me then I'm pleased for them: I am what I am when all is said and done.

Also, Natalie wasn't passing through her teenage years as effortlessly as I'd hoped she would; the machine permitted me to obsess over something other than mounting stress and steadily increasing concern for her wellbeing, even if that was only for an hour or so each day.

I finally completed the machine in 2011, a full eight years after starting it.

I won't deny that it was a strenuous undertaking, but did it give me the link with my past that

I so dearly sought?

Yes, perhaps it did, but then again perhaps not.

What is incontrovertible is that the reasons for its assembly lie firmly within that past and so, if you'd care to think of it this way, it still resides in my garage as a shrine to those tragic times.

And do I sit in it and pull on the crystal lever and pretend to be a time traveller from a bygone age like the big kid that I've always been deep down?

I do, but not as much as a certain *smaller* kid who's given me a completely new insight and perspective on what one might call the meaning of life, and love.

On August 7th 2011 the wholly-reformed Natalie gave birth to Corey, my first and, to date, only grandchild.

Three years later he's become a truly magical and beautiful little boy, and he's so bright and perceptive that there are times when I think he knows me better than I know myself.

It's uncanny, but everything I like he seems to like as well (although, as you might anticipate, the converse is not always true!).

If I'm watching something on television then, providing it's suitable of course, he'll watch it with me.

If I put on one of my favourite CD's then he'll have a crazy half-hour bopping away in the living room.

There's so much innocence and incorruptibility with him, not to mention a heart-warmingly ingenuous curiosity for the ever-changing world he's been born into.
I was reluctant at the outset to show him any of the footage from my riding career but, call it vanity if you like or possibly even the need to be seen as an all-conquering champion, the temptation to reveal my hidden self to him proved too much in the end.

So, now he thinks I'm like Superman or Spiderman because I can fly just like them.

He even copies me flicking my hair, which is something that I did at the very peak of my stunt-riding powers. The annoying thing is that the little devil can do it better than I ever could!

But he shows great pride in me for what I was and in turn I, of course, am immensely proud of him.

I see so much of myself in that boy, not only the present 'me' but also the guileless child that tried so hard to survive in Ormes Road fifty-or-so years previously.

Corey has closed that circle.

He's shown me that while artists like myself search constantly for what *we* view as the important facets of life, like fame and fortune and adulation, the things that *really* matter are considerably less complicated and will invariably come to seek *us* out instead.
You may deem that a philosophy, or a theory, or simply a subjective observation.

In truth, such sophistry isn't important.
What *is* important, however, is that *that* is a message worth conveying at the end of what I believe was a tale worth telling.

I simply *had* to get my story down on paper, and I have, and that's what you've been reading all this while, but I required momentous help to get it into the bookshop that you've subsequently rescued it from.

I needed someone who had more connections than a railway timetable.

I needed Mike Fisher.

It was a long shot I know, but would he still be willing to speak to me after the way we'd parted company back in 1997?
Was he still alive, even?

Thankfully, the answer to both of those questions was 'yes'.

Admittedly our opening conversation wasn't exactly free-flowing once I'd found the resolve to call him up, but it wasn't long before we both found the common ground and cordiality that had first brought us together.

I told him that I wanted to write my autobiography.

He replied that it sounded like a fantastic idea, adding that he thought my unusual life story would be good enough to be turned into a film.

But that was the way Mike has always been. So watch this space.

He's a go-getter and, despite our earlier separation, in my opinion he's still the best one of those in the business.

It's through his efforts, dear reader, that you're holding my story in your hands right now.

I just hope that you've enjoyed it.

CHAPTER 24: A STRANGE TWIST OF FATE

Well, I have to say that this makes a pleasant and welcome change.

You should know that, to do justice to the preceding twenty-three chapters, I've had to incarcerate myself in my study so that I could think long and hard and without interruption about all of the events I've attended, the dates I'd forgotten, the people I'd overlooked, the distances I've flown and the tragedies I've endured.

I've checked and double-checked everything as far as both my longing for exactitude and the capabilities of my search engine will allow.

Now, though, I have my feet up on the sofa with my laptop perched on my knees because I feel that I've said everything that there is to say.

Anna-Marie is sat (or rather, slumped) alongside me half-watching something-or-other on television after what appears to have been, going by the look of sheer exhaustion on her face at least, another tough day in the salon. She works bloody hard, bless her, but to cap it all today's been warm and humid and so most definitely *not* the sort of day for being stuck in there with hot water running and the dryers on full blast.

She's a remarkable woman in just about every conceivable way.

Having stuck by me through thick and thin and letting me into her life when I had absolutely nothing to give in return, it was *she* that gave me the determination of mind and strength of character to start believing in myself once again.

I simply couldn't have brought up Natalie and Natasha alone.

Of course, I would have tried my best as any doting father would if placed in such an awful situation but, without Anna-Marie, those best efforts would have probably been no more successful than anyone else's worst.

Natalie, after emerging from her own period of personal soul-searching, is the proud mother of my delightful grandson Corey (as you now know) and she's currently forging positive plans for both of their futures.

Natasha has decided to move into acting, a thoroughly natural career choice which is now starting to bear very sweet fruit and with thanks going in no small way to the tireless labours of a certain Mr Fisher.

Heaven only knows where they'd be now and what they'd be doing had it not been for Anna-Marie.

They both adore her as completely as if she'd been their own mother and, even now, with both of the girls in their twenties, that unwavering respect is still there in abundance.

That makes me feel incredibly guilty though because for the first seven years of our marriage I took Anna-Marie for granted and didn't give her the love and attention that she so indisputably warranted.

And, throughout those seven years, where was she?

The same place she's always been, that's where.

At my side, and still patiently showing the steadfast devotion that I always found so difficult to bestow upon her in return.

It might have been argued that she deserved better but she continued to stand by me and I'm so eternally grateful to her for that. She's become the glue that keeps myself and my family together and, quite simply, I couldn't be without her.

There have been a number of occasions in my life where I've discovered that love is perhaps not the easiest of emotions to get across.

Maybe it's a genetic thing.

If so, then I'm certain I would have inherited that particular trait from my father rather than from my mother.

But, as I've floated effortlessly through life's highs and plummeted to its depths in freefall, I've come to realise that he wasn't the only man who found it almost impossible to express his true feelings.

Having said that I'm aware that, throughout this book, I've possibly placed a greater emphasis on those failings which he undoubtedly possessed but, as I've grown older and perhaps a little wiser, I've begun to sense that maybe there was a decent enough man in there all along.

Do you remember me telling you about the time he took me to the pictures to see *One Million Years B.C.*, and probably showed me more fondness in that one night than he'd done in my previous ten years?

Or when he happily acted as guarantor for my first bike?

Surely, this is not the manner of character that someone can turn on and off on a whim.

It's either part of a person's make-up, or it isn't.
I believe it *was* within my father to love, but it *wasn't* within him to freely show it and that's a real regret for me because I've always held an affection for him, in spite of his frequently brutal ways, and I wish now that we could have seen that veiled side of his personality more often while he was alive.

So, and changing the subject slightly, do I have any regrets regarding my stunt-riding, now that I've retired?

I'd have to say yes because, while it's true that not breaking certain records or achieving given milestones has irked me down the years, perhaps the biggest disappointment is that my career, whilst it had 'highs' and 'lows', never really had a 'defining moment'.

It had no real peak in other words, and probably no proper tail-off either.

Please don't get me wrong here because I'm rightfully proud of all that I've done and wholly appreciative towards all those that have helped me, but sometimes I feel like someone who's tried to do a five-thousand-piece jigsaw of nothing but blue sky and, right at the very end, realised that there's one piece missing.

It's frustrating more than anything but I can't lose sight of the fact that I achieved a considerable amount during my twenty-odd years in the game.

It's just that, every so often, I've silently craved that big, juicy cherry to plonk on top.

Nevertheless, I still have much to look forward to.
Re-signing with Mike has not only given me a new lease of life but it's also provided me with the chance to get some of my latest projects off the ground.

I've written my own television series called *Daredevil Diaries – Stunts of the Silver Screen*, a series which looks at some of the technical difficulties behind getting that all-important eye-catching moment of pure magic onto the celluloid (at the time of writing we are trying to find a production company to take the project to the next stage).

Mike's not lost any of that sharpness in making things happen for people despite the fact that, like me all those years before, he's recently lost his loved one.

I'm not entirely convinced that he really understood what was going through my head when I first linked up with him in 1995 but, at the time, he did all that he reasonably could to provide support and now, because of his own touching situation, I hope that I'm in a position to give a little of that back.

He's my manager, but he's also my friend and I believe that that creates the stronger bond.

Okay, I think it's time to sign off for the last time but, before I go and leave you in peace, I'd like to impart one final sentiment to you.

I'm sure that we all have a personal tale to tell but I feel that mine is one to be shared.

Adversity, after all, is everywhere.
We can't escape it but the more we try to do so, the more it tends to close in and smother us. We're affected by it whenever we read our newspapers, turn on our televisions or walk down one of our high streets listening to the multitudes as they stomp angrily by.

Perhaps my story will provide just one person with the inspiration and the resilience to rise up against that adversity and defeat their darkest nightmares, or even chase their biggest dreams.

If *you* are that one person then you must be prepared for some disappointment because if you've formulated one plot, then you can be certain that Life will be busily drawing up another one to thwart it.

But hang in there.

Keep going, and don't be too eager to throw in the towel because our plans don't necessarily have to crumble into dust or be obliterated by forces we can't control. Instead, they can go through subtle changes and shifts which might enable us see something new that we simply didn't notice before.

We have a word for that 'something new', and that word is 'opportunity'.

So, if at the moment you're feeling that things can get no worse then you should stand up, puff your chest out and throw your shoulders back.

Face the world square on and fill yourself with courage, because *you* may just be the next deserving recipient of a strange twist of fate.

THE END

Printed in Great Britain
by Amazon